GEORGE FOX
AND THE
CHILDREN OF
THE LIGHT

GEORGE FOX AND THE CHILDREN OF THE LIGHT

Edited and introduced by
JONATHAN FRYER

KYLE CATHIE

First published in Great Britain by
Kyle Cathie Limited
3 Vincent Square London SW1P 2LX

ISBN 1 85626 024 0

A CIP catalogue record for this book is available
from the British Library

Typeset by DP Photosetting, Aylesbury, Bucks
Printed by Cox and Wyman

TO THE MEMORY OF EDITH

Acknowledgement

Friends Meeting in Saigon, Vietnam, pointed me to the spirit of George Fox in 1969. Twenty-one years later, Friends House Library, London, quietly and efficiently handled my needs regarding his work. My thanks to both.

J.F.

Contents

Introduction

A S THE founder of Quakerism, George Fox (1624–1691) has a unique position in the history of the Religious Society of Friends (as the sect is properly known). Although his teaching and writings do not enjoy any official status among modern-day Friends, the Journal, in particular, is regularly consulted as a testimony of most of the beliefs and attitudes of Quakerism as seen in one man's life. Almost all the major tenets of Quaker belief are illustrated there, such as non-violence, the rejection of religious ritual and the priesthood, and the recognition that there is something of God in everyone.

At the same time, there are many things in Fox's Journal – and in the Epistles – which rankle with Friends today. His apparent intolerance is probably the most obvious. It is certainly one reason why many twentieth-century Friends treat George Fox with a great deal of caution. They tend to be highly selective in their choice of 'quotable quotes' from Fox. But then, so they are about the Bible.

It is abundantly clear from the Journal that George Fox was not an easy man. His mission was to challenge people about the way they lived. In particular, he asked them to search their souls to see if they reached the standards set in the Christian Gospels, as he interpreted them.

Such questioning was far more common in the political and religious turmoil of seventeenth-century England than it is now. Religious argument could often be heated and took place both inside and outside places of worship. Even so, the vigour with which George Fox pursued his mission made him stand out far above other preachers and dissenters. Having agonised in his youth about what constitutes Truth, he came to the conclusion that it had very little to do with the sort of faith and practice being promulgated by any of the Churches of his age. Accordingly, he confronted ministers of religion and laymen with his vision, in a totally uncompromising fashion.

The undeniable force of George Fox's argument, and the extraordinary lengths to which he was prepared to go to continue to profess it, did indeed persuade many people that he had found the key to a kind of spiritual contentment, for which others had strived in vain. What is more, he preached the immensely appealing message that everyone – man or woman – had within him or her the potential for direct communication with God. Within every individual there was an Inner Light; one only had to identify it, nurture it and then follow its leading. In other words, irrespective of origin, everyone could gain a form of personal salvation on earth. At a time when the whole world seemed 'turned upside down', this was a very reassuring idea.

One senses that some of George Fox's 'converts' capitulated in the face of his verbal onslaught with outright relief. They were like lost sheep, only too pleased to find such a shepherd turning up in their midst. Others needed more persuading, but seem to have been moved by his obvious sincerity and the sense of spiritual power which emanated from him. Several people who encountered him directly wrote of his amazing eyes. In an age when superstition was more widespread than it is now, those eyes could be terrifying as well as impressive. Some people suspected him of witchcraft – a charge which could been fatal if 'proved'.

Yet not everyone fell under Fox's spell. Many of the people to whom he preached during his tireless travels were infuriated by what they saw as the spiritual arrogance of this man who told them they had lost their way from the Lord's path. As practised theologians found, arguing with him logically was to no avail; he did not use those methods. In fact, he was not a theologian at all. He had a comprehensive knowledge of the Bible (the Authorised

Version of which had been published in 1611) and he could rattle off any number of appropriate quotations to back his case, but his interpretation of what the Bible meant was based far more on instinct than on learning.

Unable to halt George Fox's torrent of words by argument, his opponents would often try to settle the issue with blows. The early parts of Fox's Journal are a catalogue of assault. As a pacifist, Fox refused to respond to such violence in kind. This drove many of his adversaries into greater frenzy. Yet for some people – even among his persecutors – Fox's non-violence was itself a revelation and a testimony, which finally persuaded them he might be right.

George Fox's radical originality accounts for much of his impact, both in his own day and now. Yet like most historical figures, he was largely a product of his age. His life spanned one of the great transitional periods in British history. This saw not only several re-evaluations of the role of the Monarchy, Parliament and the Church, but also the laying of the foundations of much of modern science. Fox was born just within the reign of King James I, and lived long enough to see William and Mary on the throne. It is not therefore too much of an exaggeration to say that he had a panoramic view of Stuart England.

King James had ruled Scotland for twenty years before he succeeded to the English throne in 1603, his cousin Elizabeth Tudor having died childless. Like her a Protestant, he offered both the prospect of continuity and the considerable advantage of effectively joining England to Scotland, a country with which the English had often been in conflict. Nonetheless, James was not entirely inaccurately dubbed by King Henri IV of France as 'the wisest fool in Christendom'. A man of undoubted intellectual gifts – at least by royal standards – James I also had glaring weaknesses. Financial extravagance was just one.

James's Queen, Anne of Denmark, was equally profligate and shocked the more straightlaced members of London society with her flamboyant style. On one notable occasion, she arrived at a Christmas ball dressed as a mince pie. One of George Fox's constant fears was that England would return to such frivolity; he repeatedly implored people to be sober and modest. King James also had a taste for handsome but scheming male favourites. The most notable of these was George Villiers, whom the King made Duke of Buckingham. Villiers outlived James and went on to exercise considerable influence over the foreign policy of James's son and successor Charles I – much to the disgust of Charles' young wife Henrietta Maria, the devoutly Catholic sister of the French monarch.

James I had a series of confrontations with Parliament, in particular the House of Commons, which contained many Puritans who were determined to rid the Church of England of papist ritual and hierarchy. That 'purification' process had gone much further in Scotland than it had in England, but the Puritans' hope that James would vigorously encourage it in England were soon dashed. In the Puritans' eyes, James was dangerously 'High Church', as we would call it now. He did, however, rather half-heartedly impose some restrictions on Roman Catholics (which was why Guy Fawkes was hired by Catholic plotters to try to blow up Parliament in 1605). One condition of the marriage contract drawn up for James's son Charles and Henrietta Maria was that penalties against Roman Catholics should be relaxed.

After James's death, parliamentary suspicion of the new young King gradually turned to hatred as Charles attempted to by-pass Parliament, particularly when it came to raising funds. In comparison with his father, Charles was a dismal and devious character. For the Puritans, insult was added to injury when he appointed William Laud as the new Bishop of London. They feared Laud was set on making the Church of England more like the Catholic Church than ever. Laud went on to become Archbishop of Canterbury. Altars were restored to churches, and Sunday restrictions on dancing and other entertainments and amusements – introduced by James at the Puritans' urging – were lifted. The Puritans were outraged, but had no recourse in

Parliament from 1629 to 1640 (the formative period of George Fox's youth) as Charles refused to summon it.

Matters came to a head in 1640, when a rebellion broke out in Scotland after an attempt to impose a new Laudian prayer-book there. Charles summoned what became known as the Short Parliament to ask for money, which was refused. Thereby denied a proper army, Charles organised militias which were routed by the Scots, so he had to sue for peace. Parliament was summoned again later the same year – the so-called Long Parliament, which met for the next twenty years. This passed a measure ensuring it could not be dissolved without its own consent. Working from an increasingly weak position, Charles had little choice but to accept some of Parliament's curtailments of his own powers and to see some of his closest allies brought down. Those included Archbishop Laud, who was imprisoned in the Tower of London.

Another insurrection occurred, this time in Ireland, many of whose Catholic inhabitants had little love for their foreign ruler. James I had earlier incensed them by settling Scottish Protestants on land in Ulster that had been appropriated from Catholic farmers. Those settlers now became the target of attack. The Parliament in London had little choice but to grant King Charles enough money to put together an effective army to quash the unrest. However, wrangles over the appointment of senior officers led to Puritans within Parliament introducing what was called the Grand Remonstrance, listing all their grievances at the King's handling of matters of Church and State.

The Grand Remonstrance also included a series of demands, one of which was that a special synod be called which would spearhead a full-scale religious reformation. The document was adopted by a very slender majority in the Commons. Deeply angered, Charles went to the House in January 1642 with a contingent of armed guards and in blatant defiance of parliamentary privilege installed himself in the Speaker's chair. There was uproar in the capital and within a week, Charles had to leave

London. He raised his standard at Nottingham; the Civil War had begun.

England divided between those who fought for King and Country and those who supported God and Parliament. Their armies became popularly known as the Cavaliers and the Round-heads respectively. Geographically, in very broad terms, the royalist sway covered northern England, Wales, Cornwall and the West Midlands, with Oxford – after the Battle of Edgehill – serving as Charles's capital. His opponents held most of the south and east of England, including much of the East Midlands. Yet in reality the divisions were not nearly so clear cut. Even within Parliament, the King had his supporters. Moreover, many individual families were divided in their loyalties. The two sides vied for the hearts and minds of the uncommitted through a notable series of propaganda pamphlets.

George Fox never sided openly with either of the two conflicting parties. What is more, it is quite possible to read the early parts of his Journal casually without realising that the Civil War was happening. His story is one of spiritual mission and the nurturing of what became the Religious Society of Friends, not a history of his times. Yet some knowledge of that stormy period is necessary for the modern reader to put Fox's writing in perspective.

For Fox, there was only one basic loyalty, and that was to the Lord. He remained sceptical of all men in temporal authority. Yet he recognised that such people could use their power and influence for good as well as for evil or for personal gain. Accordingly, George Fox addressed himself directly to people in authority, either in person – when he could gain access – or by letter. At first, he limited himself to the English hierarchy, but later he sent his missives worldwide. What some of the foreign potentates made of his letters (always assuming they understood them), with their frequently peremptory style, beggars the imagination. Many, understandably, did not reply, though others did. Later Quakers came to call this tactic of lobbying men of influence 'speaking Truth to Power'. Emboldened by some of

Fox's successes, a number of his followers adopted the practice themselves, with varying results, as the later parts of the Journal recount.

From Fox's point of view, one of the most successful relationships he established was with Oliver Cromwell. Like so much of what is written in the Journal, Fox's accounts of their meetings should not be taken at face value. Cromwell was a much more complex and wily character than the person who appears in these pages, and his attitude to the Quakers was far more ambivalent than Fox believed. Certainly, Cromwell had respect for dissenting religious views and he probably was impressed by George Fox's oratory and personality. Nonetheless, his seemingly positive reaction to Fox's message may have been more a matter of politeness – or at times even amusement – than of convincement. Besides, Cromwell was often warned by his advisers that the Quakers were a highly disruptive influence, liable to cause riots and hold meetings, which some people believed must mean treason or rebellion. The whole idea of an 'Inner Light', which Fox and his followers obeyed, was distinctly unsettling in a period of civil unrest. Thus Cromwell did not remain immune to the scare stories that circulated at the time, saying that Quakers might be part of some Catholic or Royalist conspiracy. Assurances of religious tolerance under Cromwell's rule sometimes proved hollow.

Cromwell was no true democrat either. Following the execution of the captured King Charles in 1649, the House of Lords was abolished and England was declared a Commonwealth. But in 1653, Cromwell followed royal precedent by dissolving parliament, which was far too disputatious for his liking. A new, politically sanitised, Parliament was summoned, which declared him Lord Protector. Some historians have tended to portray the subsequent period as an example of the virtues of benign dictatorship. Others have been less kind. Cromwell did, nevertheless, resist the pressure of sycophants who wanted to make him King. He died, though, in 1658 and only two years later, the

Stuarts were back, in the person of Charles II. The populace in London turned out in droves to welcome him, obviously relieved at the return of the monarchy. Culture bloomed again and plenty of worthy intentions of promoting religious tolerance were stated.

George Fox, typically, was an astringent critic of the new regime. It is hard to imagine his approving thoroughly of any political leader or king. During one of his many imprisonments, on this occasion in Lancaster Castle, Fox wrote to King Charles II decrying the profanity and laxity which he believed the Stuart Restoration had brought. With customary directness, his letter began with a warning: 'King Charles, thou came not into this nation by sword and not by victory of war, but by the power of the Lord. Now if thou do not live in it, thou wilt not prosper!'

It was not, of course, normal to address a monarch in that way, but George Fox took great pride in treating everyone alike. That was his way of living out the biblical observation that we are all equal before the Lord. Not surprisingly, many people took considerable offence at this apparently vulgar familiarity, particularly when it was accompanied by Fox's own brand of haughtiness.

Actually, it is obvious from the writings of some of his more intimate followers that George Fox was a much warmer, more considerate and even humble person than he appears in his own Journal. So often there – especially to the modern reader – he seems to fall into the classic trap of the latter-day evangelist: self-righteousness. Some of Fox's contemporaries seem to have found this side of him rather funny. There is more than one occasion described in the Journal when Fox was clearly being teased. Superficially, he does not appear to have realised it, but more likely he was ignoring it – or else was trying to shame those tormenting him into realising the error of their ways.

Besides, several of the many distinguished people who figure in the Journal's pages were genuinely impressed by the early Quakers' forthrightness. Nonetheless, there were times when Fox alienated even some of those people well disposed to him by his rudeness, his stubbornness and his persistence. He undoubtedly brought much of his suffering on himself, by refusing to compromise or even to be civil. Indeed, many of his imprisonments and other humiliations were the result not of convictions on the grounds of heresy (which were difficult to prove against a man who metaphorically threw the Bible back in the face of his accusers), but because of his abnormal behaviour and contempt of court.

Apart from Fox's universal use of the more intimate pronoun 'thou', instead of the more respectful 'you', two things really stuck in the gullets of the authorities. One was Fox's refusal to doff his hat, which was then an essential form of courteous behaviour. He would only do so, he said, before the Lord; in other words, at prayer. So he would stand there, in the presence of his social 'betters', or in court, his hat firmly planted on his head. Some people chose to ignore this affront, or laughed it off, but others became quite apoplectic in the face of such insolent eccentricity.

Similarly, Fox refused categorically to swear an oath, saying this was forbidden in scriptures. Time and again, he was punished or detained for sticking to this principle. Some of his followers even died for it. No amount of threats or pleading by judges or others could shake him from this stance. Throughout the long reign of Charles II (who was succeeded by his brother James II in 1685), Fox and other Quakers were accused of disloyalty to the Crown because of their refusal to swear an oath.

Reading the accounts of some of the court proceedings in which Fox and others figured, one soon discovers the extent to which they used these occasions as a platform for their highly individual message of what one might term divinely-inspired defiance. Yet, particularly in Fox's later court appearances, it becomes clear that he was using legal arguments almost as often as he was spiritual ones. This suggests that either he was being very well briefed by legal advisers at that time, or else he had used his long and frequently unpleasant sojourns in jail to work out ingenious lines of defence. Some of these hinged on legal technicalities, such as the correctness of details in charges or procedures. These arguments did not always work; some judges were determined to convict or to order the continued detention of the defendant no matter what he said. But other cases, especially when they were trials by jury, fell apart in the face of Fox's incessant legal quibbles. One could write a whole book merely on the effect of these trials on the shaping of English jurisprudence.

One of the numerous inconsistencies in George Fox's life is why he spent so much time and effort challenging the law, while at the same time doing so much to ensure that he fell foul of it. Doubtless he would say that the Spirit moved him to act this way, providing new opportunities to witness for Truth. As the years went by, though, this was no longer an individual witness, as the growing band of Friends who had followed his lead needed to be fought for as well. A large number of Fox's epistles written during the last twenty years of his life concern the trials and tribulations undergone by others.

One reason why George Fox spent so much of his latter years in the sedentary occupation of writing was that his physical health had been broken by the dreadful privations endured during his many imprisonments. One gets several glimpses of the awfulness of prison conditions in seventeenth-century England from the Journal. That wretchedness would only be overcome much later, thanks largely to the work of other Quakers, such as Elizabeth Fry. Cold, hunger, disease and brutality abounded. In several instances, the suffering was quite deliberately aggravated by prison warders who took a particular dislike to Fox and other Friends. This may sometimes have been out of sadism, but more often it stemmed from anger caused by their attitude, their preaching or – a real bone of contention – their refusal to pay for even basic facilities or privileges, on which the warder's livelihood depended.

In the most gruesome instances, Fox was incarcerated in cells lashed by cold winds or the rain. In one extreme case, he was holed up in a place used as a privy. Yet even those dreadful experiences pale in comparison with the fate suffered by some other Friends who perished under brutal conditions, or who were put to death.

Reading Fox's brief and usually rather dispassionate accounts of some of those deaths, it is all too easy to forget just what sacrifices those people made for their faith.

In contrast, Fox's language in describing his own experiences – and especially the people responsible for them – is frequently intemperate. It is hardly surprising that he should feel bitter about the way he was treated. Indeed, in many ways it is remarkable that he refused to seek redress when given the chance. Yet a number of commentators have pointed out that there are odd contradictions in Fox's accounts of some of his spells in prison. Even in some of the worst places, he appears to have been able to receive food or visits from supportive Friends, or to write letters. Part of the explanation for the inconsistencies probably lies in the concise-ness of his descriptions. Conditions must have varied from month to month, even from day to day. Pointing that out should not belittle the poignant testimony of his suffering.

Fox's unreliability as an objective reporter is even more obvious in his brief pen-portraits of various jailers, judges, soldiers and others with whom he came in contact. Many of these characters are damned in pretty strong language. This can only partly be explained by the habits of the times, which predate the English predilection for understatement. More important was Fox's own style. He used no half measures when it came to condemning evil or error, as they appeared to him. He would tell people to their face what he thought of them – even when he had never met them before. His judgements were often harsh and unsubtle, which was one reason why he found himself on numerous occasions being chased out of town.

Even more difficult for the modern reader to contend with is Fox's clear belief in divine retribution. The concept was much more prevalent in the seventeenth century than it is now. Even so, it sits uncomfortably within the general framework of beliefs that emerge from Fox's writings. Put crudely, Fox was sure that those who mistreated him and other Friends, or who put obstacles in the way of his mission, were punished by God for their wickedness.

His Journal is littered with references to people being 'cut off', or being ruined financially, or losing those they held dear, after they had wronged him. More often than not, their fate is very unspecific. Moreover, a check of independent historical records reveals that the punishment was not always as instantaneous as Fox implies. Nonetheless, there they are in great number, those accounts of uncivil people getting their just rewards. At times these are recorded by Fox with a degree of satisfaction that comes perilously close to vindictiveness.

No one bears the brunt of Fox's verbal attacks more forcefully than self-proclaimed Christians who had failed to see the Light. That goes both for 'priests' (by which he meant any paid minister of religion) and for 'professors' (lay believers). Fox had a particular horror of men who made their living from preaching, believing that this should be done out of love, not for pecuniary gain. He therefore objected to tithes, whereby the public was obliged to pay for its clergy, and indeed to churches themselves 'steeple-houses' as he called them. He far preferred to speak outdoors, or in the more intimate surroundings of people's homes. Even so, he did go into many churches, as is recorded in some of the most memorable passages in the Journal, usually to challenge the minister inside.

Odd though it may now seem, it was quite legitimate in the seventeenth century for someone to stand up at the end of a minister's sermon, to put an alternative view. Where George Fox transgressed the norm was in marching obtrusively into services long after they had begun, or actually interrupting preachers while they were in full flow. The vigour and length of his attacks on ministers for allegedly hoodwinking their congregations also caused offence. Dialogue was not one of his strong points. As a youth, he did debate religious topics with his village 'priest', Nathaniel Stephens. But the older Fox got, and the more confident he became in his own message, the more his contributions to such discussions became harangues. When truly inspired, he could keep these up for hours.

Many people have left accounts of the power of Fox's religious ministry. One of the earliest to recognise his talent was Nathaniel Stephens, who believed the young man might well go on to be ordained himself. But later, the Reverend Stephens became disturbed with the directions Fox's message and manner were taking. Certainly, it is hard to imagine his being accepted into the priesthood. But it was because what he said was so different from the words of priests that he had such a powerful effect on some of his listeners.

Not least among these was Margaret Fell, the wife of the respected Judge Thomas Fell, who was thunderstruck by Fox when she first heard him preach at Ulverston in 1652. The racy novel *The Peaceable Kingdom* by the best-selling author Jan de Hartog (which is a fictionalised account of two formative periods of Quakerism on both sides of the Atlantic) attributes a clear sexual potency to Fox's oratory, suggesting this was one reason he had such a powerful effect on women, including Margaret Fell. The historical evidence for this is slim, to say the least, though obviously there was more than just religious fervour which linked Fox to Margaret Fell. She served as a protector and benefactor, not only to him as an individual but also to the movement he formed. Long after she had been widowed and was already approaching old age, George Fox married her. In keeping with the way that Fox subjugates personal feelings and motives in his Journal, this marriage comes as a complete surprise to the uninitiated reader.

No authenticated portrait of George Fox exists, but written reminiscences imply that he was a striking rather than an attractive man. In later life, he became quite fat, which his detractors said was evidence of gluttonous living. As a young man he was undoubtedly fit; he had to be, to survive his incessant wanderings, as well as countless nights pacing the lanes or the fields in spiritual torment, or sleeping in haystacks and in hedgerows. His resultant dishevelled appearance was accentuated by the fact that he wore his hair unfashionably long (another target for unsubtle jibes) and had a very peculiar way of dressing. For many years, this included a suit made of leather, and a very large hat. Contemptuous of the finery of royalist sympathisers, Fox avoided bright colours, ribbons and adornments, but even the Puritans considered his drab outfits bizarre. Moreover, his clothes guaranteed that he would instantly be the focus of attention and curiosity when he arrived in a new place. Coupled with his unorthodox behaviour, this frequently invited ridicule.

However, Fox had several means of effectively silencing those who mocked him. The alternation of long, impenetrable silences with passionate outbursts unsettled many people. This was particularly the case when he seemed to be possessed by some unnatural bodily force. At times he would tremble with (as he put it) the power of the Lord. Hence, legend has it, the nickname 'Quaker' was accorded to him and his followers by a judge. Fox was by no means the only one who 'quaked', especially immediately before giving verbal ministry, in other words, speaking out loud what he believed the Lord was moving him to say. The phenomenon of quaking had been noted earlier among other dissident religious sects and it can still be observed occasionally in some of the more intense Quaker meetings for worship.

Fox also manifested certain physical and psychical peculiarities which some people considered miraculous and others thought positively sinister. He has left us with several descriptions of periods in which his body became completely rigid. At times it was impossible to draw blood from him. And he lists, in a very matter-of-fact way, a number of instances of what amounts to faith-healing, including one extraordinary incident in which he seems to have healed a man with a dislocated neck. There are also several accounts of his calming people who were deranged. There is no record of his having studied how to deal with such situations; probably he had an innate talent. Certainly, there are enough examples of faith-healing throughout history for us to accept that some remarkable recoveries can be made with the help of people who have considerable psychological or spiritual power, to which the patient can surrender.

Tales of Fox's 'miracles' helped build his reputation, which had already been fuelled by verbal reports from the many thousands of people who had come into contact with him during his journeyings round the country. He also featured increasingly in 'news-books', which were periodical publications, forerunners of our own current affairs magazines, though less frequent and more inaccurate.

George Fox himself wrote extensively, as did several of the growing band of Quakers: pamphlets, treatises, journals and other works, some of which were specifically designed to refute accusations levelled against the Quaker movement and its practices. As these grew in number, Fox tried – not always successfully – to ensure that he saw texts before they were published. This was not so much to act as a censor as to try to avoid embarrassing mistakes. The fact that most Quaker authors were prepared to submit their manuscripts to him is a reflection of the degree to which he was regarded as the natural leader of the movement, even though that movement specifically shied away from the notion of hierarchy.

It is said that by the time of George Fox's death, in 1691, about one per cent of the population of England were Quakers. That percentage of today's population would be nearly half a million people, whereas in fact there are now under twenty thousand Quakers, not including people who attend Quaker meetings but have not formally joined the Society of Friends. To understand how Fox was able to attract such a substantial number of followers during his own lifetime one has to realise the intense religious ferment and questioning that went on in England in the seventeenth century, especially during the Civil War.

A whole range of non-conformist groups sprang up, who differed markedly from the narrow-minded Puritans. Some challenged accepted views on individual doctrines, such as the reality of an after-life, the special nature of the Sabbath, or the validity of infant baptism. Others went much further, notably the Ranters, who appear repeatedly in Fox's Journal. He seems to have been particularly bothered by them, probably because they shared some of his analyses of where organised Christianity had gone astray, but carried their conclusions to extremes. Like Fox, the Ranters stressed each individual's ability to attain enlightenment, but they also believed that they thereby put themselves above the law. The Ranters considered themselves sinless and therefore free to act as they pleased. Their 'worship' was festive, bordering on the riotous. In the most extreme cases, some of them claimed to be Christ or even God. Fox deeply disapproved.

In many of his trials and other encounters with the authorities, Fox was himself often asked if he thought he was the Son of God. Such a claim would have left him open more often to the extremely serious charge of blasphemy, as well as associating him more closely with dangerous fringe groups. He denied any messianic role, but was sufficiently ambiguous about the relationship one could attain with God through embracing the Truth to leave many of his questioners uneasy.

For all his ability to see the fallacy of the Ranters' arguments, Fox does not appear to have realised what many theologians consider to be the fundamental flaw of his own beliefs, namely that he too was convinced that he was without sin, because he followed the Inner Light. He admitted to temptations, though he is exasperatingly vague about what they were, but he did not admit to sin. This worried many nineteenth-century Quakers, who were as cautious about Fox's writings as some Roman Catholics still are about the Old Testament. But for many modern Quakers, Fox's dismissal of the inevitability of sin (and therefore, by association, guilt) is a healthy, liberating notion.

Because Fox had had plenty of first-hand encounters with Ranters and other bizarre sects, he knew there was a danger that people who were attracted by his message might also slip into aberrant ways. This did indeed prove to be the case. The most spectacular example was the man who was virtually Fox's deputy at a formative stage in Quakerism's development: James Nayler.

Nayler's story is both colourful and tragic. Six years Fox's senior, he had also searched far and wide as a young man for spiritual fulfilment. Unlike Fox, he thought he might find this by throwing in his lot with the Parliamentary army. He served for seven years with distinction, earning wide respect both for his abilities as a quartermaster and as a man who upheld spiritual values with pride. He was tender-hearted, and filled with social concern. But he was also susceptible to the influence of others he considered to be his spiritual guides. These included far less reliable souls than George Fox.

Nayler followed Fox's example of 'speaking Truth' in steeple-houses, likewise getting thrown out and abused for his pains. In Wakefield, Yorkshire, he was roundly condemned by a Congregationalist minister for alleged theological unsoundness and adultery. In 1652, Nayler, like Fox, found hospitality and assistance at the Fells' welcoming home of Swarthmore Hall. The two men travelled together on occasions and both were consulted by 'Seekers' – non-conformists who hoped that these Quakers might have the answer to their own spiritual quest. Later, Nayler took the Quaker message to London with some success, and began to attract a following of his own. This included a number of female admirers whose self-control and level-headedness were unfortunately not equal to their fervour. Some of these started to hatch the most ambitious plans, including one to take the Quaker message overseas and convert foreign rulers to the cause. Fox himself had this as a long-term goal as well, but some of the early evangelists in Nayler's coterie (men as well as women) were both premature and ill-prepared.

Worse was to come. During one of Fox's visits to London in 1655, he saw Nayler and they had a serious disagreement. Fox refused to let Nayler kiss him and said Nayler had turned against God. Fox had grim premonitions of some impending disaster. This came in October of that year, when Nayler travelled from

Glastonbury to Bristol, accompanied by his adoring female disciples. Two of these walked at his side, spreading their garments and autumn flowers on the muddy tracks before him as he rode, loudly singing his praises. Periodically, they would stop and kneel before him. Bristol was crowded when they arrived, despite the rain, and there was excitement when one of Nayler's followers declared that he had raised her from the dead. But local magistrates, appalled by this parody of Christ's entry into Jerusalem, stepped in and had Nayler and his acolytes arrested.

The Bristol authorities considered the whole matter so complex and serious that they passed it on to London, where Nayler had to defend himself before the House of Commons. After a heated debate, he was found guilty of blasphemy and was sentenced to a cruel and protracted punishment in December 1656. He was pilloried, then dragged through the streets, being whipped all the way. A week later, back in the pillory, he had his forehead branded with 'B' for blasphemy and a red-hot wire was bored through his tongue. Another whipping then followed, in Bristol, before he was imprisoned in London, with hard labour, for the next three years. The affair threatened to do terrible damage to the Friends' cause. George Fox kept frostily distant from Nayler's sufferings, concentrating instead on trying to avoid the spread of 'Naylerism' or similar deviations among Friends around the country.

The Nayler affair happened at a highly explosive time in English history and strengthened the fears of those in authority who believed that Quakers might be linked to what were known as Fifth Monarchy men. These were religious enthusiasts who believed that 1656 would be a miraculous year, when a new era would begin. Christ would return to earth and rule for a thousand years. The passing of the four great kingdoms (Assyrian, Persian, Greek and Roman) meant a fifth was due. The Fifth Monarchy men said this was prophesised in the Book of Daniel.

The millenium would of course require the overthrow of Oliver Cromwell, which was why the government – forever nervous of rebellion – took the Fifth Monarchists more seriously than perhaps they deserved. But it was not just in Britain that people were expecting a second coming or a new Messiah. On more than one occasion, Fox had to explain to enthusiastic enquirers that although he was *a* son of God, and had even 'seen the face of God', he was not the Messiah.

During the 1660s, Fox became increasingly aware that there might be exciting possibilities for Friends on the other side of the Atlantic, where people fleeing turmoil and religious persecution had been among the early European settlers. Shortly after proposing to Margaret Fell, he had the opportunity of discussing this idea with an important young new convert, William Penn. Penn (who does not get the attention he deserves in the Journal) was the son of an admiral and had studied briefly at Oxford, before being expelled for non-conformity. He went into the army and was sent to Ireland to fight against the rebels, where he was converted to Quakerism. Back in London he heard of the existence of fertile lands in America waiting to be settled. The young man raised the issue of possible emigration by Friends with George Fox, though it was to be several years before this seed bore fruit. This would eventually lead to the settlement of what became known (largely thanks to Charles II) as Pennsylvania. There Friends were able to carry out their 'holy experiment' of a peaceable kingdom, in which all people could live harmoniously together, including the Indians.

Fox never saw the holy experiment for himself. But he did travel in America and the West Indies during the period 1671 to 1673. There he was able to gauge for himself some of the future possibilities, as well as learning more of the difficulties many pioneering Quakers had faced in areas controlled by less tolerant authorities. The passages of Fox's Journal which cover his American journey are rather disappointing and at times difficult to follow. But undoubtedly the visit was crucial in helping establish Quakerism in America, where its adherents now far outnumber their counterparts in Europe and elsewhere.

Although Fox lived until 1691, reaching what was in

seventeenth-century England the ripe old age of sixty-six, he was already suffering long bouts of illness during his travels across the Atlantic. A less hectic lifestyle was clearly called for. From then on, Fox spent a great deal of his time writing, with the help of a series of secretaries and assistants. One of the first and most important of these was a doctor who moved into Swarthmore, Thomas Lower. From the end of 1675, Fox dictated to Lower what was to become his spiritual autobiography, the Journal, as a record of his personal development in the service of the Lord.

Fox's opening years received deliberately scant treatment in this Journal. This makes it rather a frustrating document for those schooled in the modern tradition of biographical study, which puts much store in ancestry and the subject's formative years. But as far as George Fox was concerned, what was important was what happened after his spiritual awakening at the age of nineteen, not before.

Fox and Lower had a large number of letters and documents at Swarthmore to which they could refer to check details of Fox's life story and the birth of the Society of Friends. But Fox's own memory was the principal source of the Journal. What this lacked in accuracy was made up for in the undeniable power and immediacy of subjective recollection in some of the Journal's passages. Nonetheless, it is a highly uneven text. For every page of moving testimony there are at least two more of tedious, repetitious material. Some of the most significant events and people get very brief treatment in the Journal, while less interesting organisational or legal procedures are gone over in inordinate detail. Moreover, there are some strange contrasts in style. These doubtless reflect the fact that many hands were responsible for the editing and even writing of much of the text, as it has been handed down.

If Fox's epistles are anything to go by, then his own writing style was often elliptical and at times cryptic. Yet he was also a master of powerful phrases. There are times when the reader of the Journal feels that it is indeed George Fox talking, while at others, it is as if some much more conventional and educated hand has taken over.

Reading the whole Journal – which runs to over a thousand pages of closely-printed text – is a daunting task, though rewarding for the serious student of Quakerism and its origins. However, a selected edition of the work makes it far more accessible, not least for those people for whom it may be the first in-depth encounter with Quaker beliefs. I have found considerable inspiration in the preparation of the present volume from earlier selected editions, not least that by the great American scholar Rufus M. Jones. But I felt it right to go much further in reducing the book's length and in dividing up the text into small sections, which make the narrative easier to follow. The Journal is by its nature episodic, and I felt it was better to try to make a virtue of that, rather than sticking to the earlier practice of presenting the Journal in chapters. Similarly, I have taken out many lists of names and passing references to places visited in Fox's itinerary, as these are more often confusing than illuminating. Some purists will doubtless object; so be it.

I have worked from the two-volume 1901 corrected eighth edition of the Journal, published by Headley Brothers, which can be found at Friends House Library in London and in some other Quaker collections. That edition helpfully used standardised spelling, but I have had no qualms about altering the punctuation radically in places, to bring it more into line with modern usage. More importantly, I have deliberately included in my selection passages which I suspect the editors of earlier selected editions left out because they highlighted sides to George Fox's character which they found difficult to take, or which appeared inconsistent with generally-accepted Quaker attitudes. In contrast, I wanted to show George Fox warts and all. He was by no means the only spiritual leader in history to have had some unpleasant traits.

My approach to the Epistles has broken with tradition, in that I have selected freely not only from the many hundreds of letters sent to Friends meetings and individual Friends (which are what are usually referred to as his Epistles), but also from letters and documents which are interspersed verbatim in the Journal. I think this gives a much fuller picture of both his concerns and his style. I have been quite ruthless in cutting down extracts, as many of the originals are very long and – to modern tastes – rambling. I have been helped in this by consulting an American edition of the pastoral letters of George Fox, *The Power of the Lord Is Over All*, edited by T. Canby Jones (Friends United Press, 1989).

Two things, I hope, emerge from this new selected edition of the Journal and Epistles. One is a self-portrait of a quite extraordinary individual, possessed of phenomenal power and natural authority. George Fox was no saint. His shortcomings are all too apparent from these pages. Yet his very humanity makes him all the more fascinating and impressive. Secondly, Fox's Journal and Epistles between them provide a unique blend of spirituality and common sense, which has lessons for everyone, no matter how sympathetic or hostile they may be to the general thrust of Quaker beliefs and practice. That is largely why Fox's writing has endured. Quakers themselves draw great strength from the example of past members of the Society of Friends, as set down in numerous books and pamphlets, or remembered from personal encounters. Within that tradition, George Fox and his writings have a very special place.

Three hundred years have elapsed since George Fox died, yet he still, as Quakers say, 'speaks to our condition'. No matter how much circumstances in seventeenth-century England may have differed from those we live in today, the fundamental questions of human existence remain the same. Living in peace and integrity with both God and the world still remains a goal worth striving to attain.

Chronology

1624		Birth of George Fox
1625	Death of James I Charles I accedes	
1629	Parliament dissolved	
1640	Parliament re-summoned	
1642	Civil War begins	
1645	Battle of Naseby	
1649	Charles I beheaded	Fox's first imprisonment (Nottingham)
1650		Second imprisonment (Derby)
1652		Pendle Hill vision Blasphemy trial
1653	Cromwell 'Lord Protector'	Third imprisonment (Carlisle)
1655		Fox first meets Cromwell
1656		Fourth imprisonment (Launceston)
1657		Journey to Scotland
1658	Death of Oliver Cromwell	
1660	Stuart Restoration (Charles II)	Fifth imprisonment (Lancaster)

1662		Sixth imprisonment (Leicester)
1664		Seventh imprisonment (Lancaster)
1665	The Plague	In Scarborough Castle
1666	Great Fire of London	
1669		Visit to Ireland Marries Margaret Fell
1671–73		Travels in West Indies and America
1673		Eighth imprisonment (Worcester/London)
1675–77		Based at Swarthmore
1677–78		On the continent
1684		Second visit to Holland
1684–1691		London
1685	Charles II dies; brother James II accedes	
1688	The Glorious Revolution	
1689	William and Mary crowned	
1690	Battle of the Boyne	
1691		George Fox dies

THE JOURNAL

The Preacher

BOYHOOD

I WAS BORN in the month called July 1624, at Drayton-in-the-Clay[1] in Leicestershire. My father's name was Christopher Fox. He was by profession a weaver, an honest man; and there was the seed of God in him. The neighbours called him Righteous Christer. My mother was an upright woman; her maiden name was Mary Lago, of the family of the Lagos and of the stock of the martyrs.[2]

In my very young years I had a gravity and stayedness of mind and spirit not usual in children; insomuch that when I saw old men behave lightly and wantonly towards each other, I had a dislike thereof raised in my heart and said within myself: 'if ever I come to be a man, surely I shall not do so, nor be so wanton.'

When I came to eleven years of age, I knew pureness and righteousness; for while a child I was taught how to walk to be kept pure. The Lord taught me to be faithful in all things, and to act faithfully two ways, viz. inwardly to God and outwardly to Man; and to keep to Yea and Nay in all things. And that my words should be few and savoury, seasoned with grace; and that I might not eat and drink to make myself wanton, but for health, using the creatures[3] in their service as servants in their places, to the glory of Him that created them; they being in their covenant, and I being brought up into the covenant, as sanctified by the Word which was in the beginning, by which all things are upheld; wherein is the unity with the creation.

But people being strangers to the covenant of life with God, they eat and drink to make themselves wanton with the creatures, wasting them upon their own lusts, and living in all filthiness, loving foul ways, and devouring the creation; and all this in the world, in the pollutions thereof, without God. Therefore I was to shun all such.

Afterwards, as I grew up, my relations thought to make me a priest,[4] but others persuaded to the contrary. Whereupon I was put to a man, a shoemaker by trade, but who dealt in wool and was a grazier and sold cattle. And a great deal went through my hands. While I was with him, he was blessed. But after I left him, he broke, and came to nothing. I never wronged man or woman in all that time; for the Lord's power was with me and over me to preserve me. While I was in that service, I used in my dealings the word 'verily', and it was a common saying among people that knew me: 'If George says verily, there is no altering him'. When boys and rude people would laugh at me, I left them alone and went my way. But people had generally a love to me for my innocency and honesty.

THE BREAK WITH HOME

When I came towards nineteen years of age, being upon a business at a fair, one of my cousins, a professor,[5] and having another professor with him, came to me and asked me to drink part of a jug of beer with them, and I, being thirsty, went in with them. For I loved any that had a sense of good, or that sought after the Lord. When we had drunk each a glass, they began to drink healths, calling for more and agreeing together that he that would not drink should pay all. I was grieved that any who made profession of religion should do so. They grieved me very much, having never had such a thing put to me before, by any sort of people. Wherefore, I rose up to go, and putting my hand in my pocket, laid a groat on the table before them and said: 'If it be so, I will leave you.'

So I went away. And when I had done what business I had to do, I returned home, but did not go to bed that night. Nor could I sleep, but sometimes walked up and down, and sometimes prayed and cried to the Lord, who said unto me: 'Thou seest how young people go together into vanity, and old people into the earth. Thou must forsake all, both young and old, and keep out of all, and be as a stranger unto all.'

Then at the command of God, on the ninth day of the seventh month[6] 1643, I left my relations, and broke off all familiarity or fellowship with old or young. I passed to Lutterworth, thence to Northampton, then to Newport Pagnell, whence I went to Barnet, in the fourth month, called June, in 1644. As I thus travelled through the country, professors took notice and sought to be acquainted with me. But I was afraid of them, for I was sensible they did not possess what they professed.

TEMPTATION AND DESPAIR

Now during the time that I was at Barnet, a strong temptation to despair came upon me. Then I saw how Christ was tempted, and mighty troubles I was in. Sometimes I kept myself retired in my chamber, and often walked solitary in the chase, to wait upon the Lord. I wondered why these things should come to me; and I looked upon myself and said: 'was I ever so before?' Then I thought because I had forsaken my relations, I had done amiss against them. So I was brought to call to my mind all the time that I had spent, and to consider whether I had wronged any. But temptations grew more and more, and I was tempted almost to despair. And when Satan could not effect his designs upon me that way, he laid snares for me, and baits to draw me to commit some sin, whereby he might take advantage to bring me to despair. I was about twenty years of age when these exercises came upon me. And I continued in that condition some years, in great trouble, and fain would have put it from me. I went to many a priest to look for comfort, but found no comfort from them.

From Barnet I went to London, where I took a lodging, and was under great misery and trouble there. For I looked upon the great professors of the city and I saw all was dark and under the chain of darkness. I had an uncle there, one Pickering, a Baptist – and they were tender[7] then – yet I could not impart my mind to him, nor join to them. For I saw all, young and old, where they were. Some tender people would have had me stay, but I was fearful and returned homewards into Leicestershire again, having a regard upon my mind unto my parents and relations, lest I should grieve them; who, I understood, were troubled by my absence.

When I was come down into Leicestershire, my relations would have had me marry, but I told them I was but a lad and I must get wisdom. Others would have had me into the auxiliary band among the soldiery, but I refused. And I was grieved that they proffered such things to me, being a tender youth.

DISENCHANTMENT WITH PRIESTS

The priest of Drayton, the town of my birth, whose name was Nathaniel Stephens, came often to me and I went often to him. And this priest Stephens asked me a question, viz. why Christ cried upon the Cross 'My God, my God, why hast thou forsaken me?' And why he said: 'If it be possible, let this cup pass from me; yet not my will, but thine be done?' I told him that at the time the sins of all mankind were upon Him, and their iniquities and transgressions with which He was wounded, which He was to bear, and to be an offering for, as He was man, but He died not as He was God; and so, in that He died for all men, and tasted death for every man, He was an offering for the sins of the whole world.

This I spoke, being at that time in a measure sensible of Christ's sufferings, and what He went through. And the priest said it was a very good, full answer and such a one as he had not heard. At that time he would applaud and speak highly of me to others. And what I said in discourse to him on the weekdays, he would preach on the First-days,[8] for which I did not like him. This priest afterwards became my great persecutor.

After this I went to another ancient priest at Mancetter, in Warwickshire, and reasoned with him about the ground of despair and temptations. But he was ignorant of my condition. He bade me take tobacco and sing psalms. Tobacco was a thing I did not love, and psalms I was not in a state to sing; I could not sing. Then he bid me come again and he would tell me many things. But when I came, he was angry and pettish, for my former words had displeased him. He told my troubles, sorrows and griefs to his servants, which grieved me that I had opened my mind to such a one. I saw they were all miserable comforters and this brought my troubles more upon me.

I heard also of one called Dr Cradock, of Coventry, and went to him. I asked him the ground of temptations and despair, and how troubles came to be wrought in man. He asked me: 'Who was Christ's father and mother?' I told him: 'Mary was His mother, and that He was supposed to be the son of Joseph, but He was the son of God.' Now, as we were walking together in his garden, the alley being narrow, I chanced, in turning, to set my foot on the side of a bed, at which the man was in a rage, as if his house had been on fire. Thus all our discourse was lost, and I went away in sorrow, worse than I was when I came.

After this, I went to another, one Macham, a priest in high account. He would needs give me some physic, and I was to have been let blood. But they could not get one drop from me, either in arms or head (though they endeavoured to do so), my body being as it were dried up with sorrows, grief and troubles, which were so great upon me that I could have wished I had never been born, or that I had been born blind, that I might never have seen wickedness or vanity; and deaf, that I might never have heard vain and wicked words, or the Lord's name blasphemed.

When the time called Christmas came, while others were feasting and sporting themselves, I looked out poor widows from house to house and gave them some money. When I was invited to marriages (as I sometimes was), I went to none at all. But the next day, or soon after, I would go and visit them; and if they were poor, I gave them money. For I had wherewith both to keep myself from being chargeable to others and to administer something to the necessities of those who were in need.

EVERYONE CAN FIND GOD

About the beginning of the year 1646, as I was going to Coventry, and approaching towards the gate, a consideration arose in me, how it was that all Christians are believers, both Protestants and Papists. And the Lord opened to me that if all were believers, then they were all born of God, and passed from death to life. And that none were true believers but such; and though others said they were believers, yet they were not.

At another time, as I was walking in a field on a First-day morning, the Lord opened to me that being bred at Oxford or Cambridge was not enough to fit and qualify men to be ministers of Christ. And I wondered at it, because it was the common belief of people. But I saw clearly as the Lord opened it to me and was satisfied, and admired the goodness of the Lord who had opened this thing unto me that morning.

But my relations were much troubled that I would not go with them to hear the priest. For I would get into the orchards or the fields, with my Bible by myself. I asked them: 'Did not the apostle say to believers that they needed no man to teach them, but as the anointing teacheth them?' And though they knew this was Scripture, and that it was true, yet they were grieved because I could not be subject in this matter, to go to hear the priest with them. I saw that to be a true believer was another thing than they looked upon it to be. And I saw that being bred at Oxford or Cambridge did not quality or fit a man to be a minister of Christ. What then should I follow such for? So neither these, nor any of the Dissenting people, could I join with, but was a stranger to all, relying wholly upon the Lord Jesus Christ.

At another time it was opened to me that God, who made the world, did not dwell in temples made with hands. This at first seemed a strange word, because both priests and people used to call their temples or churches dreadful places, holy ground, and the temples of God. But the Lord showed me clearly that He did not dwell in these temples which men set up, but in people's hearts. His people were His temple and He dwelt in them.

ON WOMEN AND DREAMS

I met with a sort of people that held women have no souls, adding in a light manner: no more than a goose! But I reproved them, and told them that was not right. For Mary said: 'My soul doth magnify the Lord, and my spirit hath rejoiced in God my Saviour.'

Removing to another place, I came upon a people that relied much on dreams. I told them, except they could distinguish between dream and dream, they would confound all together. For there were three sorts of dreams; multitude of business sometimes caused dreams; and there were whisperings of Satan in man in the night-season; and there were speakings of God to man in dreams. But these people came out of these things and at last became Friends.[9]

BARREN WILDERNESS, FRUITFUL FIELD

Now though I had great openings, yet great troubles and temptation came many times upon me; so that when it was day, I wished for night, and when it was night I wished for day. And by reason of the openings I had in my troubles, I could say as David said: 'Day unto day uttereth speech, and night unto night showeth knowledge.' When I had openings, they answered one another, and answered the Scriptures. For I had great openings of the Scriptures, and when I was in troubles, one trouble also answered to another.

I fasted much, and walked abroad in solitary places many days, and often took my Bible, and went and sat in hollow trees and lonesome places till night came on. And frequently in the night walked mournfully about by myself; for I was a man of sorrows in the times of the first workings of the Lord in me.

During all this time, I was never joined in profession of religion with any, but gave myself up to the Lord, having foresaken all evil company, and taken leave of father and mother and all other relations, and travelled up and down as a stranger in the earth, which way the Lord inclined my heart; taking a chamber to myself in the town where I came, and tarrying sometimes a month, more or less, in a place. For I durst not stay long in any place, being afraid both of professor and profane, lest, being a tender young man, I should be hurt by conversing much with either. For which reason I kept myself much as a stranger, seeking heavenly wisdom and getting knowledge from the Lord; and was brought off from outward things, to rely wholly on the Lord alone.

Though my exercises and troubles were very great, yet they were not continual but that I had some intermissions, and was sometimes brought into such a heavenly joy, that I thought I had been in Abraham's bosom. As I cannot declare the misery I was in, it was so great and heavy upon me; so neither can I set forth the mercies of God unto me in all my misery. O, the everlasting love of God to my soul, when I was in great distress! When my troubles and torments were great, then was His love exceedingly great. 'Thou, Lord, makest a fruitful field a barren wilderness, and a barren wilderness a fruitful field. Thou bringest down and settest up. Thou killest and makest alive. All honour and glory be to thee, O Lord of glory. The knowledge of thee in the Spirit is life; but that knowledge which is fleshly works death.'

CHRIST HAS THE KEY, IS THE WAY

As I had foresaken the priests, so I left the separate preachers also, and those esteemed the most experienced people; for I saw there was none among them all that could speak to my condition. When all my hopes in them and in all men were gone, so that I had nothing outwardly to help me, nor could I tell what to do; then O then I heard a voice which said: 'There is one, even Christ Jesus, that can speak to thy condition.' And when I heard it, my heart did leap for joy. Then the Lord let me see why there was none upon the earth that could speak to my condition, namely that I might give Him all the glory. For all are concluded under sin, and shut up in unbelief, as I had been, that Jesus Christ might have the pre-eminence, who enlightens and gives grace and faith and power.

My desire after the Lord grew stronger, and zeal in the pure knowledge of God, and of Christ alone, without the help of any man, book or writing. For though I read the Scriptures that spoke of Christ and of God, yet I knew Him not but by revelation; as He who hath the key did open, and as the Father of Life drew me to His Son by His Spirit. Then the Lord gently led me along and let me see His love, which was endless and eternal, surpassing all the knowledge that men have in the natural state, or can obtain from history or books. And that love let me see myself, as I was without Him. I was afraid of all company, for I saw them perfectly where they were, through the love of God, which let me see myself. I had not fellowship with any people, priests or professors, or any sort of separated people, but with Christ, who hath the key, and opened the door of Light and Life unto me.

I was afraid of all carnal talk and talkers, for I could see nothing but corruptions, and the life lay under the burthen of corruptions. When I myself was in the deep, shut up under all, I could not believe that I should ever overcome. My troubles, my sorrows and my temptations were so great that I thought many times I should have despaired, I was so tempted. But when Christ opened to me, how He was tempted by the same devil, and overcame him and bruised his head, and that through Him and His power, light, grace and Spirit I should overcome also, I had confidence in Him. So He it was that opened to me, when I was shut up and had no hope nor faith.

Christ, who had enlightened me, gave me His light to believe in. He gave me hope, which He Himself revealed in me, and He gave me His Spirit and grace, which I found sufficient in the deeps and in weakness. Thus, in the deepest miseries, and in the greatest sorrows and temptations that many times beset me, the Lord in His mercy did keep me.

Therefore, all wait patiently upon the Lord, whatsoever condition you be in; wait in the grace and truth that comes by Jesus. For if ye so do, there is a promise to you, and the Lord God will fulfil it for you. Blessed are all they that do indeed hunger and thirst after righteousness; they shall be satisfied with it.

But while people's minds run in the earthly, after the creatures and changeable things – changeable ways and religions and changeable, uncertain teachers – their minds are in bondage. They are brittle and changeable, tossed up and down with windy doctrines and thoughts, and notions and things. Their minds being out of the unchangeable truth in the inward parts, the Light of Jesus Christ, which would keep them in the unchangeable. He is the way to the Father; and in all my troubles He preserved me by His Spirit and power. Praised be His holy name for ever!

THE CHILDREN OF LIGHT

The pure and perfect law of God is over the flesh, to keep it and its works, which are not perfect, under, by the perfect law; and the law of God that is perfect answers the perfect principle of God in every one. This law the Jews and the prophets and John were to perform and do. None know the giver of this law but by the Spirit of God. Neither can they truly read it, or hear its voice, but by the Spirit of God; he that can receive it, let him. John, who was the greatest prophet that was born of a woman, did bear witness to the light, which Christ, the great heavenly prophet, hath enlightened every man that cometh into the world withal; that they might believe in it, and become children of light, and so have the light of life, and not come into condemnation. For the true belief stands in the light that condemns all evil and the Devil, who is the prince of darkness, and would draw out of the light into condemnation. They that walk in this light come to the mountain of the house of God, established above all mountains, and to God's teaching, who will teach them His ways. These things were opened to me in the light.

OPENINGS FOR MINISTRY

About this time [1647], there was a great meeting of the Baptists at Broughton, in Leicestershire, with some that had separated from them. And people of other notions went thither, and I went also. Not many Baptists came, but many others were there. The Lord opened my mouth, and the everlasting truth was declared among them, and the power of the Lord was over them all. For in that day the Lord's power began to spring, and I had great openings in the Scriptures. Several were convinced in those parts and were turned from darkness to light, from the power of Satan unto God; and many were raised up to praise God. When I reasoned with professors and other people, some became convinced.

I went back into Nottinghamshire, and there the Lord showed me that the natures of these things which were hurtful without were within, in the hearts and minds of wicked men. The natures of dogs, swine, vipers, of Sodom and Egypt, Pharaoh, Cain, Ishmael, Esau etc. The natures of these I saw within, though people had been looking without. I cried unto the Lord saying 'Why should I be thus, seeing I was never addicted to commit those evils?' And the Lord answered that it was needful I should have a sense of all conditions; how else would I speak to all conditions? And in this I saw the infinite love of God.

And as I was walking by the steeple-house[10] in Mansfield the Lord said unto me: 'That which people trample upon must be thy food'. And as the Lord spoke, He opened it up to me that people and professors trampled upon the life, even the life of Christ. They fed upon words, and fed one another with words. But they trampled upon the life; trampled underfoot the blood of the Son of God, which blood was my life, and lived in their airy notions, talking of Him. It seemed strange to me at first, that I should feed on that which the high professors trampled upon. But the Lord opened it clearly to me by His eternal Spirit and Power.

Then came people from far and near to see me; but I was fearful of being drawn out by them. Yet I was made to speak and open things to them. There was one Brown, who had great prophecies and sights of me upon his death-bed. He spoke openly of what I should be made instrumental by the Lord to bring forth. When this man was buried, a great work of the Lord fell upon me, to the admiration of many, who thought I had been dead. And many came to see me for about fourteen days. I was very much altered in countenance and person, as if my body had been new moulded or changed.

When I was in that condition, I had a sense and discerning given me by the Lord, through which I saw plainly that when many people talked of God and of Christ etc., the serpent spoke in them.

But this was hard to be borne. Yet the work of the Lord went on in some, and my sorrows and troubles began to wear off, and tears of joy dropped from me, so that I could have wept night and day with tears of joy to the Lord, in humility and brokenness of heart. I saw that which was without end, and things which cannot be uttered, and of the greatness and infinitude of the love of God, which cannot be expressed by words.

I had been in spiritual Babylon, Sodom, Egypt and the grave. But by the eternal power of God I was come out of it, and was brought over it, and the power of it, into the power of Christ. I saw the harvest white and the seed of God lying thick on the ground, as ever did wheat that was sown outwardly, and none to gather it. For this I mourned with tears.

A report went abroad of me that I was a young man that had a discerning spirit; whereupon many came to me, from far and near: professors, priests and people. The Lord's power broke forth; and I had great openings and prophecies; and spoke unto them of the things of God, which they heard with attention and silence, and went away and spread the fame thereof.

THE POWER TO SHAKE

[In 1648] I went again to Mansfield, where was a great meeting of professors and people. Here I was moved to pray; and the Lord's power was so great that the house seemed to be shaken. When I had done, some of the professors said it was now as in the days of the apostles, when the house was shaken where they were. After I had prayed, one of the professors would pray, which brought deadness and a veil over them. And others of the professors were grieved at him and told him it was temptation upon him. Then he came to me and desired that I would pray again; but I could not pray in man's will.

THE LIVING CHURCH

I heard of a great meeting to be at Leicester, for a dispute, wherein Presbyterians, Independents, Baptists and Common-prayer-men[11] were said to be all concerned. The meeting was in a steeple-house; and thither I was moved by the Lord God to go and be amongst them. I heard their discourse and reasonings, some being in pews, and the priest in the pulpit, abundance of people being gathered together. At last one woman asked a question out of Peter: what that birth was, viz. a being born again of incorruptible seed, by the word of God, that liveth and abideth together?

And the priest said to her: 'I permit not a woman to speak in the church', though he had before given liberty to any to speak. Whereupon I was wrapped up, as in a rapture, in the Lord's power. And I stepped up and asked the priest: 'Dost thou call this (the steeple-house) a church? Or dost thou call this mixed multitude a church?' For the woman asking a question, he ought to have answered it, having given liberty for any to speak. But instead of answering me, he asked me what a church was. I told him the church was the pillar and the ground of truth, made up of living stones, living members, a spiritual household, which Christ was the head of. But He was not the head of a mixed multitude or of an old house made up of lime, stones and wood.

This set them all on fire. The priest came down out of his pulpit, and others out of their pews, and the dispute there was marred. But I went to a great inn, and there disputed the thing with the priests and professors of all sorts. And they were all on fire. But I maintained the true church, and the true head thereof, over the heads of them all, till they all gave out and fled away.

One man seemed loving, and appeared for a while to join with me. But he soon turned against me, and joined with a priest in pleading for infant baptism, though he himself had been a Baptist before, and so left me alone. Howbeit, there were several convinced that day. And the woman that asked the question was convinced, and her family. And the Lord's power and glory shone over all.

TREATING SERVANTS FAIRLY

At a certain time, when I was at Mansfield, there was a sitting of the justices about the hiring of servants; and it was upon me from the Lord to go and speak to the justices, that they should not oppress the servants in their wages. So I walked towards the inn where they sat. But finding a company of fiddlers there, I did not go in, but thought to come in the morning, when I might have a more serious opportunity to discourse with them, not thinking that a seasonable time. But when I came again in the morning, they were gone, and I was struck even blind, that I could not see. I inquired of the innkeeper where the justices were to sit that day, and he told me at a town eight miles off. My sight began to come to me again, and I went and ran thitherward as fast as I could.

When I was come to the house where they were, and many servants with them, I exhorted the justices not to oppress the servants in their wages, but to do which was right and just to them. And I exhorted the servants to do their duties and serve honestly etc. They all received my exhortations kindly, for I was moved of the Lord therein.

Moreover, I was moved to go to several courts and steeple-houses in Mansfield, and other places, to warn them to leave off oppression and oaths, and to turn from deceit to the Lord and do justly. Particularly in Mansfield, after I had been at a court there, I was moved to go and speak to one of the most wicked men in the country, one who was a common drunkard, a noted whore-master and a rhyme-maker. And I reproved him in the dread of the mighty God, for his evil courses. When I had done speaking and left him, he came after me, and told me that he was so smitten when I spoke to him that he had scarcely any strength left in him. So this man was convinced and turned from his wickedness, and remained an honest, sober man, to the astonishment of the people who had known him before.

Thus the work of the Lord went forward, and many were turned from the darkness to the light, within the compass of these three years 1646, 1647 and 1648. Divers meetings of Friends, in several places, were then gathered in God's teaching, by His light, Spirit and power. For the Lord's power broke forth more and more, wonderfully.

PURENESS, INNOCENCY AND RIGHTEOUSNESS

Now was I come up in Spirit through the flaming sword, into the paradise of God. All things were new. And all of the creation gave another smell unto me than before, beyond what words can utter. I knew nothing but pureness and innocency and righteousness, being renewed into the image of God by Christ Jesus, to the state of Adam, which he was in before he fell. The creation was opened to me; and it was showed me how all things had their names given them, according to their nature and virtue. I was at a stand in my mind, whether I should practise physic for the good of mankind, seeing the nature and virtue of things were so opened to me by the Lord.

But I was immediately taken up in Spirit to see into another or more steadfast state of Adam's innocency, even into a state in Christ Jesus, that should never fall. And the Lord showed me that such as were faithful to Him, in the power and light of Christ, should come up into that state in which Adam was before he fell, in which the admirable works of creation, and the virtues thereof, may be known, through the openings of that divine Word of wisdom and power, by which they were made. Great things did the Lord lead me into, and wonderful depths were opened unto me, beyond what can by words be declared. But as people come into subjection to the Spirit of God and grow up in the image and power of the Almighty, they may receive the Word of Wisdom that opens all things, and come to know the hidden unity in the Eternal Being.

ON PHYSICIANS, PRIESTS AND LAWYERS

While I was [in the Vale of Beavoir]*, the Lord opened to me three things, relating to those three great professions in the world: physic, divinity (so called) and law. He showed me that the physicians were out of the wisdom of God, by which the creatures were made; and so knew not their virtues, because they were out of the Word of Wisdom, by which they were made. He showed me that the priests were out of the true faith, which Christ is the author of: the faith which purifies and gives victory, and brings people to have access to God, by which they please God; which mystery of faith is held in a pure conscience. He showed me also that the lawyers were out of the equity, and out of the true justice, and out of the law of God, which went over the first transgression, and over all sin, and answered the Spirit of God, that was grieved and transgressed in man. And that these three, the physicians, the priests and the lawyers, ruled the world out of the wisdom, out of the faith, and out of the equity and law of God: the one pretending the cure of the body, the other the cure of the soul, and the third the property of the people.

But I saw they were all out of wisdom, out of the faith, out of the equity and perfect law of God. And as the Lord opened these things unto me, I felt His power went forth over all, by which all might be reformed, if they would receive and bow unto it. The priests might be reformed, and brought unto the true faith, which

* Vale of Belvoir today

was the gift of God. The lawyers might be reformed, and brought into the law of God, which answers that of God, which is transgressed, in every one, and brings to love one's neighbour as himself. This lets man see, if he wrongs his neighbour he wrongs himself. And this teaches him to do unto others as they would they should do unto him. The physicians might be reformed, and brought into the wisdom of God, by which all things were made and created; that they might receive a right knowledge of them and understand their virtues, which the Word of Wisdom, by which they were made and are upheld, hath given them.

Abundance was opened concerning these things; how all lay out of the wisdom of God, and out of the righteousness and holiness that man at the first was made in. But as all believe in the light, and walk in the light, which Christ hath enlightened every man that cometh into the world withal, and so become the children of the light, and of the day of Christ. In His day, all things are seen, visible and invisible, by the divine light of Christ, the spiritual, heavenly man, by whom all things were made and created.

THE DIVINE LIGHT OF CHRIST

Now the Lord God opened to me by His invisible power that every man was enlightened by the divine light of Christ. And I saw it shine through all; and that they that believed in it came out of the condemnation to the light of life, and became the children of it. But they that hated it, and did not believe in it, were condemned by it, though they made a profession of Christ. This I saw in the pure openings of the light, without the help of any man. Neither did I then know where to find it in the Scriptures, though afterwards, searching the Scriptures, I found it. For I saw in that Light and Spirit which was before the Scriptures were given forth, and which led the holy men of God to give them forth, that all must come to that Spirit if they would know God, or Christ, or the Scriptures aright, which they that gave them forth were led and taught by.

THE MISSION

On a certain time, as I was walking in the fields, the Lord said unto me: 'Thy name is written in the Lamb's book of life, which was before the foundation of the world'. And as the Lord spoke it, I believed, and saw in it the new birth. Then, some time after, the Lord commanded me to go abroad into the world, which was like a briery, thorny wilderness. And when I came, in the Lord's mighty power, with the word of life into the world, the world swelled and made a noise like the great raging waves of the sea. Priests and professors, magistrates and people, were all like a sea, when I came to proclaim the day of the Lord amongst them, and to preach repentance to them.

I was sent to turn people from darkness to the light, that they might receive Christ Jesus. For, to as many as should receive Him in His light, I saw that He would give power to become the sons of God, which I had obtained by receiving Christ. I was to direct people to the Spirit, that gave forth the Scriptures, by which they might be led into all truth, and so up to Christ and God, as they had been who gave them forth. I was to turn them to the grace of God, and to the truth in the heart, which came by Jesus; that by this grace they might be taught, which would bring them salvation, that their hearts might be established by it, and their words might be seasoned, and all might come to know their salvation nigh.

I had no slight esteem of the holy Scriptures, but they were very precious to me, for I was in that Spirit by which they were given forth, and what the Lord opened to me, I found very agreeable to them. I could speak much of these things, and many volumes might be written, but all would prove too short to set forth the infinite love, wisdom and power of God, in preparing, fitting and furnishing me for the service He had appointed me to; letting me see the depths of Satan on the one hand, and opening to me, on the other hand, the divine mysteries of His own everlasting kingdom.

Now, when the Lord God and His son Jesus Christ sent me forth into the world, to preach His everlasting gospel and kingdom, I was glad that I was commanded to turn people to that inward light, Spirit and grace, by which all might know their salvation and their way to God. Even that divine Spirit, which would lead them into all truth, which I infallibly knew would never deceive any.

I was to bring people off from all the world's religions, which are vain, that they might know the pure religion, might visit the fatherless, the widows and the strangers, and keep themselves from the spots of the world. Then there would not be so many beggars, the sight of whom often grieved my heart, as it denoted so much hard-heartedness amongst them that professed the name of Christ.

I was to bring them off from all the world's fellowships and prayings and singings, which stood in forms without power; that their fellowship might be in the Holy Ghost, and in the Eternal Spirit of God. That they might pray in the Holy Ghost, and sing in the Spirit, and with the grace that comes by Jesus, making melody in their hearts to the Lord, who hath sent His beloved Son to be their Saviour, and caused His heavenly sun to shine upon all the world, and through them all; and His heavenly rain to fall upon the just and the unjust (as His outward rain doth fall and His outward sun doth shine on all), which is God's unspeakable love to the world.

I was to bring people off from Jewish ceremonies, and from heathenish fables, and from men's inventions and windy doc-trines, by which they blew the people about this way and the other way, from sect to sect; and from all their beggarly rudiments, with their schools and colleges for making ministers of Christ, who are indeed ministers of their own making, but not Christ's; and from all their images and crosses, and sprinkling of infants, with all their holy days (so called) and all their vain traditions, which they had instituted since the apostles' days, which the Lord's power was against. In the dread authority of which I was moved to declare against them all, and against all that preached and not freely, as being such as had not received freely from Christ.

TREATING ALL ALIKE

When the Lord sent me forth into the world, He forbade me to put off my hat to any, high or low. And I was required to Thee and Thou all men and women, without any respect to rich or poor, great or small. And as I travelled up and down, I was not to bid people Good morrow or Good evening. Neither might I bow or scrape with my leg to anyone. And this made the sects and professions to rage. But the Lord's power carried me over all to His glory, and many came to be turned to God in a little time. For the heavenly day of the Lord sprung from on high, and broke forth apace, by the light of which many came to see where they were.

But O! the rage that then was in the priests, magistrates, professors and people of all sorts. But especially in priests and professors! For although 'Thou' to a single person was according to their own learning, their accidence and grammar rules, and according to the Bible, yet they could not bear it. And as to the hat-honour, because I could not put off my hat to them, it set them all into a rage. But the Lord showed me that it was an honour below, which He would lay in the dust, and stain. An honour which proud flesh looked for, but sought not the honour which came from God only.

O! the rage and scorn, the heat and fury that arose! O! the

blows, punchings, beatings and imprisonments that we underwent, for not putting off our hats to men! For that soon tried all men's patience and sobriety what it was. Some had their hats violently plucked off and thrown away, so that they quite lost them. The bad language and evil usage we received on this account are hard to be expressed, besides the danger we were sometimes in, of losing our lives for this matter, and that by the great professors of Christianity, who thereby evinced that they were not true believers. And though it was but a small thing in the eye of man, yet a wonderful confusion it brought among all professors and priests. But blessed be the Lord, many came to see the vanity of that custom of putting off the hat to men and felt the weight of Truth's testimony against it.

TEACHING THE PURE LIFE

About this time [1649], I was sorely exercised in going to their courts to cry for justice, and in speaking and writing to judges and justices to do justly; in warning such as kept public-houses for entertainment that they should not let people have more drink than would do them good. And in testifying against their wakes or feasts, May-games, sports, plays and shows, which trained up people to vanity and looseness, and led them from the fear of God. And the days they had set forth for holy-days were usually the times wherein they most dishonoured God by these things.

In fairs, also, and in markets, I was made to declare against their deceitful merchandise, cheating and cozening; warning all to deal justly, to speak the truth, to let their yea be yea and their nay be nay. And to do unto others as they would have others do unto them, forewarning them of the great and terrible day of the Lord, which would come upon them all. I was moved also to cry against all sorts of music, and against the mountebanks playing tricks on their stages, for they burthened the pure life, and stirred up people's minds to vanity.

I was much exercised, too, with school-masters and school-mistresses, warning them to teach their children sobriety in the fear of the Lord, that they might not be nursed and trained up in lightness, vanity and wantonness. Likewise, I was made to warn masters and mistresses, fathers and mothers in private families, to take care that their children and servants might be trained up in the fear of the Lord. And that they themselves should be therein examples and patterns of sobriety and virtue to them.

For I saw that as the Jews were to teach their children the law of God and the old covenant, and to train them up in it, and their servants, yea, the very strangers were to keep the Sabbath amongst them and be circumcised, before they might eat of their sacrifices, so all Christians, and all that made a profession of Christianity, ought to train up their children and servants in the new covenant of light, Christ Jesus, who is God's salvation to the ends of the earth, that all may know their salvation.

But the earthly spirit of the priests wounded my life. And when I heard their bell toll to call people together to the steeple-house, it struck at my life. For it was just like a market-bell, to gather people together, that the priest might set forth his ware to sale. O! the vast sums of money that are gotten by the trade they make of selling the Scriptures and by their preaching, from the highest bishop to the lowest priest! What one trade else in the world is comparable to it? Notwithstanding the Scriptures were given forth freely and Christ commanded His ministers to preach freely, and the prophets and apostles denounced judgement against all covetous hirelings and diviners for money. But in this free Spirit of the Lord Jesus was I sent forth to declare the Word of life and reconciliation freely, that all might come to Christ, who gives freely, and who renews up into the image of God, which man and woman were in before they fell, that they might sit down in heavenly places in Christ Jesus.

DISRUPTING A SERVICE

Now as I went towards Nottingham on a First-day in the morning, with Friends to a meeting there, when I came on the top of a hill in sight of the town, I espied the great steeple-house. And the Lord said unto me: 'Thou must go cry against yonder great idol and against the worshippers therein'. I said nothing of this to the Friends that were with me, but went on with them to the meeting, where the mighty power of the Lord was amongst us; in which I left Friends sitting in the meeting, and I went away to the steeple-house.

When I came there, all the people looked like fallow-ground, and the priest (like a great lump of earth) stood in his pulpit above. He took for his text these words of Peter: 'We have also a more sure Word of prophecy, whereunto ye do well that ye take heed, as unto a light that shineth in a dark place, until the day dawn, and the day-star arise in your hearts'. And he told the people that this was the Scriptures, by which they were to try all doctrines, religious and opinions. Now the Lord's power was so mighty upon me, and so strong in me, that I could not hold, but was made to cry out and say: 'O no, it is not the Scriptures'. And I told them what it was, namely, the Holy Spirit, by which the holy men of God gave forth the Scriptures, whereby opinions, religions and judgements were to be tried. For it led into all truth and so gave the knowledge of all truth.

The Jews had the Scriptures, and yet resisted the Holy Ghost, and rejected Christ, the bright morning-star. They persecuted Christ and His apostles, and took upon them to try their doctrines by the Scriptures, but erred in judgement, and did not try them outright, because they tried without the Holy Ghost. As I spoke thus amongst them, the officers came and took me away, and put me into a nasty, stinking prison, the smell whereof got so into my nose and throat that it very much annoyed me.

But that day the Lord's power sounded so in their ears that they were amazed at the voice, and could not get it out of their ears for some time after, they were so reached by the Lord's power in the steeple-house. At night, they took me before the mayor, aldermen and sheriffs of the town. And when I was brought before them, the mayor was in a peevish, fretful temper; but the Lord's power allayed him. They examined me at large, and I told them how the Lord had moved me to come. After some discourse between them and me, they sent me back to prison again. But some time after, the head sheriff, whose name was John Reckless, sent for me to his house.

When I came in, his wife met me in the hall and said: 'Salvation is come to our house!' She took me by the hand, and was much wrought upon by the power of the Lord God. And her husband and children and servants were much changed, for the power of the Lord wrought upon them. I lodged at the sheriff's, and great meetings we had at his house. Some persons of considerable condition in the world came to them, and the Lord's power appeared eminently amongst them.

The Lord's power was with this friendly sheriff and wrought a mighty change in him, and great openings he had. The next market-day, as he was walking with me in the chamber, in his slippers, he said: 'I must go into the market and preach repentance to the people'. And accordingly, he went into the market, and into several streets, and preached repentance to the people. Several others also in the town were moved to speak to the mayor and magistrates, and to the people, exhorting them to repent.

Hereupon the magistrates grew very angry, and sent for me from the sheriff's house, and committed me to the common prison. When the assize came on, there was one moved to come and offer up himself for me, body for body; yea, life also. But when I should have been brought before the judge, the sheriff's man being somewhat long in fetching me to the sessions-house, the judge was risen before I came. At which I understand the judge was somewhat offended and said he would have admonished the youth, if he had been brought before him. For I was then imprisoned by the name of 'a youth'. So I was returned to prison again and put into the common jail.

The Lord's power was great among Friends. But people began to be very rude, wherefore the governor of the castle sent down soldiers and dispersed them. And after that they were quiet. But both priests and people were astonished at the wonderful power that broke forth. And several of the priests were made tender, and some did confess to the power of the Lord.

A WOMAN'S MIND IS MENDED

After I was released from Nottingham jail, where I had been kept prisoner some time, I travelled as before, in the work of the Lord. Coming to Mansfield-Woodhouse, there was a distracted woman under a doctor's hand, with her hair loose all about her ears. He was about to bleed her, she being first bound, and many people being about her, holding her by violence. But he could get no blood from her. I desired them to unbind her, and let her alone, for they could not touch the spirit in her, by which she was tormented. So they unbound her and I was moved to speak to her, and in the name of the Lord to bid her be quiet and still. And she was so. The Lord's power settled her mind, and she mended. And afterwards she received the truth and continued in it to her death. The Lord's name was honoured, to whom the glory of all His works belongs.

A BEATING

Now while I was at Mansfield-Woodhouse, I was moved to go to the steeple-house there, and declare the truth to the priest and people. But the people fell upon me in great rage, struck me down, and almost stifled and smothered me. And I was cruelly beaten and bruised by them with their hands, Bibles and sticks. Then they hauled me out, though I was hardly able to stand, and put me into the stocks, where I sat some hours. And they brought dog-whips and horse-whips, threatening to whip me.

After some time they had me before the magistrates, at a knight's house, where were many great persons, who, seeing how evilly I had been used, after much threatening set me at liberty. But the rude people stoned me out of the town, for preaching the word of life to them. I was scarcely able to move or stand, by reason of the ill-usage I had received. Yet with considerable effort I got about a mile from the town, and then I met with some people who gave me something to comfort me, because I was inwardly bruised. But the Lord's power soon healed me again. That day some people were convinced of the Lord's truth, and turned to His teaching, at which I rejoiced.

RANTERS

I heard of a people that were in prison in Coventry for religion. And as I walked towards the jail, the word of the Lord came to me saying: 'My love was always to thee, and thou art in my love'. And I was ravished with the sense of the love of God, and greatly strengthened in my inward man. But when I came into the jail, where the prisoners were, a great power of darkness struck at me and I sat still, having my spirit gathered into the love of God. At last these prisoners began to rant and vapour and blaspheme, at which my soul was greatly grieved.

They said they were God, but that we could not bear such things. When they were calm, I stood up and asked them whether they did such things by motion, or from Scripture; and they said: from Scripture. A Bible being at hand, I asked them to point out that Scripture. And they showed me the place where the sheet was let down to Peter, and it was said to him, what was sanctified he should not call common or unclean. When I had showed them that that Scripture proved nothing for their purpose, they brought another, which spoke of God's reconciling all things to Himself: things in heaven and things in earth. I told them I owned that Scripture also, but showed them that that was nothing to their purpose either.

Then seeing they said they were God, I asked them if they knew whether it would rain tomorrow. They said they could not tell. I told them God could tell. Again, I asked them if they thought they should be always in that condition, or should change. And they answered they could not tell. Then said I unto them, God can tell, and God doth not change. You say you are God, and yet you cannot tell whether you shall change or not.

So they were confounded, and quite brought down for the time. After I had reproved them for their blasphemous expressions, I went away. For I perceived they were Ranters. I had met with none before. And I admired the goodness of the Lord in appearing so unto me before I went amongst them. Not long after this, one of these Ranters, whose name was Joseph Salmon, put forth a paper or book of recantation, upon which they were all set at liberty.

DENOUNCED AS MAD

I went to Market-Bosworth and there was a lecture there. He that preached that day was Nathaniel Stephens, who was priest of the town where I was born. He raged much when I spoke to him and to the people, and told them I was mad. He had said before, to one Colonel Purfoy, that there was never such a plant bred in England; and he bid the people not to hear me. So the people, being stirred up by this deceitful priest, fell upon me and stoned us out of the town. Yet they did not do us much hurt. Howbeit, some people were made loving that day, and others were confirmed, seeing the rage of both priests and professors. And some cried out that the priest durst not stand to prove his ministry.

A NAKED RAPIER

As I travelled through markets, fairs and divers places, I saw death and darkness in all people, where the power of the Lord God had not shaken them. As I was passing on in Leicestershire, I came to Twy-Cross, where there were excise-men. I was moved of the Lord to go to them, and warn them to take heed of oppressing the poor. And people were much affected with it.

There was in that town a great man, that had long lain sick and was given up by the physician. And some Friends in the town desired me to go to see him. I went up to him in his chamber and spoke the word of life to him; and was moved to pray by him. And the Lord was entreated and restored him to health.

But when I was come downstairs, into a lower room, and was speaking to the servants, and to some people that were there, a serving-man of his came raving out of another room, with a naked rapier in his hand, and set it just to my side. I looked steadfastly on him and said: 'Alack for thee, poor creature! What wilt thou do with thy carnal weapon? It is no more to me than a straw'. The standers-by were much troubled and he went away in a rage and full of wrath. But when the news of it came to his master, he turned him out of his service. Thus the Lord's power preserved me.

A LIFE WITHOUT SIN

Coming to Derby, I lay at a doctor's house, whose wife was

convinced. And so were several more in the town. As I was walking
in my chamber, the [steeple-house] bell rung, and it struck at my
life at the very hearing of it. So I asked the woman of the house
what the bell rung for. She said there was to be a great lecture
there that day, and many of the officers of the army and priests and
preachers were to be there, and a colonel that was a preacher. Then
was I moved of the Lord to go up to them. And when they had
done I spoke to them what the Lord commanded me and they
were pretty quiet.

But there came an officer and took me by the hand, and said I
must go before the magistrates, and the other two that were with
me. It was about the first hour after noon that we came before
them. They asked me why we came thither. I said God moved us to
do so. And I told them: 'God dwells not in temples made with
hands'. I told them also all their preaching, baptism and sacrifices
would never sanctify them. And bid them look unto Christ in
them and not unto men. For it is Christ that sanctifies.

Then they ran into many words. But I told them they were not
to dispute of God and Christ, but to obey Him. The power of God
thundered amongst them and they flew like chaff before it. They
put me in and out of the room often, hurrying me backward and
forward. For they were from the first hour till the ninth at night in
examining me. Sometimes they would tell me in a deriding
manner that I was taken up in raptures. At last they asked me
whether I was sanctified. I answered 'Yes'; for I was in the paradise
of God.

Then they asked me if I had no sin. I answered: 'Christ my
Saviour has taken away my sin, and in Him there is no sin'. They
asked how we knew that Christ did abide in us. I said, by His
Spirit, that He had given us. They temptingly asked if any of us
were Christ. I answered nay, we were nothing, Christ is all. They
said, if a man steal, is it no sin? I answered, all unrighteousness is
sin. So when they had wearied themselves in examining me, they
committed me and one other man to the House of Correction in

Derby for six months, as blasphemers, as appears by the following mittimus:-

To the Master of the House of Correction in Derby, greeting.

We have sent you herewithal the bodies of George Fox, late of Mansfield, in the county of Nottingham, and John Fretwell, late of Stainsby, in the county of Derby, husbandman, brought before us this present day and charged with the avowed uttering and broaching of divers blasphemous opinions contrary to a late Act of Parliament, which, upon their examination before us, they have confessed. These are therefore to require you forthwith, upon sight thereof, to receive them, the said George Fox and John Fretwell, into your custody, and them therein safely to keep during the space of six months, without bail or mainprize, or until they shall find sufficient security to be of good behaviour, or be thence delivered by order from ourselves. Hereof you are not to fail. Given under our hands and seals this 30th day of October 1650. Ger. Bennett; Nath. Barton.

A LETTER FROM JAIL

Having written to the justices and to the priests, it was upon me to write to the Mayor of Derby also, who, though he did not sign the mittimus, had a hand with the rest in sending me to prison. To him I wrote after this manner:-

Friend,

Thou art set in place to do justice. But in imprisoning my body thou hast done contrary to justice, according to your own law. O take heed of pleasing men more than God, for that is the way of the Scribes and the Pharisees; they sought the praise of men more than God. Remember who said 'I was a stranger and ye took Me not in; I was in prison and ye visited Me not'. O friend, thy envy is not against me, but against the power of truth. I had no envy to you, but love. O take heed of oppression, 'for the day of the Lord is coming, that shall burn us as an oven; and all the proud, and all that do wickedly, shall be as stubble; and the day that cometh shall burn them up, saith the Lord of Hosts; it shall leave them without root nor branch'. O friend, if the love of God were in thee, thou wouldst love the truth, hear the truth spoken, and not imprison unjustly. The love of God beareth and suffereth, and envieth no man. If the love of God had broken your hearts, you would show mercy. But you show forth what ruleth you. Every tree doth show forth its fruit; you do show your fruits openly. For drunkenness, swearing, pride and vanity rule among you, from the teacher to the people. O friend, mercy and true judgement and justice are cried for in your streets! Oppression, unmercifulness, cruelty, hatred, pride, pleasures, wantonness and foulness are in your streets. But the poor are not regarded. O! take heed: 'Woe be to the crown of pride! Woe be to them that drink wine in bowls, and the poor is ready to perish'. O! remember Lazarus and Dives! One fared deliciously every day and the other was a beggar. O friend, mind these things, for they are near. And see whether thou be not in Dives' state.

THE KEEPER OF DERBY JAIL

Now the keeper of the prison, being a high professor, was greatly enraged against me, and spoke very wickedly of me. But it pleased the Lord one day to strike him so, that he was in great trouble and under great terror of mind. As I was walking in my chamber I heard a doleful noise; and standing still, I heard him say to his wife: 'Wife, I have seen the day of judgement, and I saw George there, and I was afraid of him, because I had done such wrong, and spoken so much against him to the ministers and professors, and to the justices, and in taverns and ale-houses'.

After this, towards the evening, he came up into my chamber and said to me: 'I have been as a lion against you, but now I come like a lamb, and like the jailer that came to Paul and Silas trembling'. And he desired that he might lodge with me. I told him that I was in his power; he might do what he would. But he said nay, he would have my leave, and he could desire to be always with me, but not to have me as a prisoner. And he said he had been plagued and his house had been plagued for my sake.

So I suffered him to lodge with me. And then he told me all his heart, and said he believed what I had said of the true faith and hope to be true. And he wondered that the other man that was put into prison with me did not stand to it; and said that man was not right, but I was an honest man. He confessed also to me, that at those times when I had asked him to let me go forth to speak the word of the Lord to the people, and he had refused to let me, and I had laid the weight thereof upon him, that he used to be under great trouble, amazed and almost distracted for some time after; and in such a condition that he had little strength left him.

When the morning came, he rose and went to the justices and told them that he and his house had been plagued for my sake. And one of the justices replied (as he reported to me) that the plagues were on them too for keeping me. This was Justice Bennet of Derby, who was the first that called us Quakers,[12] because I bid them tremble at the word of the Lord. This was in the year 1650.

After this, the justices gave leave that I should have liberty to walk a mile. I perceived their end and told the jailer if they would show me how far a mile was, I might walk it sometimes. For I believed they thought I would go away. And the jailer confessed afterwards that they did it with that intent, to have me escape, to ease them of their plague. But I told him I was not of that spirit.

MINISTRY IN JAIL

While I was in the House of Correction, my relations came to see me. And being troubled for my imprisonment, they went to the justices that cast me into prison and desired to have me home with them, offering to be bound in one hundred pounds, and others of Derby with them in fifty pounds each, that I should come no more thither to declare against the priests. So I was had up before the justices. And because I would not consent that they, or any, should be bound for me (for I was innocent from any ill behaviour, and had spoken the word of life and truth unto them), Justice Bennet rose up in a rage. And as I was kneeling down to pray to the Lord to forgive him, he ran upon me and struck me with both his hands crying: 'Away with him, jailer! Take him away, jailer!' Whereupon I was had again to prison and there kept, until the time of my commitment for six months was expired.

But I had now my liberty of walking a mile by myself, which I made use of, as I felt freedom. Sometimes I went into the market and streets, and warned the people to repent of their wickedness; and so returned to prison again. And there being persons of several sorts of religion in the prison, I sometimes went and visited them in their meetings on First-days.

While I was yet in the House of Correction, there came unto me a trooper and said: as he was sitting in the steeple-house hearing the priest, exceeding great trouble came upon him. And the voice of the Lord came to him saying: 'Dost thou not know that my servant is in prison? Go to him for direction'. So I spoke to his condition and his understanding was opened. I told him that which showed him his sins, and troubled him for them, would show him his salvation; for He that shows a man his sin is the same that takes it away. While I was speaking to him, the Lord's power opened him, so that he began to have a good understanding in the Lord's truth and to be sensible of God's mercies; and began to speak boldly in his quarters amongst the soldiers, and to others, concerning truth (for the scriptures were very much opened to him), insomuch that he said his colonel was as blind as Nebuchad-nezzar, to cast the servant of the Lord into prison.

Upon this, his colonel had a spite against him. And at Worcester fight,[13] the year after, when the two armies were lying near one another, two came out of the King's army and challenged any two of the Parliament army to fight with them. His colonel made choice of him and another to answer to the challenge. And when in the encounter his companion was slain, he drove both his enemies within musket-shot of the town, without firing a pistol at them. This, when he returned, he told me with his own mouth. But when the fight was over, he saw the deceit and hypocrisy of the officers. And being sensible how wonderfully the Lord had preserved him, and seeing also to the end of the fighting, he laid down his arms.

Now the time of my commitment to the House of Correction being nearly ended, and there being many new soldiers raised, the commissioners would have made me captain over them. And the soldiers said they would have none but me. So the keeper of the House of Correction was commanded to bring me before the commissioners and soldiers in the market-place. And there they offered me that preferment, as they called it, asking me if I would not take up arms for the Commonwealth against Charles Stuart. I told them I knew from whence all wars rose, even from the lust, according to James's doctrine; and that I lived in the virtue of that life and power that took away the occasion of all wars.

But they courted me to accept their offer and thought I did but compliment them. But I told them I was come into the covenant of peace, which was before wars and strifes were. They said they offered it in love and kindness to me, because of my virtue; and such like flattering words they used. But I told them if that was their love and kindness, I trampled it under my feet. Then their rage got up and they said: 'Take him away, jailer, and put him into the dungeon amongst the rogues and felons'.

So I was had away and put into a lousy, stinking place, without any bed, amongst thirty felons, where I was kept almost half a year, unless it were at times; for they would sometimes let me walk in the garden, having a belief that I would not go away. Now when they got me into Derby dungeon, it was the belief and saying of people that I should never come out. But I had faith in God and believed I should be delivered in His time. For the Lord had said to me before that I was not to be removed from that place yet, being set there for a service which He had for me to do.

While I was here in prison, there was a young woman in the jail for robbing her master of some money. When she was about to be tried for her life, I wrote to the judge and to the jury about her, showing them how it was contrary to the law of God in old time to put people to death for stealing, and moving them to show mercy. Yet she was condemned to die and a grave was made for her. And at the time appointed, she was carried forth for execution. Then I wrote a few words, warning all people to beware of greediness or covetousness, for it leads from God; and exhorting all to fear the Lord, to avoid all earthly lusts and to prize their time while they have it. This I gave to be read at the gallows. And though they had her upon the ladder, with a cloth bound over her face, ready to be turned off, yet they did not put her to death, but brought her back again to prison. And in the prison, she afterwards came to be convinced of God's everlasting truth.

Now the time of the Worcester fight coming on, Justice Bennet sent the constables to press me for a soldier, seeing I would not voluntarily accept of a command. I told them that I was brought off from outward wars. They came down again to give me press-money, but I would take none. After a while, the constables fetched me up again and brought me before the commissioners, who said I should go for a soldier. But I told them that I was dead to it. They said I was alive. I told them where envy and hatred are, there is confusion. They offered me money twice, but I would not take it. Then they were angry and committed me to close prisoner, without bail or mainprize. Whereupon I wrote to them again, directing my letter to Colonel Barton (who was a preacher) and the rest that were concerned in my commitment. I wrote thus:

You who are without Christ, and yet use the words which He and His saints have spoken, consider: neither He nor His apostles did ever imprison any. But my Saviour is merciful even to the unmerciful and rebellious. He brings out of prison and bondage; but men, while the carnal mind rules, oppress and imprison. My Saviour saith: 'Love your enemies and do good to them that hate you, and pray for them that despitefully use you and persecute you'. For the love of God doth not persecute any, but loveth all where it dwelleth. 'He that hateth his brother is a murderer'. You profess to be Christian, and one of you a minister of Jesus Christ. Yet you have imprisoned me, who am a servant of Jesus Christ. The apostles never imprisoned any, but were imprisoned themselves. Take head of speaking of Christ in words, and denying Him in life and power. O friends, the imprisoning of my body is to satisfy your wills; but take heed of giving way to your wills, for that will hurt you. If the love of God had broken your hearts, ye would not have imprisoned me. But my love is to you, as to all my fellow-creatures. And that you may weigh yourselves, and see how you stand, is this written.

DERBY DAMNED

Great was my exercise and travail in spirit, during my imprisonment here, because of the wickedness that was in this town. For though some were convinced, yet the generality were a hardened people. And I saw the visitation of God's love pass from them. I mourned over them. And it came upon me to give forth the following lamentation for them:

O Derby! as the waters run away when the floodgates are up, so doth the visitation of God's love pass away from thee, O Derby! Therefore look where thou art, and how thou art grounded; and consider, before thou art utterly foresaken. O Derby! thy profession and preaching stink before the Lord. Ye profess a Sabbath in words, and meet together, dressing yourselves in fine apparel. You uphold pride. Thy women go with stretched-forth necks and wanton eyes, etc., which the true prophet of old cried against. Your assemblies are odious and an abomination to the Lord. Pride is set up and bowed down to. Covetousness abounds. And he that doeth wickedly is honoured. So deceit bears with deceit, and yet they profess Christ in words. O the deceit that is within thee! It doth even break my heart to see how God is dishonoured in thee, O Derby!

There was a great judgement on the town, and the magistrates were uneasy about me. But they could not agree what to do with me. One while they would have me sent up to the parliament; another while they would have banished me to Ireland. At first, they called me a deceiver and seducer, and a blasphemer. Afterwards, when God had brought His plagues upon them, they said I was an honest, virtuous man. But their good report or bad report, their good-speaking or ill-speaking, was nothing to me. For the one did not lift me up, nor the other cast me down. Praised be the Lord! At length they were made to turn me out of jail, about the beginning of the Winter, in the year 1651, after I had been a prisoner in Derby almost a year: six months in the House of Correction, and the rest of the time in the common jail and dungeon.

BLOODY LICHFIELD

Thus being set at liberty again, I went on as before, in the work of the Lord, passing through the country. As I was walking along with several Friends, I lifted up my head and saw three steeple-house spires, and they struck at my life. I asked them what place that was, and they said Lichfield. Immediately the word of the Lord came to me that I must go thither. Being come to the house we were going to, I wished the Friends that were with me to walk into the house, saying nothing to them whither I was to go.

As soon as they were gone, I stepped away and went by my eye over hedge and ditch, till I came within a mile of Lichfield; where, in a great field, there were shepherds keeping their sheep. Then I was commanded by the Lord to pull off my shoes. I stood still, for it was Winter. And the word of the Lord was like a fire in me. So I put off my shoes and left them with the shepherds; and the poor shepherds trembled and were astonished.

Then I walked on about a mile, and as soon as I was within the city, the word of the Lord came to me again saying: 'Cry "Woe until the bloody city of Lichfield!"' So I went up and down the streets, crying with a loud voice: 'Woe to the bloody city of Lichfield!' It being market-day, I went into the market-place, and to and fro in the several parts of it, and made stands, crying as before: 'Woe to the bloody city of Lichfield!' And no one laid hands on me. But as I went thus crying through the streets, there seemed to me to be a channel of blood running down the streets, and the market-place appeared like a pool of blood.

When I had declared what was upon me, and felt myself clear, I went out of the town in peace. And returning to the shepherds, gave them some money, and took my shoes of them again. But the fire of the Lord was so in my feet, and all over me, that I did not matter to put on my shoes any more, and was at a stand whether I should or not, till I felt freedom from the Lord so to do. And then, after I had washed my feet, I put on my shoes again.

After this, a great consideration came upon me, why or for what reason I should be sent to cry against that city and call it 'the bloody city'. For though the Parliament had the minster one while, and the King another, and much blood had been shed in the town, during the wars between them, yet that was no more than had befallen many other places. But afterwards I came to understand that in the Emperor Diocletian's time, a thousand Christians were martyred in Lichfield. So I was to go, without my shoes, through the channel of their blood, and into the pool of their blood in the market-place, that I might raise up the memorial of the blood of those martyrs which had been shed above a thousand years before, and lay cold in their streets. So the sense of this blood was upon me, and I obeyed the word of the Lord.

JUSTICE HOTHAM

I went to Cranswick, to Captain Pursloe's, who accompanied me to Justice Hotham's. This Justice Hotham was a tender man, one that had some experience of God's working in his heart. After some discourse with him of the things of God, he took me into his closet; where, sitting together, he told me he had known of that principle these ten years, and was glad that the Lord did now publish it abroad to the people.

While I was here, there came a great woman of Beverley to speak to Justice Hotham about some business. And in discourse, she told him that the last Sabbath-day (as she called it) there came an angel or spirit into the church at Beverley, and spoke the wonderful things of God, to the astonishment of all that were there. And when it had done, it passed away, and they did not know whence it came, nor whither it went. But it astonished all, both priests, professors and magistrates of the town. This relation Justice Hotham gave me afterwards, and then I gave him an account how I had been that day at Beverley steeple-house, and had declared truth to the priest and the people there.

When the First-day of the week was come, Justice Hotham walked out with me into the field. And Captain Pursloe coming up after us, Justice Hotham left us and returned home; but Captain Pursloe went with me into the steeple-house. When the priest had done, I spoke both to priest and people; declared to them the word of life and truth, and directed them where they might find their teacher: the Lord Jesus Christ. Some were convinced, received the truth, and stand fast in it; and have a fine meeting to this day.

In the afternoon, I went to another steeple-house about three miles off, where preached a great high-priest, called a Doctor. I went into the steeple-house and stayed till the priest had done. The words which he took for his text were these: 'Ho, every one that thirsteth, come ye to the waters; and he that hath no money, come ye, buy and eat, yea come; buy wine and milk without money and without price'.

Then was I moved of the Lord to say unto him: 'Come down, thou deceiver! Dost thou bid people come freely and take of the water of life freely, and yet thou takest three hundred pounds a year of them, for preaching the Scriptures to them? Mayest thou not blush for shame? Did the prophet Isaiah and Christ do so, who spoke the words and gave them forth freely? Did not Christ say to His ministers, whom He sent to preach: "Freely ye have received, freely give"?'

The priest, like a man amazed, hastened away. After he had left his flock, I had as much time as I could desire to speak to the people. And I directed them from the darkness to the light, and to the grace of God, that would teach them and bring them salvation; to the Spirit of God in their inward parts, which would be a free teacher unto them.

Having cleared myself amongst the people, I returned to Justice Hotham's house that night, who, when I came in, took me in his arms and said his house was my house. For he was exceedingly glad at the work of the Lord and that His power was revealed. Then he told me why he went not with me to the steeple-house in the morning. For he thought if he had gone with me to the steeple-house, the officers would have put me to him. And then he should have been so put to it that he should not have known what to do.

A LIAR EXPOSED

From hence I passed on through the country, and came at night to an inn where was a company of rude people. I bid the woman of the house, if she had any meat, to bring me some. But because I said Thee and Thou to her she looked strangely on me. Then I asked her if she had any milk, and she said 'no'. I was sensible she spoke falsely, and being willing to try her further, I asked her if she had any cream. She denied that she had any. Now there stood a churn in the room, and a little boy playing about it put his hands into it, and pulled it down and threw all the cream on the floor before my eyes. Thus was the woman manifested to be a liar. She was amazed, and blessed herself, and taking up the child whipped it sorely. But I reproved her for her lying and deceit. After the Lord had thus discovered her deceit and perverseness, I walked out of the house, and went away till I came to a stack of hay, and lay in the hay-stack that night in rain and snow, it being but three days before the time called Christmas.

A CONFRONTATION WITH RANTERS

[The Ranters] sent word that they would have a dispute with me [at Staithes]. A day was fixed, and the [leader of the Ranters locally] came with his company. Philip Scafe, who had been a priest, and was convinced, was with me; and a great number of people met. When we were settled, the Ranter – whose name was T. Bushel – told me had had a vision of me: that I was sitting in a great chair, and that he was to come and put off his hat and bow down on the ground before me. And he did so. And many other flattering words he spoke. I told him it was his own figure, and said unto him: 'Repent, thou beast!'

He said it was jealousy in me to say so. Then I asked him the ground of jealousy and how it came to be bred in man; and the nature of a beast, what made it, and how it was bred in man. For I saw him directly in the nature of the beast; and therefore I wished to know of him how that nature came to be bred in him. I told him he should give me an account of the things done in the body, before we came to discourse of things done out of the body. So I stopped his mouth, and all his fellow Ranters were silenced.

I laid open the Ranters, ranking them with the old Ranters of Sodom. The priests I manifested to be of the same stamp with their fellow-hirelings, the false prophets of old; and the priests that then bore rule over the people by their means, seeking for their gain from their quarter, divining for money and teaching for filthy lucre.

I brought all the prophets and Christ and the apostles over the heads of the priests, showing how the prophets, Christ and the apostles had long since discovered them by their marks and fruits. Then I directed the people to their inward teacher, Christ Jesus their Saviour. And I preached up Christ in the hearts of His people, when all these mountains were laid low. The people were all quiet and the gainsayers' mouths were stopped. For though they broiled inwardly, yet the power bound them down, that they could not break out.

After the meeting, [a] Scotch priest desired me to walk with him on the top of the cliffs. Whereupon I called a brother-in-law of his, who was in some measure convinced, and desired him to go with me, telling him I desired to have somebody by to hear what was said, lest the priest, when I was gone, should report anything of me which I did not say. We went together, and as we walked, the priest asked me many things concerning the light and concerning the soul; to all which I answered fully.

When he had done questioning, we parted, and he went his way. And meeting with Philip Scafe, he broke his cane against the ground in madness, and said if ever he met with me again he would have my life, or I should have his, adding that he would give his head if I were not knocked down within a month. By this, Friends suspected that his intent was, in desiring me to walk with him alone, either to thrust me down from off the cliff, or to do me some other mischief. And that when he saw himself frustrated in that, by my having one with me, it made him rage. I feared neither his prophecies nor his threats; for I feared God Almighty.

FEAR STRIKES THE PRIESTS

Another priest sent to have a dispute with me, and Friends went with me to the house where he was. But when he understood we were come, he slipped out of the house and hid himself under a hedge. The people went to seek him, and found him, but could not get him to come to us.

Then I went to a steeple-house hard by, where the priest and people were in a great rage. This priest had threatened Friends what he would do. But when I came, he fled; for the Lord's power came over him and them. Yea, the Lord's everlasting power was over the world, and reached to the hearts of people, and made both priests and professors tremble. It shook the earthly and airy spirit, in which they held their profession of religion and worship, so that it was a dreadful thing unto them when it was told them: 'the man in leather breeches is come!'[14] At the hearing thereof, the priests in many places would get out of the way; they were so struck with the dread of the eternal power of God. And fear surprised the hypocrites.

GRATITUDE FROM JUSTICE HOTHAM

Now I came towards Cranswick, to Captain Pursloe's and Justice Hotham's, who received me kindly, being glad that the Lord's power had so appeared; that truth was spread and so many had received it. Justice Hotham said if God had not raised up this principle of light and life, which I preached, the nation had been overrun with Ranterism, and all the justices in the nation could not have stopped it with all their laws. Because (said he) they would have said as we said, and done as we commanded, and yet have kept their own principle still. But this principle of truth, said he, overthrows their principle, and the root and ground thereof.

And therefore he was glad the Lord had raised up this principle of life and truth.

UPROAR IN PATRINGTON

One day, I came towards night into a town called Patrington. And as I walked along the town, I warned both priest and people (for the priest was in the street) to repent and turn to the Lord. It grew dark before I came to the end of the town. And a multitude of people gathered about me, to whom I declared the word of life.

When I had cleared myself, I went to an inn and desired them to let me have a lodging, but they would not. Then I desired them to let me have a little meat or milk and I would pay them for it, but they would not. So I walked out of the town. After I had gone some distance, I came to another house, and desired the people to let me have a little meat and drink and lodging for my money; but they denied me. Then I went to another house and desired the same; but they refused me also. By this time it was grown so dark that I could not see the highway. But I discerned a ditch and got a little water and refreshed myself. Then I got over the ditch and, being weary with travelling, sat down among the furze-bushes till it was day.

About break of day, I got up and passed over the fields. A man came after me with a great pike-staff and went along with me to a town. And he raised the town upon me, with the constable and chief constable, before the sun was up. I declared God's everlasting truth amongst them, warning them of the day of the Lord that was coming upon all sin and wickedness; and exhorted them to repent. But they seized me and had me back to Patrington, about three miles, guarding me with pikes, staves and halberds.

Now when I was come back to Patrington, all the town was in an uproar, and the priest and people were consulting together. So I had another opportunity to declare the word of life amongst them, and warn them to repent. At last a professor, a tender man, called me into his house, and there I took a little milk and bread, not having eaten for some days before. Then they guarded me about nine miles to a justice. The men that guarded me said it was well if the justice were not drunk before we got to him, for he used to be drunk early.

When I was brought in before him, because I did not put off my hat, and said Thou to him, he asked whether I was not mazed or fond.[15] But [someone] told him no, it was my principle. Then I warned him to repent and come to the light, which Christ had enlightened him with, that by it he might see all his evil words and actions. 'Ay, ay,' said he, 'the light that is spoken of in the third [chapter] of John.' I desired him that he would mind it and obey it. As I admonished him, I laid my hand upon him and he was brought down by the power of the Lord. And all the watchmen stood amazed. Then he took me into a little parlour and desired to see what I had in my pockets, of letters or intelligence. I plucked out my linen, and showed him that I had no letters. He said: 'He is not a vagrant by his linen.' And then he set me at liberty.

SLANDER

[In 1652], when I came to Gainsborough, where a Friend had been declaring truth in the market, the town and the market-people were all in an uproar. I went into a friendly man's house, and the people rushed in after me. This false accuser came in and charged me openly before all the people, that I said I was Christ, and he had got witnesses to prove it. This set the people into such a rage that they had much to do to keep their hands off me. Then I was moved of the Lord God to stand up on the table and, in the eternal power of God, to tell the people that Christ was in them, except that they were reprobates. And that it was Christ the eternal power of God that spoke in me at that time unto them, not that I was Christ.

And the people were generally satisfied, except himself, a professor and his own false witness. I called the accuser Judas, and was moved to tell him that Judas's end would be his. And that that was the word of the Lord and of Christ, through me, to him. So the Lord's power came over all and quieted the minds of the people and they departed in peace. But this Judas went away and shortly after hanged himself, and a stake was driven into his grave.

Afterwards, the wicked priests raised a scandal upon us and reported that a Quaker had hanged himself in Lincolnshire, and had a stake driven through him. This falsehood they printed to the nation, adding sin to sin; which the truth and we were clear of, for he was no more a Quaker than the priest that printed it, but was one of their own people.

BLOODED WITH A BIBLE

I went to Tickhill, whither the Friends of that side gathered together, and in the meeting a mighty brokenness by the power of God was amongst the people. I went out of the meeting, being moved of God to go to the steeple-house. And when I came there, I found the priest and most of the chief of the parish together in the chancel. So I went up to them and began to speak. But they immediately fell upon me, and the clerk took up his Bible as I was speaking, and struck me on the face with it, so that it gushed out with blood, and I bled exceedingly in the steeple-house. Then the people cried: 'Let us have him out of the church!' And when they had got me out, they beat me exceedingly and threw me down, and over a hedge. And afterwards they dragged me through a house into the street, stoning and beating me as they drew me along, so that I was besmeared all over with blood and dirt. They got my hat from me, which I never obtained again. Yet when I was got upon my legs again, I declared to them the word of life, and showed them the fruits of their teacher and how they dishonoured Christianity.

After a while, I got into the meeting again amongst Friends; and the priest and people coming by the house, I went forth with Friends into the yard, and there I spoke unto the priest and people. The priest scoffed at us and called us Quakers. But the Lord's power was so over them, and the word of life was declared in such authority and dread to them, that the priest began trembling himself. And one of the people said: 'Look how the priest trembles and shakes! He is turned a Quaker also!'

When the meeting was over, Friends departed. And I went without my hat to Balby, about seven or eight miles. Friends were much abused that day by the priest and his people; insomuch that some moderate justices hearing of it, two or three of them came and sat at the town, to hear and examine the business. And he that had shed my blood was afraid of having his hand cut off, for striking me in the church (as they called it). But I forgave him, and would not appear against him.

THE VISION ON PENDLE HILL

As we travelled, we came near a very great hill, called Pendle Hill, and I was moved of the Lord to go up to the top of it; which I did with difficulty, it was so very steep and high. When I was come to the top, I saw the sea bordering upon Lancashire. From the top of this hill the Lord let me see in what places He had a great people to be gathered.

As I went down, I found a spring of water in the side of the hill, with which I refreshed myself, having eaten or drunk but little for several days before.

At night, we came to an inn and declared truth to the man of the house, and wrote a paper to the priests and professors, declaring the day of the Lord, and that Christ was come to teach people Himself, by His power and Spirit in their hearts, and to bring people off from all the world's ways and teachers, to His own free teaching, who had brought them and was the Saviour of all them that believed in Him. The man of the house spread the paper abroad and was mightily affected with the truth. Here the Lord opened unto me and let me see a great people in white raiment by a river side, coming to the Lord. And the place that I saw them it was about Wensleydale and Sedbergh.

I went to a meeting at Justice Benson's, where I met a people that were separated from the public worship. This was the place that I had seen, where a people came forth in white raiment. A large meeting it was, and the people were generally convinced and continue a large meeting still of Friends near Sedbergh; which was then first gathered through my ministry in the name of Jesus.

A MAN OF AUTHORITY

In the same week, there was a great fair, at which servants used to be hired. And I declared the day of the Lord through the fair. After I had done so, I went into the steeple-house yard and many of the people of the fair came thither to me and abundance of priests and professors. There I declared the everlasting truth of the Lord and the word of life for several hours. I exhorted the people to come off from the temples made with hands, and wait to receive the Spirit of the Lord, that they might know themselves to be the temples of God.

Not one of the priests had power to open his mouth against what I declared. But at last a captain said: 'Why will you not go into the church? This is not a fit place to preach in'. I told him I denied their church. Then stood up one Francis Howgill, who was a preacher to a congregation. He had not seen me before, yet he undertook to answer the captain and soon put him to silence.

Then said Francis Howgill of me: 'This man speaks with authority, and not as the scribes'.

The next First-day, I came to Firbank Chapel, in Westmoreland, where Francis Howgill had been preaching in the morning. The chapel was full of people, so that many could not get in. Francis Howgill said he thought I looked into the chapel and his spirit was ready to fail; the Lord's power did so surprise him. But I did not look in.

While the others were gone to dinner, I went to a brook and got a little water; and then came and sat down on the top of a rock hard by the chapel. In the afternoon, the people gathered about me, with several of their preachers. It was judged there were about a thousand people, amongst whom I declared God's everlasting truth and word of life freely and largely, for about the space of three hours, directing all to the Spirit of God in themselves, that they might be turned from darkness to the light, and believe in it, that they might become the children of it.

Now there were many old people, who went into the chapel and looked out at the windows, thinking it a strange thing to see a man preach on a hill, and not in their church, as they called it. Whereupon I was moved to open to the people that the steeple-house, and the ground whereon it stood, were no more holy than that mountain. I declared unto them that the Lord God had sent me to preach the everlasting gospel and word of life amongst them, and to bring them off from all these temples, tithes, priests and rudiments of the world, which had been instituted since the apostles' days, and had been set up by such as had erred from the Spirit and the power the apostles were in.

Very largely was I opened at this meeting, and the Lord's convincing power accompanied my ministry and reached the hearts of the people, whereby many were convinced. And all the teachers of that congregation (who were many) were convinced of God's everlasting truth.

COMPASSION, NOT WINGS

I went to Underbarrow, to one Miles Bateman's. At night the priest and many professors came to the house, and much disputing I had with them. Supper being provided for the priest and the rest of the company, I had not freedom to eat with them, but told them if they would appoint a meeting for the next day at the steeple-house, and acquaint the people with it, I might meet them. They had a great deal of reasoning about it, some being for it and some against it.

In the morning, I went out, after I had spoken again to them concerning the meeting. And as I walked upon a bank by the house, there were several poor people, travellers, asking relief, who I saw were in necessity. And they gave them nothing, but said they were cheats. It grieved me to see such hard-heartedness amongst professors. So, when they were gone in to their breakfast, I ran after the poor people about a quarter of a mile and gave them some money. Meanwhile, some of them that were in the house, coming out again and seeing me a quarter of a mile off, said I could not have gone so far in such an instant if I had not had wings. Hereupon the meeting was like to have been put by; for they were filled with such strange thoughts about me that many of them were against having a meeting with me.

I told them I ran after those poor people to give them some money, being grieved at their hard-heartedness, who gave them nothing. Then came Miles and Stephen Hubbersty, who, being more simple-hearted men, would have the meeting held. So to the chapel I went and the priest came. A great meeting there was, and the way of life and salvation was opened. And after a while, the priest fled away.

FIRST ENCOUNTER WITH MARGARET FELL

I went to Ulverstone, and so to Swarthmore to Judge Fell's, whither came up one Lampitt, a priest who was a high notionist. With him I had much reasoning; for he talked of high notions and perfection, and thereby deceived the people. He would have owned me, but I could not own nor join with him, he was so full of filth. He said he was above John, and made as though he knew all things. But I told him death reigned from Adam to Moses, that he was under death and knew not Moses, for Moses saw the paradise of God; but he knew neither Moses nor the prophets nor John. For that crooked and rough nature stood in him, and the mountain of sin and corruption; and the way was not prepared in him for the Lord. He confessed he had been under a cross in things, but now he could sing psalms and do anything. I told him now he could see a thief and join hand in hand with him, but he could not preach Moses, nor the prophets, nor John, nor Christ, except he were in the same spirit that they were in.

Margaret Fell had been absent in the day-time, and at night her children told her that priest Lampitt and I had disagreed, which somewhat troubled her, because she was in profession with him. But he hid his dirty actions from them. At night we had much reasoning, and I declared the truth to her and her family.

The next day Lampitt came again, and I had much discourse with him, before Margaret Fell, who then clearly discerned the priest. A convincement of the Lord's truth came upon her and her family. Soon after a day was to be observed for a humiliation, and Margaret Fell asked me to go with her to the steeple-house in Ulverstone, for she was not wholly come off from them. I replied: 'I must do as I am ordered by the Lord'. So I left her, and walked into the fields. And the word of the Lord came to me saying: 'Go to the steeple-house after them'.

When I came, Lampitt was singing with his people. But his spirit was so foul, and the matter they sung so unsuitable to their states, that after they had done singing I was moved of the Lord to speak to him and the people. The word of the Lord to them was: 'He is not a Jew that is one outwardly, but he is a Jew that is one inwardly, whose praise is not of man, but of God'. Then, as the Lord opened further, I showed them that God was come to teach His people by His Spirit, and to bring them off from their old ways, religions, churches and worships. For all their religions, worships and ways were but talking with other men's words; but they were out of the life and Spirit, which they were in who gave them forth.

Then cried out one, called Justice Sawrey: 'Take him away!' But Judge Fell's wife said to the officers: 'Let him alone. Why may he not speak as well as any other?' Lampitt also, the priest, in deceit said: 'Let him speak'. So at length, when I had declared some time, Justice Sawrey caused a constable to put me out. And then I spoke to the people in the grave-yard.

JUDGE FELL

I returned to Swarthmore. After I had stayed a few days, and most of the family were convinced, I went again into Westmoreland, where priest Lampitt had been amongst the professors on Kendal side, and had mightily incensed them against me, telling them I held many strange things. I met with those he had so incensed, and sat up all night with them, and answered their objections. They were both thoroughly satisfied with the truth that I had declared and dissatisfied with him and his lies, so that he clearly lost the best of his hearers and followers, who thus came to see his deceit and forsook him.

Soon after, Judge Fell being come home, Margaret Fell his wife sent for me, desiring me to return thither. And feeling freedom from the Lord to do so, I went back to Swarthmore. I found the priest and professors, and that envious Justice Sawrey, had much incensed Judge Fell and Captain Sands against the truth by their lies. But when I came to speak with him, I answered all his objections, and so thoroughly satisfied him by the Scriptures that he was convinced in his judgement. He asked me if I was that George Fox whom Justice Robinson spoke so much in commendation of amongst many of the parliament men. I told him I had been with Justice Robinson, and with Justice Hotham in Yorkshire, who were very civil and loving to me; and that they were convinced in their judgement by the Spirit of God, that the principle which I bore testimony to was the truth; and that they saw over and beyond the priests of the nation, so that they – and many others – were now come to be wiser than their teachers.

After we had discoursed some time together, Judge Fell himself was satisfied also, and came to see, by the openings of the Spirit of God in his heart, over all the priests and teachers of the world; and did not go to hear them for some years before he died. For he knew it was the truth I declared, and that Christ was the teacher of his people, and their Saviour.

[One day] came that envious justice John Sawrey. I told him his heart was rotten and he was full of hypocrisy to the brim. Several other people also came, whose states the Lord gave me a discerning of; and I spoke to their condition. While I was in these parts, Richard Farnsworth[16] and James Nayler[17] came to see me and the family. And Judge Fell, being satisfied that it was the way of truth, notwithstanding all their opposition, suffered the meeting to be kept at this house. And a great meeting was settled there in the Lord's power, which continued near forty years, until the year 1690, that a new meeting-house was erected near it.

CONFOUNDING THE PRIESTS

I heard of a great meeting the priests were to have at Ulverstone, on a lecture-day. I went to it and into the steeple-house in the dread and power of the Lord. When the priest had done, I spoke among them the word of the Lord, which was as a hammer, and as a fire amongst them. And though Lampitt, the priest of the place, had been at variance with most of the priests before, yet against the truth they all joined together. But the almighty power of the Lord was over all. And so wonderful was the appearance thereof that priest Bennett said the church shook, insomuch that he was afraid and trembled. And when he had spoken a few confused words, he hastened out, for fear it should fall on his head. Many priests got together there; but they had not power as yet to persecute.

When I had cleared my conscience towards them, I went up to Swarthmore again, whither came four or five of the priests. Coming to discourse, I asked them whether any of them could say he ever had the word of the Lord to go and speak to such or such a people. None of them durst say he had. But one of them burst out into a passion, and said he could speak his experience as well as I. I told him experience was one thing, but to receive and go with a message, and to have a word from the Lord, as the prophets and apostles had and did, and as I had done to them, this was another thing. Then I told them the false prophets, the false apostles and antichrists could use the words of the true prophets, the true apostles and of Christ, and would speak of other men's experiences, though they themselves never knew or heard the voice of God or Christ; and such as they might obtain the good words and experiences of others. This puzzled them much, and laid them open.

[Such occasions] very much confirmed Judge Fell in the persuasion he had that the priests were wrong. For he had thought formerly, as the generality of the people then did, that they were sent from God.

PERSECUTION AND MINISTRY

Now began the priests to rage more and more, and as much as they could to stir up persecution. James Nayler and Francis Howgill were cast into prison in Appleby jail, at the instigation of the malicious priests; some of whom prophesied that within a month we should all be scattered again and come to nothing.

But blessed for ever be the worthy name of the Lord, the work of the Lord went on and prospered. For about this time, John Audland, Francis Howgill, Richard Hubberthorn, Miles Hubbersty and several others, being endued with power from on high, came forth in the work of the ministry, and approved themselves faithful labourers therein, travelling up and down, and preaching the gospel freely; by means whereof multitudes were convinced and many effectually turned to the Lord.

A RIOT IN ULVERSTONE

Now when meetings were set up and we met in private houses, Lampitt the priest began to rage. And he said we forsook the temple and went to Jeroboam's calves' houses.

After this, on a lecture-day, I was moved to go to the steeple-house at Ulverstone, where were abundance of professors, priests and people. I went up near to priest Lampitt, who was blustering on in his preaching. And after the Lord had opened my mouth to speak, John Sawrey the justice came to me and said if I would speak according to the Scriptures, I should speak. I wondered at his speaking so to me, for I did speak according to the Scriptures. And I told him I should speak according to the Scriptures and bring the Scriptures to prove what I had to say; for I had something to speak to Lampitt and to them. Then he said I should not speak, contradicting himself.

The people were quiet and heard me gladly, until this Justice

Sawrey (who was the first stirrer-up of cruel persecution in the North) incensed them against me, and set them on to hale, beat and bruise me. Suddenly, the people were in a rage, and fell upon me in the steeple-house before his face; knocked me down, kicked me and trampled on me. And so great was the uproar that some tumbled over their seats for fear.

At last he came and took me from the people, led me out of the steeple-house and put me into the hands of the constables and other officers, bidding them whip me and put me out of the town. They led me about a quarter of a mile, some taking hold of my collar, and some by my arms and shoulders, and shook and dragged me along. Many friendly people being come to the market, and some of them to the steeple-house to hear me, divers of these they knocked down also, and broke their heads, so that the blood ran down from several of them. And Judge Fell's son running after, to see what they would do with me, they threw him into a ditch of water, some of them crying: 'Knock the teeth out of his head!'

Now when they had haled me to the common moss-side, a multitude of people following, the constables and other officers gave me some blows over my back with their willow-rods, and so thrust me among the rude multitude who, having furnished themselves, some with staves, some with hedge-stakes, and others with holm or holly-bushes, fell upon me and beat me on my head, arms and shoulders, till they had deprived me of sense, so that I fell down upon the wet common.

When I recovered again and saw myself lying in a watery common, and the people standing about me, I lay still a little while. And the power of the Lord sprang through me, and the Eternal Refreshings refreshed me, so that I stood up again in the strengthening power of the Eternal God. And stretching out my arms amongst them, I said with a loud voice: 'Strike again! Here are my arms, my head and my cheeks'.

There was in the company a mason, a professor, but a rude fellow. He with his walking rule-staff gave me a blow with all his might, just over the back of my hand, as it was stretched out; with which blow my hand was so bruised and my arm so benumbed that I could not draw it unto me again. So that some of the people cried out: 'he hath spoiled his hand for ever having use of it any more'. But I looked at it in the love of God (for I was in the love of God to them all, that had persecuted me). And after a while the Lord's power sprang through me again, and through my hand and arm, so that in a moment I recovered strength in my hand and arm, in the sight of them all. Then they began to fall out among themselves, and some of them came to me and said if I would give them money, they would secure me from the rest. But I was moved of the Lord to declare to them the word of life, and showed them their false Christianity, and the fruits of the priest's ministry, telling them they were more like heathens and Jews than true Christians.

Then I was moved of the Lord to come up again through the midst of the people and go into Ulverstone market. As I went, there met me a soldier, with his sword by his side. 'Sir,' he said to me, 'I see you are a man, and I am ashamed and grieved that you should be thus abused.' And he offered to assist me in what he could. But I told him the Lord's power was over all. So I walked through the people in the market and none of them had power to touch me then. But some of the market-people abusing some Friends in the market, I turned about and saw this soldier among them with his naked rapier, whereupon I ran in amongst them, and catching hold of his hand that his rapier was in, I bid him put up his sword again, if he would go along with me; for I was willing to draw him out from the company, lest some mischief should be done.

A few days after, seven men fell upon this soldier and beat him cruelly, because he had taken part with Friends and me. For it was the manner of the persecutors of that country for twenty or forty people to run upon one man. And they fell so upon Friends in many places, that they could hardly pass the highways; stoning, beating and breaking their heads.

When I came to Swarthmore, I found the friends there dressing the heads and hands of Friends and friendly people, which had been broken or hurt that day by the professors and hearers of Lampitt, the priest. My body and arms were yellow, black and blue with the blows and bruises I received amongst them that day. Now began the priests to prophesy again that within half a year we should be all put down and gone.

A LIFE PRESERVED BY THE LORD

About two weeks after this I went into Walney Island, and James Nayler went with me. We stayed one night at a little town on this side, called Cockan. After a while there came a man with a pistol, whereupon the people ran out of doors. He called for me, and when I came out to him, he snapped his pistol at me, but it would not go off. This caused the people to make a great bustle about him. And some of them took hold of him, to prevent his doing mischief. But I was moved in the Lord's power to speak to him. And he was so struck by the power of the Lord that he trembled for fear, and went and hid himself.

Next morning I went over in a boat to James Lancaster's. As soon as I came to land, there rushed out about forty men with staves, clubs and fishing poles, who fell upon me, beating and punching me, and endeavouring to thrust me backward into the sea. When they had thrust me almost into the sea, and I saw they would have knocked me down in it, I went up into the midst of them. But they laid at me again and knocked me down and stunned me.

When I came to myself, I looked up and saw James Lancaster's wife throwing stones at my face, and her husband, James Lancaster, was lying over me, to keep the blows and the stones off me. For the people had persuaded James Lancaster's wife that I had bewitched her husband; and had promised her that if she would let them know when I came hither, they would be my death.

And having got knowledge of my coming, many of the town rose up in this manner with clubs and staves to kill me. But the Lord's power preserved me, that they could not take away my life.

At length I got up on my feet, and they beat me down again into the boat; which James Lancaster observing, he presently came into it and set me over the water from them. But while we were on the water within their reach, they struck at us with long poles and threw stones after us. But the time we were come to the other side, we saw them beating James Nayler. For whilst they had been beating me, he walked up into a field and they never minded him until I was gone. Then they fell upon him, and all their cry was: 'Kill him! Kill him!'

When I was come over to the town again, on the other side of the water, the townsmen rose up with pitchforks and staves, to keep me out of the town, crying: 'Kill him, knock him on the head, bring the cart and carry him away to the churchyard!' So after they had abused me, they drove me some distance out of the town, and there left me.

Then went James Lancaster back to look after James Nayler. And I being now left alone, went to a ditch of water, and having washed myself (for they had besmeared my face, hands and clothes with miry dirt), I walked about three miles to Thomas Hutton's house. When I came in, I could hardly speak to them, I was so bruised. Only I told them where I left James Nayler. So they took each of them a horse and went and brought him thither that night.

The next day, Margaret Fell, hearing of it, sent a horse for me. But so sore I was with bruises I was not able to bear the shaking of the horse without much pain. When I was come to Swarthmore, Justice Sawrey and one Justice Thompson of Lancaster granted a warrant against me. But Judge Fell coming home, it was not served upon me. For he was out of the country all this time, that I was thus cruelly abused. When he came home, he sent forth warrants into the Isle of Walney, to apprehend all those riotous persons, whereupon some of them fled the country.

James Lancaster's wife was afterwards convinced of the truth, and repented of the evils she had done me. And so did others of those bitter persecutors also. But the judgements of God fell upon some of them, and destruction is come upon many of them since.

Judge Fell asked me to give him a relation of my persecution. But I told him they could do no otherwise in the spirit wherein they were, and that they manifested the fruits of their priest's ministry. So he told his wife I made light of it, and that I spoke of it as a man that had not been concerned. For indeed, the Lord's power healed me again.

AT LANCASTER SESSIONS

The time for the sessions at Lancaster being come, I went thither with Judge Fell, who on the way told me he had never had such a matter brought before him before, and he could not tell what to do in the business. I told him, when Paul was brought before the rulers, and the Jews and priests came down to accuse him, and laid many false things to his charge, Paul stood still at that while. And when they had done, Festus, the governor, and King Agrippa beckoned him to speak for himself; which Paul did, and cleared himself of all those false accusations. So he might do with me.

Being come to Lancaster, Justice Sawrey and Justice Thompson having granted a warrant to apprehend me – though I was not apprehended by it, yet hearing of it – I appeared at the sessions; where there appeared against me about forty persons. These had chosen one Marshall, priest of Lancaster, to be their orator. And had provided one young priest and two priests' sons to bear witness against me, who had sworn beforehand that I had spoken blasphemy.

When the justices were sat, they heard all that the priests and their witnesses could say and charge against me; their orator Marshall sitting by, and explaining their sayings for them. But the witnesses were so confounded that they discovered themselves to be false witnesses. For when the court had examined one of them upon oath, and then began to examine another, he was at such loss he could not answer directly, but said the other could say it. Which made the justices say to him: 'have you sworn it and given it in already upon your oath, and now say that he can say it? It seems you did not hear those words spoken yourself, though you have sworn it.'

There were then in court several people who had been at that meeting, wherein the witnesses swore I spoke those blasphemous words, which the priests accused me of. And these being men of integrity and reputation in the country, declared and affirmed in court that the oath, which the witnesses had taken against me, was altogether false. And that no such words as they had sworn against me were spoken by me at that meeting.

This was taken notice of by Colonel West who, being a justice of the peace, was then upon the bench. And having long been weak in body, blessed the Lord, and said the Lord had healed him that day; adding that he never saw so many sober people and good faces together in all his life. And then, turning himself to me, he said in the open sessions: 'George, if thou hast anything to say to the people thou mayst freely declare it'.

I was moved of the Lord to speak. And as soon as I began, priest Marshall, the orator for the rest of the priests, went away. That which I was moved to declare was this: that the Holy Scriptures were given forth by the Spirit of God and all people must first come to the Spirit of God in themselves, by which they might know God and Christ, of whom the prophets and the apostles learnt; and by the same Spirit know the Holy Scriptures. For as the Spirit of God was in them that gave forth the Scriptures, so the same Spirit of God must be in all them that come to understand the Scriptures; by which Spirit they might have fellowship with the Son and with the Father, and with the Scriptures, and with one another. And without this Spirit they can know neither God nor Christ, nor the Scriptures, nor have right fellowship one with another.

I had no sooner spoken these words than about half a dozen priests that stood behind me burst into a passion. And one of them, named Jackus, amongst other things that he spake against the truth, said that the Spirit and the letter were inseparable. I replied: 'then every one that hath the letter hath the Spirit, and they might buy the Spirit with the letter of the Scriptures'.

This plain discovery of darkness in the priest moved Judge Fell and Colonel West to reprove them openly, and tell them that according to that position they might carry the Spirit in their pockets, as they did the Scriptures. Upon this the priests, being confounded and put to silence, rushed out in a rage against the justices, because they could not have their bloody ends upon me. The justices, seeing the witnesses did not agree, and perceiving that they were brought to answer the priests' envy, and finding that all their evidences were not sufficient in law to make good their charge against me, discharged me.

And after Judge Fell had spoken to Justice Sawrey and Justice Thompson concerning the warrant they had given forth against me, and showed them the errors thereof, he and Colonel West granted a supersedeas to stop the execution of it. Thus was I cleared of all those lying accusations which the malicious priests had laid to my charge. And multitudes of people praised God that day, for it was a joyful day to many. Several friendly people and professors reproved the priests in their inns and in the streets, so that they fell, like an old rotten house. And the cry was among the people that the Quakers had got the day, and the priests were fallen.

ACCUSED OF WITCHCRAFT

I went to visit Justice West, Richard Hubberthorn accompanying me. Not knowing the way, or the danger of the sands, we rode where – as we were afterwards told – no man ever rode before, swimming our horses over a very dangerous place. When we were come in, Justice West asked us if we did not see two men riding over the sands. 'I shall have their clothes anon,' said he, 'for they cannot escape drowning, and I am the coroner.'

But when we told him that we were the men, he was astonished, and wondered how we escaped drowning. Upon this the envious priests and professors raised a slanderous report concerning me, that neither water could drown me, nor could they draw blood of me; and that therefore surely I was a witch. Indeed, sometimes when they beat me with great staves, they did not much draw my blood, though they bruised my body oftimes very sorely. But all these slanders were nothing to me with respect to myself, though I was concerned on the truth's behalf, which I saw they endeavoured by these means to prejudice people against. But the Lord's power carried me above their slanderous tongues, and their bloody murderous spirits; who had the ground of witchcraft in themselves, which kept them from coming to God and to Christ.

THE END OF JUSTICE SAWREY

I was moved to write several letters to the magistrates, priests and professors thereabouts, who had raised persecution before. That which I sent to Justice Sawrey was after this manner:

Friend,
Thou wast the first beginner of all the persecution in the North. Thou wast the beginner and the maker of the people tumultuous. Thou wast the first stirrer of them up against the righteous seed, and against the truth of God; the first strengthener of the hands of evil-doers against the innocent and harmless. And thou shalt not prosper.

Instead of stirring up the pure mind in people, thou hast

stirred up the wicked, malicious and envious, and taken hand with the wicked. Thou hast made the people's minds envious up and down the country. This was thy work. But God hath shortened thy days, and limited thee; hath set thy bounds and broken thy jaw. How is thy habitation fallen, and become the habitation of devils! How is thy beauty lost, and thy glory withered! View thy ways and take notice with whom thou hast taken part. That of God in thy conscience will tell thee; the Ancient of days will reprove thee. How like a madman and blind man didst thou turn thy sword backward against the saints, against whom there is no law! How wilt thou be gnawed and burned one day, when thou shalt feel the flame and have the plagues of God poured upon thee, and thou begin to gnaw thy tongue for pain, because of the plagues!

Thou canst not escape. The Lord's righteous judgement will find thee out. How hast thou caused the heathen to blaspheme, gone on with the multitude to do evil, and joined hand in hand with the wicked! How is thy latter end worse than thy beginning, who art come with the dog to bite and art turned as a wolf, to devour the lambs!

Thy ill savour, John Sawrey, the country about have smelled, and of thy unchristian carriage all that fear God have been ashamed. And to them, thou hast been a grief; in the day of account thou shalt know it, even in the day of thy condemnation. Thou wast mounted up, and hadst set thy nest on high, but never gottest higher than the fowls in the air. Now thou art run amongst the beast of prey, and art fallen into the earth, so that earthliness and covetousness have swallowed thee up.

Thy conceitedness would not carry thee through, in whom was found the selfish principle, which hath blinded thy eye. Thy back must be bowed down always; for thy table is already become thy snare. G.F.

This Justice Sawrey, who was the first persecutor in that country, was afterwards drowned.

A PROPHECY

It was now about the beginning of the year 1653, when I returned to Swarthmore. Great openings I had from the Lord, not only of divine and spiritual matters, but also of outward things, relating to the civil government. For being one day in Swarthmore Hall, when Judge Fell and Justice Benson were talking of the news, and of the parliament then sitting – which was called the Long Parliament – I was moved to tell them that before that day two weeks the Parliament should be broken up, and the Speaker plucked out of his chair. And that day two weeks Justice Benson, coming thither again, told Judge Fell that now he saw George was a true prophet: for Oliver [Cromwell] had broken up the parliament.

THE HEALER

I went to a meeting at Arnside, where Richard Meyer was, who had been long lame of one of his arms. I was moved of the Lord to say unto him, amongst all the people: 'Stand up on thy legs' (for he was sitting down). And he stood up and stretched out his arm that had been lame a long time and said: 'Be it known unto you, all people, that this day I am healed'. Yet his parents could hardly believe it. But after the meeting, they had him aside, took off his doublet and then saw it was true.

He came soon after to Swarthmore meeting, and then declared how the Lord had healed him. Yet after this the Lord commanded him to go to York with a message from Him, but he disobeyed the Lord. And the Lord struck him again, so that he died about three-quarters of a year after.

AMONG THE SOLDIERS AT CARLISLE

We came to Carlisle, and the pastor of the Baptists, with most of his hearers, came to me to the abbey, where I had a meeting and declared the word of life amongst them. And many of the Baptists and of the soldiers were convinced. After the meeting, the pastor of the Baptists – a high notionist and a flashy man – came to see me and asked me what must be damned. I was moved immediately to tell him that which spoke in him was to be damned. This stopped his mouth. And the witness of God was raised up in him.

Then I went up to the castle among the soldiers, who beat a drum and called the garrison together. I preached the truth amongst them, directing them to the Lord Jesus Christ to be their teacher, and to the measure of His Spirit in themselves, by which they might be turned from the darkness to the light, and from the power of Satan unto God. I warned them all that they should do no violence to any man, but should show forth a Christian life; telling them that He who was to be their teacher would be their condemner, if they were disobedient to Him. So I left them having no opposition from any of them except the sergeants, who afterwards came to be convinced.

On the market-day I went up into the market, to the market-cross. Now the magistrates had both threatened and sent their sergeants. And the magistrates' wives had said that if I came there, they would pluck the hair off my head; and that the sergeants should take me up. Nevertheless, I obeyed the Lord God and went upon the Cross, and there declared unto them that the day of the Lord was coming upon all their deceitful ways and doings, and deceitful merchandize. And that they should put away all cozening and cheating, and keep to yea and nay, and speak the truth one to another. So the truth and power of God was set over them.

After I had declared the word of life to the people, the throng became so great that the sergeants could not get to me, nor the magistrates' wives come at me. I passed away quietly. Many people and soldiers came to me, and some Baptists that were bitter contenders; amongst whom one of their deacons, being an envious man, and finding the Lord's power was over them, cried out from very anger. Whereupon I set my eyes upon him, and spoke sharply to him in the power of the Lord. And he cried: 'Do not pierce me so with thy eyes! Keep thy eyes off me!'

On the First-day following, I went into the steeple-house; and after the priest had done, I preached the truth to the people and declared the word of life amongst them. The priest got away, and the magistrates desired me to go out of the steeple-house. But I still declared the way of the Lord unto them, and told them I came to speak the word of life and salvation amongst them. The power of the Lord was dreadful amongst them in the steeple-house.

The magistrates' wives were in a rage and strove mightily to be at me. But the soldiers and friendly people stood thick about me. At length the rude people of the city rose, and came with staves and stones into the steeple-house, crying: 'Down with these round-headed rogues!' And they threw stones. Whereupon the Governor sent a file or two of musketeers into the steeple-house to appease the tumult, and commanded all the other soldiers out. So those soldiers took me by the hand in a friendly manner, and said they would have me along with them.

When we came forth into the street, the city was in an uproar, and the governor came down. And some of those soldiers were put in prison for standing by me, and for me, against the town's-people. A lieutenant, that had been convinced, came and brought me to his house, where there was a Baptists' meeting, and thither came Friends also, and we had a very quiet meeting. They heard the word of life gladly and many received it.

The next day, the justices and magistrates being gathered in the town hall, they granted a warrant against me, and sent for me to come before them. I went up to the hall to them, where many rude people were, some of whom had sworn strange, false things against me. I had much discourse with the magistrates, wherein I laid open the fruits of their priests' preaching, and showed them how void they were of Christianity. And that, though they were such great professors (for they were Independents and Presbyterians), they were without the possession of that which they professed. After a large examination they committed me to prison as a blasphemer, a heretic and a seducer; though they could not justly charge any such thing against me.

CARLISLE JAIL

The jail at Carlisle had two jailers, an upper and an under, who looked like two great bear-wards. Now when I was brought in, the upper jailer had me up into a great chamber, and told me I should have what I would in that room. But I told him he should not expect any money from me, for I would neither lie in any of his beds nor eat any of his victuals. Then he put me into another room, where, after a while, I got something to lie upon. There I lay till the assizes came; and then all the talk was that I was to be hanged. The high sheriff, whose name was William Lawson, stirred them much up to take away my life, and said he would guard me to my execution himself. They were in a great rage, and set three musketeers for a guard upon me: one at my chamber door, another at the stairs' foot, and a third at the street door. And they would let none come at me, except one sometimes, to bring me some necessary things.

At night, they would bring up priests to me, sometimes as late as the tenth hour, who were exceedingly rude and devilish. There was a company of bitter Scotch priests, Presbyterians, made up of envy and malice, who were not fit to speak of the things of God, they were so foul-mouthed. But the Lord, by His power, gave me dominion over them all, and I let them see both their fruits and their spirits. Great ladies also (as they were called) came to see the man that they said was to die.

Now, while both the judge, justices and sheriff were contriving together how they might put me to death, the Lord disappointed their design by an unexpected way. For the judge's clerk (as I was informed) started a question among them, which confounded all their counsels; so that after that they had not power to call me before the judge.

The judges, reviling and scoffing at me behind my back, left me to the magistrates of the town, giving them what encouragement they could to exercise their cruelty upon me. Whereupon an order was sent to the jailer to put me down into the dungeon among the moss-troopers,[18] thieves and murderers, which accordingly he did. A filthy, nasty place it was, where men and women were put together in a very uncivil manner, and not even a house of convenience to it; and the prisoners so lousy that one woman was almost eaten to death with lice. Yet, as bad as the place was, the prisoners were all very loving and subject to me. And some of them were convinced of the truth, as the publicans and harlots of old, so that they were able to confound any priest that might come to the grates to dispute.

But the jailer was very cruel and the under-jailer very abusive to me, and to Friends that came to see me. For he would beat Friends with a great cudgel, that did but come to the window to look in upon me. I could get up to the grate, where sometimes I took in my meat, at which the jailer was often offended. One time, he came in a great rage and beat me with a great cudgel, though I was not at the grate at that time. And as he beat me, he cried: 'Come out of the window!', though I was then far enough from it. While he struck me, I was made to sing in the Lord's power. And that made him rage the more. Then he fetched a fiddler, and brought him in where I was and set him to play, thinking to vex me thereby. But while he played, I was moved in the everlasting power of the Lord God to sing. And my voice drowned the noise of the fiddle, and struck and confounded them, and made them give over fiddling and go their way.

JAMES PARNELL

Whilst I was in the dungeon at Carlisle, James Parnell, a little lad of about sixteen years of age, came to see me and was convinced. And the Lord quickly made him a powerful minister of the word of life. And many were turned to Christ by him, though he lived not long. For travelling into Essex, in the work of the ministry, in the year 1655, he was committed to Colchester Castle, where he endured very great hardships and sufferings; being put by the cruel jailer into a hole in the castle wall, called the oven, so high from the ground that he went up to it by a ladder which, being six feet too short, he was obliged to climb from the ladder to the hole by a rope that was fastened above.

And when Friends would have given him a cord and a basket, to draw up his victuals in, the inhuman jailer would not suffer them, but forced him to go down and up by that short ladder and rope, to fetch his victuals (which for a long time he did), or else he might have famished in the hole. At length, his limbs being much benumbed with lying in that place, yet being constrained to go down to take up some victuals, as he came up the ladder again with his victuals in one hand, and caught the rope with the other, he missed the rope and fell down from a very great height upon the stones. By which fall he was exceedingly wounded in his head and arms, and his body was so much bruised that he died a short time after.

When he was dead, the wicked professors, to cover their own cruelty, wrote a book of him, and said he fasted himself to death; which was an abominable falsehood, and was manifested so to be by another book, which was written in answer to that, and was called 'The Lamb's Defence against Lies'.

INTERCESSION

While I lay in the dungeon at Carlisle, the report raised at the time of the assize that I should be put to death was gone far and near; insomuch that the parliament then sitting (which, I think, was called the Little Parliament), hearing that a young man at Carlisle was to die for religion, caused a letter to be sent to the sheriff and magistrates concerning me.

Gervase Benson and Anthony Pearson, though they had been justices of the peace, were not permitted to come to me in prison. Whereupon they jointly wrote a letter to the magistrates, priests and people at Carlisle, concerning my imprisonment, which was thus:-

Him, who is called George Fox, who is persecuted by rulers and magistrates, by justices, by priests and by people, and who suffers imprisonment of his body at this present, as a blasphemer and a heretic, and a seducer, him do we witness, who in measure are made partakers of the same life that lives in him, to be a minister of the eternal World of God, by whom the everlasting gospel is preached; by the powerful preaching whereof the eternal Father of the saints hath opened the blind eyes, hath unstopped the deaf ears, hath let the oppressed go free, and hath raised up the dead out of the graves.

Because he lives up out of the fall, and testifies against the works of the world, that the deeds thereof are evil, he suffers by you magistrates; not as an evil-doer. For thus it was ever, where the seed of God is kept in prison under the cursed nature, that nature sought to imprison them in whom it was raised. The Lord will make him to you as a burdensome stone. For the sword of the spirit of the Almighty is put into the hands of the saints, which shall wound all the wicked, and shall not be put up till it hath cut down all corrupt judges, justices, magistrates, priests and professors. Therefore fear the Lord God Almighty, ye judges, justices, commanders, priests and people. Ye that forget God, suddenly will the Lord come and destroy you with utter destruction, and will sweep your names out of the earth, and will restore His people's judges, as at the first, and counsellors, as at the beginning.

We are not suffered to see our friend in prison, whom we witness to be a messenger of the living God. Now, all people, consider whether this be according to law, or from the wicked, perverse, envious will of the envious rulers and magistrates, who are of the same generation that persecuted Jesus Christ. For, said He: 'as they have done to me, so will they do to you'.

Now are your hearts made manifest to be full of envy against the living truth of God, which is made manifest in His people, who are condemned and despised of the world, and scornfully called Quakers. You are worse than the heathens, that put Paul in prison, for none of his friends or acquaintances were hindered to come to him by them; therefore they shall be witnesses against you. Ye are made manifest to the saints to be of the same generation that put Christ to death, and that put the apostles in prison on the same pretence that you act under, in calling truth error, and the ministers of God blasphemers, as they did. But the day is dreadful and terrible that shall come upon you, ye evil magistrates, priests and people, who profess the truth in words outwardly, and yet persecute the power of truth and them that stand in and for the truth. While ye have time prize it, and remember what is written, Isa. liv. 17.[19]

Not long after this, the Lord's power came over the justices and they were made to set me at liberty. But some time previous, the governor and Anthony Pearson came down into the dungeon, to see the place where I was kept and understand what usage I had. They found the place so bad, and the savour so ill, that they cried shame on the magistrates for suffering the jailer to do such things. They called for the jailers into the dungeon, and required them to find sureties for their good behaviour. And the under-jailer, who had been such a cruel fellow, they put into the dungeon with me, among the moss-troopers.

ON PERFECTION

After I was set at liberty, I went into the country and had mighty great meetings. The everlasting gospel and word of life flourished, and thousands were turned to the Lord Jesus Christ, and to His teaching.

In Northumberland, many came to dispute, of whom some pleaded against perfection; unto whom I declared that Adam and Eve were perfect before they fell. And all that God made was perfect. And that the imperfection came by the Devil, and the fall. But Christ, that came to destroy the Devil, said: 'Be ye perfect!'. One of the professors alleged that Job said: 'Shall mortal man be more pure than his Maker? The heavens are not clean in His sight. God charged His angels with folly'. But I showed him his mistake and let him see that it was not Job that said so, but one of those that contended against Job. For Job stood for perfection, and held his integrity; and they were called miserable comforters.

Then these professors said the outward body was the body of death and sin. I showed them their mistake in that also, for Adam and Eve had each of them an outward body, before the body of death and sin got into them: and that man and woman will have bodies, when the body of sin and death is put off again; when they are renewed up into the image of God again by Christ Jesus, which they were in before they fell. So they ceased at that time from opposing further. And glorious meetings we had in the Lord's power.

A SILENT MEETING

We came through the country into Cumberland, where we had a general meeting of many thousands of people at the top of a hill near Langlands. A glorious and heavenly meeting it was, for the glory of the Lord did shine over all. And there were as many as one could well speak over, the multitude was so great. Their eyes were fixed on Christ their teacher, and they came to sit under their own vine; insomuch that Francis Howgill, coming afterwards to visit them, found they had no need of words. For they were sitting under their teacher Christ Jesus; in the sense whereof, he sat down amongst them, without speaking anything.

FRIENDS MULTIPLY AND PROSPER

About this time [1653], the priests and professors fell to prophesying against us afresh. They had said long before that we should be destroyed within a month; and after that, they prolonged the time to half a year. But that time being long expired, and we mightily increased in number, they now gave forth that we would eat out one another. For often after meetings, many tender people having a great way to go, tarried at Friends' houses by the way, and sometimes more than there were beds to lodge in; so that some have lain on the hay-mows.

Hereupon Cain's fear possessed the professors and world's people. For they were afraid that when we had eaten one another out, we would all come to be maintained by the parishes and be chargeable to them. But after a while, when they saw that the Lord blessed and increased Friends, as He did Abraham, both in the field and in the basket, at their goings forth and comings in, at their risings up and lyings down, and that all things prospered with them, then they saw the falseness of all their prophesies against us. And that it was vain to curse where God had blessed.

At the first convincement, when Friends could not put off their hats to people, or say 'you' to a single person, but 'thou' and 'thee'; when they could not bow, or use flattering words in salutations, or adopt the fashions and customs of the world, many Friends that were tradesmen of several sorts lost their customers. For the people were shy of them and would not trade with them, so that for a time some Friends could hardly get money enough to buy bread. But afterwards, when people came to have experience of Friends' honesty and faithfulness, and found that their yea was yea, and their nay was nay; that they kept to a word in their dealings, and that they would not cozen and cheat them; that if they sent a child to their shops for anything, they were as well used as if they had come themselves; the lives and conversations of Friends did preach, and reached to the witness of God in the people.

Then things altered so that all the inquiry was: 'where is there a draper, or shopkeeper, or tailor or shoemaker, or any other tradesman that is a Quaker?' Insomuch that Friends had more trade than many of their neighbours, and if there was any trading, they had a great part of it. Then the envious professors altered their note and began to cry out: 'if we let these Quakers alone, they will take the trade of all the nation out of our hands'.

This has been the Lord's doing to and for His people!

OBEDIENCE TO THE TRUTH

About this time the oath or engagement to Oliver Cromwell was tendered to the soldiers, many of whom were disbanded because, in obedience to Christ, they could not swear. John Stubbs was one, who was convinced when I was in Carlisle prison and became a good soldier in the Lamb's war, and a faithful minister of Christ Jesus, travelling much in the service of the Lord in Holland, Ireland, Scotland, Italy, Egypt and America. And the Lord's power preserved him out of the hands of the Papists, though many times he was in great danger of the Inquisition.

But some of the soldiers who had been convinced, but had not come into obedience to the truth, took Cromwell's oath; and going afterwards into Scotland, and coming before a garrison there, the garrison thinking they had been enemies, fired at them and killed many of them; which was a sad judgement.

THE VALIANT SIXTY

About this time did the Lord move upon the spirits of many whom He had raised up and sent forth to labour in His vineyard, to travel southwards and spread themselves, in the service of the gospel, to the eastern, southern and western parts of the nation: as Francis Howgill and Edward Burrough to London, John Camm and John Audland to Bristol, Richard Hubberthorn and George Whitehead towards Norwich, Thomas Holmes into Wales and others different ways. For above sixty ministers had the Lord raised up and now sent abroad out of the North country.

The sense of their service being very weighty upon me, I was moved to give forth to Friends in the Ministry: 'All Friends that are turned to the Light, which cometh from Him by whom the world was made, who was before it was made Christ Jesus, the Saviour of your Souls: abide in the light and you will see your salvation to be walls and bulwarks against that which the light discovers to be contrary to it. Waiting in the light, you will receive the power of God, which is the gospel of peace. That you may be shod with it, and know that in one another which raiseth up the seed of God, sets it over the world and the earth and crucifies the affections and lusts. Then the truth comes to reign, which is the girdle.'

DISCOURSE ON HOME GROUND

[In 1654] I went to Drayton in Leicestershire, to visit my relations. As soon as I was come in, Nathaniel Stephens the priest, having got another priest and given notice to the country, sent to me to come to them, as they could not do anything till I came. Having been three years away from my relations, I knew nothing of their design. But at last I went into the steeple-house yard, where the two priests were. And they had gathered abundance of people. When I came there, they would have me go into the steeple-house. I asked them what I should do there. And they said Mr Stephens could not bear the cold. I told them he might bear the cold as well as I.

At last we went into a great hall, Richard Farnsworth being with me. And a great dispute we had with these priests concerning their practices, how contrary they were to Christ and His apostles. The priests would know whether tithes were forbidden or ended. I showed them out of the seventh chapter of Hebrews that not only tithes but the priesthood that took tithes was ended. And the law was ended and disannulled, by which the priesthood was made and tithes were commanded to be paid.

Then the priests stirred up the people to some lightness and rudeness. I had known Stephens from a child, therefore I laid open his condition and the manner of his preaching, and how that he, like the rest of the priests, did apply the promises to the first birth, which must die. But I showed that the promises were to the Seed, not to the many seeds, but to one Seed: Christ, who was one in male and female. For all were to be born again before they could enter into the kingdom of God.

Then he said I must not judge so. But I told him he that was spiritual judged all things. Then he confessed that that was a full Scripture. 'But, neighbours,' said he, 'this is the business: George Fox is come to the light of the sun. And now he thinks to put out my star-light.' I told him I would not quench the least measure of God in any, much less put out his star-light, if it were true star-light – light from the morning star. But I told him if he had anything from Christ or God, he ought to speak it freely, and not take tithes from the people for preaching, seeing Christ commanded His ministers to give freely, as they had received freely.

After a while, the people began to be vain and rude, so we broke up. Yet some were made loving to the truth that day. Before we parted, I told them that, if the Lord would, I intended to be at the town again that day week.

Against that time, this priest had got seven priests to help him. For priest Stephens had given notice at a lecture on a market-day at Atherstone that such a day there would be a meeting and a dispute with me. I knew nothing of it, but had only said I should be in town that day week again. These eight priests had gathered several hundreds of people, even most of the country thereabouts, and they would have had me into the steeple-house. But I would not go in, but got on a hill and there spoke to them and the people.

There were with me Thomas Taylor, who had been a priest, James Parnell and several other Friends. The priests thought that day to trample down truth; but the truth came over them. Then they grew light and the people rude. And the priests would not stand trial with me, but would be contending here and there a little, with one Friend or other. At last one of the priests brought his son to dispute with me. But his mouth was soon stopped. When he could not tell how to answer, he would ask his father. And his father was confounded also, when he came to answer for his son. So after they had toiled themselves they went away in a rage to priest Stephens' house to drink. As they went away, I said I never came to a place where so many priests together would not stand trial with me. Whereupon they and some of their wives came about me, laid hold of me and fawningly said what might I have been, if I had not been for the Quakers!

Then they began to push Friends to and fro, to thrust them from me and to pluck me to themselves. After a while, several lusty fellows came, took me up in their arms and carried me into the steeple-house porch, intending to carry me into the steeple-house by force. But the door being locked, they fell down on a heap, having me under them. As soon as I could, I got up from under them and went to the hill again. Then they took me from that place to the steeple-house wall, and set me on something like a footstool; and all the priests coming back, stood under with the people.

The priests cried: 'Come, to argument, to argument!' I said I denied all their voices, for they were the voices of hirelings and strangers. And they cried: 'Prove it, prove it!' Then I directed them to the tenth [chapter] of John, where they might see what Christ said of such. He declared He was the true shepherd that laid down His life for His sheep, and His sheep heard His voice and followed Him. But the hireling would fly when the wolf came, because he was a hireling. I offered to prove that they were such hirelings. Then the priests plucked me off from the stool again, and they themselves got up on footstools under the steeple-house wall.

Then I felt the mighty power of God arise over all and told them if they would but give audience and hear me quietly, I would show them by the Scriptures why I denied those eight priests or teachers that stood before me, and all the hireling teachers of the world whatsoever. And I would give them Scriptures for what I said. Whereupon both priests and people consented.

Then I showed them out of the prophets Isaiah, Jeremiah, Ezekiel, Micah, Malachi and others that they were in the steps of such as God sent his true prophets to cry against. Then coming to the New Testament, I showed them from thence that they were like the chief priests and scribes and Pharisees of old, such as Christ cried against. When I had largely quoted the Scriptures and showed them wherein they were like the Pharisees, loving to be called of men masters, and to go in long robes, and to stand praying in the synagogues, and to have the uppermost rooms at feasts, and the like; and when I had thrown them out in the sight of the people amongst the false prophets, deceivers, scribes and Pharisees, and showed at large how such as they were judged and condemned by the true prophets, by Christ and by the apostles: I directed them to the light of Christ Jesus, who enlightens every man that cometh into the world, that by it they might see whether these things were not true, as had been spoken. When I appealed to that of God in their consciences, the light of Christ Jesus in them, they could not bear to hear of it. They were all quiet till then; but then a professor said: 'George, what! Wilt thou never have done?'

I told him I should have done shortly. So I went on a little longer and cleared myself of them in the Lord's power. When I had done, all the priests and people stood silent for a time. At last one of the priests said they would read the Scriptures that I had quoted. I told them, with all my heart.

Then the priests whispered together. And priest Stephens came to me and desired that my father and brother and I might go aside with him, that he might speak to me in private. And the rest of the priests should keep the people from coming to us. I was very loath to go aside with him. But the people cried: 'Go, George. Do, George, go aside with him'. I was afraid if I did not go they would say I was disobedient to my parents. So I went, and the rest of the priests were to keep the people off. But they could not, for the people being willing to hear drew close to us.

I asked the priest what he had to say. And he said if he was out of the way, I should pray for him. And if I was out of the way, he would pray for me. And he would give me a form of words to pray for him by. I replied: 'It seems thou dost not know whether thou art in the right way or not. But I know that I am in the everlasting way, Christ Jesus, which thou art out of. And thou wouldst give me a form of words to pray by, and yet thou deniest the Common Prayer-Book to pray by, as well as I. And I deny thy form of words as well as it. If thou wouldst have me pray for thee by a form of words, is not this to deny the apostles' doctrine and practice of praying by the Spirit, as it gave words and utterance?'

Here the people fell a-laughing; but I was moved to speak more to him. And when I had cleared myself to him and them, we parted, after I had told them that I should (God willing) be in the town that day week again. So the priests packed away, and many people were convinced. For the Lord's power came over all. Though they thought to have confounded truth that day, many were convinced of it. And many that were convinced before were at that day's work confirmed in the truth, and abode in it. And a great shake it gave to the priests.

My father, though he was a hearer and follower of the priest, was so well satisfied that he struck his cane upon the ground and said: 'Truly I see, he that will but stand to the truth, it will carry him out'.

STEPHENS BRINGS IN THE TROOPERS

I passed about the country till that day week and then came again. For we had appointed a meeting at my relations' house. Now priest Stephens had notice beforehand thereof, [and] had got another priest to him. And they got a company of troopers with them and sent for me to come to them. But I sent them word our meeting was appointed, and they might come to it, if they would. The priests came not. But the troopers came and many rude people. They had laid their plot that the troopers should take everyone's name and then command them to go home. And such as would not go they should take, and carry them away with them.

Accordingly they began and took several names, charging them to go home. But when they came to take my name, my relations told them I was at home already; so they could not take me away that time. Nevertheless, they took my name. But the Lord's power was over them and they went away, both the professors and the troopers, crossed and vexed, because they obtained not their end.

This was that priest Stephens, who once said of me: 'never was such a plant bred in England'. Yet afterwards he reported that I was carried up into the clouds and found again full of gold and silver; and many lies and false reports he raised respecting me. But the Lord swept them all away.

COLONEL HACKER

After this I went to Whetstone. There came about seventeen troopers of Colonel Hacker's[20] regiment, with his marshal, and took me up before the meeting, though Friends were beginning to gather together; for several Friends [had] come from various parts. I told the marshal he might let all the Friends go; I would answer for them all. So he took me and let them go, except Alexander Parker, who went with me.

At night they had me before Colonel Hacker, his major and captains – a great company of them. And much discourse we had about the priests and meetings. For at this time there was a rumour of a plot against Oliver Cromwell. Much reasoning I had with them about the light of Christ, which enlighteneth every man that cometh into the world. Colonel Hacker asked whether it was not the light of Christ that made Judas betray his master, and afterwards led him to hang himself. I told him: 'No. That was the spirit of darkness, which hated Christ and His light.'

Then Colonel Hacker said I might go home, and keep there, and not go abroad to meetings. I told him I was an innocent man, free from plots, and denied all such work. His son Needham said: 'Father, this man hath reigned too long. It is time to have him cut off.' I asked him for what? What had I done? Or whom had I wronged from a child? For I was bred and born in that country [Leicestershire], and who could accuse me of any evil from a child?

Then Colonel Hacker asked me again if I would go home and stay there. I told him if I should promise him that, it would manifest that I was guilty of something; to go home and make my home a prison. And if I went to meetings, they would say I broke their order. I told them I should go to meetings, as the Lord should order me, and therefore could not submit to their requirings. But I said we were a peaceable people. 'Well then,' said Colonel Hacker, 'I will send you to my Lord Protector [Oliver Cromwell] by Captain Drury, one of his life-guards.'

That night I was kept a prisoner at the Marshalsea. And the next morning, by six o'clock, I was delivered to Captain Drury. I desired he would let me speak with Colonel Hacker before I went, and he had me to his bedside. Colonel Hacker set upon me presently again, to go home and keep no further meetings. I told him I could not submit to that, but must have my liberty to serve God and go to meetings. 'Then,' said he, 'you must go before the Protector.'

Whereupon I kneeled by his bedside and besought the Lord to forgive him, for he was as Pilate, though he would wash his hands. And when the day of his misery and trial should come upon him, I bid him then remember what I had said to him. But he was stirred up and set on by priest Stephens and the other priests and professors, wherein their envy and baseness was manifest. Who, when they could not overcome me by disputes and arguments, nor resist the Spirit of the Lord that was in me, then they got soldiers to take me up.

Afterwards, when this Colonel Hacker was in prison in London, a day or two before he was executed, he was put in mind of what he had done against the innocent. And he remembered it and confessed it to Margaret Fell, saying he knew well whom she meant. And he had a trouble upon him for it. So his son, who told his father I had reigned too long, and that it was time to have me cut off, might observe how his father was cut off afterwards, he being hanged at Tyburn.

A MEETING WITH OLIVER CROMWELL

Now I was carried up a prisoner by Captain Drury from Leicester, who brought me to London, and lodged me at the Mermaid, over against the mews at Charing Cross. He left me there and went to give the Protector an account of me. When he came to me again, he told me the Protector required that I should promise not to take up a carnal sword or weapon against him or the government, as it then was. And I should write it in what words I saw good, and set my hand to it. I said little in reply to Captain Drury.

But the next morning, I was moved of the Lord to write to the Protector, Oliver Cromwell, wherein I did in the presence of the Lord God declare that I denied the wearing or drawing of a carnal sword, or any other outward weapon against him or any man; and that I was sent of God to stand a witness against all violence, and against the works of darkness; and to turn people from darkness to light; and to bring them from the causes of war and fighting to the peaceable gospel, and from being evil-doers, which the magistrates' swords should be a terror to. When I had written what the Lord had given me to write, I set my name to it and gave it to Captain Drury to hand to Oliver Cromwell, which he did.

After some time, Captain Drury brought me before the Protector himself at Whitehall. It was in a morning, before he was dressed; and one Harvey, who had come a little among Friends, but was disobedient, waited upon him. When I came in I was moved to say: 'Peace be in this house'. And I exhorted him to keep in the fear of God, that he might receive wisdom from Him, that by it he might be directed and order all things under his hand to God's glory. I spoke much to him of truth, and much discourse I had with him about religion. Wherein he carried himself very moderately. But he said we quarrelled with priests, whom he called ministers. I told him I did not quarrel with them, but they quarrelled with me and my friends. 'But,' said I, 'if we own the prophets, Christ and the apostles, we cannot hold up such teachers, prophets and shepherds as the prophets, Christ and the apostles declared against; but we must declare against them by the same power and Spirit.'

Then I showed him that the prophets, Christ and the apostles declared freely, and against them that did not declare freely, such as preached for filthy lucre, and divined for money, and preached for hire, and were covetous and greedy, that can never have enough. And that they that have the same Spirit that Christ and the apostles and the prophets had, could not but declare against all such now, as they did then. As I spoke, he several times said it was very good, and it was truth. I told him that all Christendom (so called) possessed the Scriptures, but wanted the power and the Spirit that they had who gave forth the Scriptures, and that was the reason they were not in fellowship with the Son, nor with the Father, nor with the Scriptures, nor with another.

Many more words I had with him, but people coming in, I drew a little back. And as I was turning, he caught me by the hand and with tears in his eyes said: 'Come again to my house. For if thou and I were but an hour a day together, we should be nearer one to the other'; adding that he wished me no more ill than he did his own soul. I told him if he did, he wronged his own soul. And I bid him harken to God's voice, that he might stand in His counsel and obey it. And if he did so, that would keep him from hardness of heart. But if he did not hear God's voice, his heart would be hardened. He said it was true.

Then I went out. And when Captain Drury came out after me, he told me his Lord Protector said I was at liberty, and might go whither I would. Then I was brought into a great hall, where the Protector's gentlemen were to dine. And I asked them what they brought me thither for. They said it was by the Protector's order that I might dine with them. I bid them let the Protector know I would not eat of his bread, nor drink of his drink. When he heard this, he said: 'Now I see there is a people risen and come up that I cannot win either with gifts, honours, offices or places. But all other sects and people I can.'

THE TRUTH SPREADS IN LONDON

When I came from Whitehall to the Mermaid at Charing Cross, I stayed not long there, but went into the city of London, where we had great and powerful meetings. So great were the throngs of people that I could hardly get to and from the meetings for the crowds. And the truth spread exceedingly.

After a while, I went to Whitehall again, and was moved to declare the day of the Lord amongst them, and that the Lord was come to teach His people Himself. So I preached truth both to the officers and to them that were called Oliver's gentlemen, who were of his guard. But a priest opposed while I was declaring the word of the Lord amongst them. For Oliver had several priests about him, of which this was his news-monger: an envious priest, and a light, scornful, chaffy man. I bid him repent. And he put it in his newspaper the next week that I had been at Whitehall and had bid a godly minister there repent.

When I went thither again, I met with him. An abundance of people gathered about me. I manifested the priest to be a liar in several things that he had affirmed. And so he was silenced. He put in the news that I wore silver buttons, which was false, for they were but alchymy.[21] Afterwards he said in the news that I hung ribands on people's arms, which made them follow me. This was another of his lies, for I never wore or used ribands in my life.

Three Friends went to examine this priest that gave forth this false intelligence, and to know of him where he had that information. He said it was a woman that told him so. And if they would come again, he would tell them her name. When they returned, he said it was a man, but would not mention his name then. But if they would come again, he would tell them his name and where he lived. They went the third time and then he would not say who told him, but offered, if I would give it under my hand, that there was no such thing, he would put that into the news. Thereupon the Friends carried it to him under my hand. But when they came, he broke his promise and would not insert it, but was in a rage, and threatened them with the constable. This was the deceitful thing of this forger of lies, which he spread over all the nation in the news, to render truth odious, and to put evil into people's minds against Friends.

The God of Heaven carried me over all in His power, and His

blessed power went over the nation; insomuch that many Friends about this time were moved to go up and down to sound forth the everlasting gospel in most parts of it, and also in Scotland. And the glory of the Lord was felt over all to His everlasting praise.

A great convincement there was in London, and some in the Protector's house and family. I went to see him again, but could not get access to him, the officers were grown so rude.

AGAINST FASHION

My spirit was greatly burdened to see the pride that existed in the nation, even among professors. And in the sense thereof I was moved to give forth the following paper, directed to such as follow the World's Fashions:-

What a world is this! How doth the devil garnish himself! And how obedient are people to do his will and mind! They are altogether so carried away with fooleries and vanities, both men and women, that they have lost the hidden man of the heart, and the meek and quiet spirit, which with the Lord is of great price. They have lost the adorning of Sarah. They are putting on gold and gay apparel; women plaiting the hair, men and women powdering it; making their backs look like bags of meal. They look so strange that they can scarce look at one another, they are so lifted up in pride.

Pride is flown up into their head, and hath so lifted them up that they snuff up, like wild asses. Like Ephraim, they feed upon the wind, and are like wild heifers, who feed upon the mountains. Pride hath puffed up every one of them. They are out of the fear of God, men and women, young and old; one puffs up another. They must be in the fashion of the world, else they are not in esteem; else they shall not be respected, if they have not gold or silver upon their backs, or if the hair be not powdered.

But if he have store of ribands hanging about his waist and

at his knees, and in his hat, of divers colours – red, white, black or yellow – and his hair is powdered, then he is a brave man. Then he is accepted. He is no Quaker, because he has ribands on his back and front and knees, and his hair powdered. This is the array of the world. But is not this from the lust of the eye, the lust of the flesh, or the pride of life?

HOSTILE STUDENTS AT CAMBRIDGE

[One evening in 1655] I passed to Cambridge. When I came into the town, the scholars hearing of me were up, and were exceedingly rude. I kept on my horse's back and rode through them in the Lord's power. But they unhorsed Amor Stoddart before he could get to the inn. When we were in the inn, they were so rude in the courts and in the streets that miners, colliers and carters could never be ruder. The people of the house asked us what we would have for supper. 'Supper!' said I. 'Were it not that the Lord's power is over them, these rude scholars look as if they would pluck us to pieces and make a supper of us!' They knew I was so against the trade of preaching, which they were there as apprentices to learn, that they raged as much as ever Diana's craftsmen did against Paul.

When it was within night, the mayor of the town, being friendly, came and fetched me to his house. And as we walked through the streets, there was a bustle in the town. But they did not know me, it being darkish. They were in a rage, not only against me, but against the mayor also; so that he was almost afraid to walk the streets with me, for the tumult. We sent for the friendly people and had a fine meeting there in the power of God. And I stayed there all night.

Next morning, having ordered our horses to be ready by six, we passed peaceably out of town. And the destroyers were disappointed. For they thought I would have stayed longer, and intended to do us mischief. But our passing away early in the morning frustrated their evil purposes against us.

A WARNING TO SCOFFERS

[Back in London] I was moved to give forth a paper to those that made a scorn of trembling and quaking:

> The word of the Lord to all you that scorn trembling and quaking, who scoff at, scorn, stone and belch forth oaths against those who are trembling and quaking; threatening them and beating them. Strangers ye are to all the apostles and prophets; and are of the generation that stoned them and mocked them in those ages. Ye are the scoffers of whom they spoke, that are come in the last times. Be ye witnesses against yourselves. To the light in all your consciences I speak, that with it you may see yourselves to be out of the life of the holy men of God.
>
> Moses, who was judge over all Israel, trembled, feared and quaked when the Lord said unto him: 'I am the God of Abraham, the God of Isaac and the God of Jacob'. Then Moses trembled and durst not behold. This, which makes to tremble now, ye teachers and people scoff at, and scorn them in your streets who witness the power of the Lord.
>
> David, a king, trembled. He was mocked. They made songs on him. They wagged their heads at him. Will you profess David's words, and Moses's words, who are in the generation of your fathers, mockers, scoffers, wonderers and despisers, who are to perish? O blush! Be ashamed of all your profession, and be confounded!
>
> Job trembled; his flesh trembled. And they mocked him. So you now mock them in whom the same power of God is made manifest. And yet you profess Job's words. O deceitful hypocrites! Will ye not own Scripture?
>
> The prophet Jeremiah trembled. He shook; his bones quaked. He reeled to and fro, like a drunken man, when he saw

the deceits of the priests and prophets, who were turned from the way of God. They were not ashamed, neither could they blush. Such were gone from the light. And such were they that ruled over the people. But he was brought to cry: 'O foolish people, that had eyes and could not see; that had ears and could not hear; that did not fear the Lord'.

Habakkuk, the prophet of the Lord, trembled. And Joel, the prophet of the Lord, said: 'Blow the trumpet in Zion, and let all the inhabitants of the earth tremble'.

And now this trembling is witnessed by the power of the Lord. This power of the Lord is come. The trumpet is sounding. The earth is shaking. The inhabitants of the earth are trembling. The dead are arising, and the living are praising God. The world is raging and the scoffers are scorning. And they that witness trembling and quaking wrought in them by the power of the Lord can scarcely pass up and down the streets, but with stones and blows, fists and sticks, or dogs set at them. Or they are pursued with mockings and reproaches. Thus you vent forth your malice against them that witness the power of the Lord.

Take warning, all ye powers of the earth, how ye persecute them whom the world nickname and call Quakers, who dwell in the eternal power of God; lest the hand of the Lord be turned against you, and ye be all cut off. To you this is the word of God. Fear and tremble, and take warning!

THE PROTECTOR HARDENS

This year [1655] came out the Oath of Abjuration, by which many Friends suffered. And several went to speak to the Protector about it. But he began to harden. And suffering increasing upon Friends, by reason that envious magistrates made use of that oath as a snare to catch Friends in, who, they knew, could not swear at all, I was moved to write to the Protector.

But sufferings and imprisonments continuing and increasing,

and the Protector (under whose name they were inflicted) hardening himself against the complaints that were made to him, I was moved to issue the following amongst Friends, to bring the weight of their sufferings more heavy upon the heads of the persecutors:

Who is moved by the power of the Lord to offer himself to the justice for his brother or sister that lies in prison, and to go lie there in their stead, that his brother or sister may come out of prison, and so offer his life for his brother or sister? Where any lie in prison for tithes, witnessing the priesthood changed that took tithes, and the unchangeable priesthood come; if any brother in the light, who witnesseth a change of the old priesthood that took tithes, be moved of the Lord to go to the priest or impropriator, to offer himself to lie in prison for his brother, and to lay down his life, that he may come forth, he may cheerfully do it, and heap up coals of fire upon the head of the adversary of God.

Likewise, if any Friends be moved of the Lord to go to the magistrate, judge, general or Protector, and offer up themselves to lay down their lives for the brethren, as Christ hath laid down His life for you, so lay down your lives one for another. Here you may go over the heads of the persecutors, and reach the witness of God in all. And this shall rest a judgement upon them all for ever, and be witnessed to by that which is of God in their conscience. Given forth from the Spirit of the Lord through G.F.

The Organiser

A PREMONITION

I WENT TO Drayton, my native town, where so many priests and professors had formerly gathered together against me. But now not a priest or professor appeared. I asked some of my relations where all the priests and professors were. They said the priest of Nuneaton was dead, and eight or nine of them were seeking to get his benefice. 'They will let you alone now,' said they, 'for they are like a company of crows when a sheep is dead; they all gather together to pull out the puddings. So do the priests for a fallen benefice.' These were some of their own hearers that said so of them. But they had spent their venom against me, and the Lord delivered me by His power out of their snares.

In Derbyshire, James Nayler met me, and told me seven or eight priests had challenged him to a dispute. I had a travail in my spirit for him, and the Lord answered me, and I was moved to bid him go on, and God Almighty would be with him, and give him the victory in His power. And the Lord did so; insomuch that the people saw the priests were foiled and they cried: 'a Nailer, a Nailer hath confuted them all!'

After the dispute, he came to me again, praising the Lord. Thus was the Lord's day proclaimed and set over all their heads, and people began to see the apostasy and slavery they had been under to their hireling teachers for means. And they came to know their teacher, the Lord Jesus, who had purchased them and made their place between God and them. While we were here, Friends came out of Yorkshire to see us, and were glad of the prosperity of truth.

[Later,] after I had tarried some time in London, and had visited Friends in their meetings, I went out of town, leaving James Nayler in the city. As I passed from him, I cast my eyes upon him, and a fear struck me concerning him; but I went away.

A CONFRONTATION WITH BAPTISTS

We went to Dorchester, and alighted at an inn, a Baptist's house. We sent into the town to the Baptists, to let us have their meeting-house to meet in, and to invite the sober people to the meeting. But they denied it us. We sent to them again, to know why they would deny us their meeting-house. So the thing was noised in the town. Then we sent them word, if they would not let us come to their house, they, or any people that feared God, might come to our inn, if they pleased.

They were in a great rage. And their teacher and many of them came up, and slapped their Bibles on the table. I asked them why they were so angry; were they angry with the Bible? But they fell into a discourse about their water-baptism. I asked them whether they could say they were sent of God to baptise people, as John was; and whether they had the same Spirit and power that the apostles had. They said they had not. Then I asked them how many powers there are; whether there are any more than the power of God and the power of the devil? They said there was not any other power than those two. Then said I: 'if you have not the power of God that the apostles had, then you act by the power of the devil.'

Many sober people were present who said: 'they have thrown themselves on their backs.' Many substantial people were convinced that night; a precious service we had there for the Lord, and His power came over all.

Next morning, as we were passing away, the Baptists, being in a rage, began to shake the dust off their feet after us. 'What,' said

I, 'in the power of darkness! We, who are in the power of God, shake off the dust of our feet against you.'

AN END TO MIRTH

Leaving Dorchester, we came to Weymouth. There was a captain of horse in the town, who sent to me, and would fain have had me to stay longer. But I was not to stay. He and his man rode out of town with me about seven miles, Edward Pyot also being with me. This captain was the fattest, merriest man, the most cheerful and the most given to laughter, that ever I met with; insomuch that I was several times moved to speak in the dreadful power of the Lord to him. And yet it was become so customary to him that he would presently laugh at anything he saw. But I still admonished him to come to sobriety, sincerity and the fear of the Lord.

We stayed at an inn that night. And in the morning I was moved to speak to him again, when he parted from us. Next time I saw him, he told me that when I spoke to him at parting, the power of the Lord so struck him that before he got home he was serious enough, and had discontinued his laughing. He afterwards was convinced, and became a serious and good man, and died in the truth.

A CONTROVERSIAL PAPER

We passed into Cornwall, to Market Jew [Marazion]. And having taken up our lodging at an inn, we went out over-night to inquire for such as feared the Lord. Next morning, the mayor and aldermen gathered together, with the high-sheriff of the country, and they sent first the constables to bid us come before them. We asked them for their warrant. And they saying they had none, we told them we should not go along with them without.

Upon the return of the constables without us, they sent their sergeants, and we asked them for their warrant. They said they had none. But they told us the mayor and aldermen stayed for us. We told them the mayor and his company did not well to trouble us in our inn, and we should not go with them without a warrant. So they went away and came again. And when we asked them for their warrant, one of them pulled his mace from under his cloak. We asked them whether this was their custom, to molest and trouble strangers in their inns and lodgings?

After some time Edward Pyot went to the mayor and aldermen, and had much discourse with them. But the Lord's power gave him dominion over them all. When he had returned, several of the officers came to us, and we laid before them the incivility and unworthiness of their conduct towards us, who were the servants of the Lord God, thus to stop and trouble us in our lodgings; and what an unchristian act it was. Before we left the town, I wrote a paper, to be sent to the seven parishes at the Land's End. A copy of which follows:-

The mighty day of the Lord is come, and coming, wherein all hearts shall be made manifest, and the secrets of everyone's heart shall be revealed by the light of Jesus, who lighteth every man that cometh into the world, that all men through Him might believe, and that the world might have life through Him who saith 'Learn of Me'; and of whom God saith 'This is My beloved Son; hear ye Him'. Christ is come to teach His people Himself. And everyone that will not hear this Prophet, which God hath raised up, and which Moses spoke of when he said: 'Like unto me will God raise you up a Prophet, Him shall you hear'; every one (I say) that will not hear this Prophet is to be cut off.

They that despised Moses's law died under the hand of two or three witnesses. But how much greater punishment will come upon them that neglect this great salvation, Christ Jesus, who saith 'Learn of me: I am the way, the truth and the life', who lighteth every man that cometh into the world; and by His light lets him see his evil ways and his evil deeds. But if you hate this light, and go on in evil, this light will be your condemnation.

Therefore, now ye have time, prize it. For this is the day of your visitation and salvation offered to you. Every one of you hath a light from Christ, which lets you see you should not lie, nor do wrong to any, nor swear, nor curse, nor take God's name in vain, nor steal. It is the light that shows you these evil deeds; which, if you love, and come unto it and follow it, will lead you to Christ, who is the way to the Father, from whom it comes; where no unrighteousness enters, nor ungodliness. If you hate this light, it will be your condemnation. But if you love it and come to it, you will come to Christ. And it will bring you off from all the world's teachers and ways, to learn of Christ, and will preserve you from the evils of the world, and all the deceivers in it. G.F.

This paper a Friend who was then with me had. And when we were gone three or four miles from Market Jew towards the west, he meeting with a man upon the road, gave him a copy of the paper. This man proved to be a servant to one Peter Ceely, major in the army, and a justice of the peace in that county. And he riding before us to a place called St Ives, showed the paper to his master, Major Ceely.

When we came to Ives, Edward Pyot's horse having cast a shoe, we stayed to have it set. And while he was getting his horse shod, I walked down to the sea-side. When I returned, I found the town in an uproar. And they were hailing Edward Pyot and the other Friend before Major Ceely. I followed them into the justice's house, though they did not lay hands upon me. When we came in, the house was full of rude people. Whereupon I asked whether there were not an officer among them to keep the people civil. Major Ceely said he was a magistrate. I told him he should show forth gravity and sobriety then, and use his authority to keep the people civil. For I never saw any people ruder. The Indians were more like Christians than they.

After a while, they brought forth the paper aforesaid, and asked whether I would own it. I said yes. Then he tendered the oath of abjuration to us. Whereupon I put my hand in my pocket and drew forth the answer to it, which had been given to the Protector. After I had given him that, he examined us severally, one by one. He had with him a silly young priest, who asked us many frivolous questions. And amongst the rest, he desired to cut my hair, which then was pretty long. But I was not to cut it though many times many were offended at it. I told them I had no pride in it, and it was not my own putting on.

At length the justice put us under guard of soldiers, who were hard and wild, like the justice himself. Nevertheless we warned people of the day of the Lord and declared the truth to them. The next day he sent us, guarded by a party of horse with swords and pistols, to Redruth.

On First-day, the soldiers would have taken us away. But we told them it was their Sabbath, and it was not usual to travel on that day. Several of the town's people gathered about us and whilst I held the soldiers in discourse, Edward Pyot spoke to the people. And afterwards, he held the soldiers to discourse whilst I spoke to the people. And in the meantime, the other Friend got out the back way and went to the steeple-house to speak to the priest and people. The people were exceedingly desperate, in a mighty rage against him and abused him. The soldiers, also missing him, were in a great rage, ready to kill us. But I declared the day of the Lord and the word of eternal life to the people that gathered about us.

In the afternoon, the soldiers were resolved to have us away, so we took horse. When we were got to the town's end, I was moved of the Lord to go back again, to speak to the old man of the house. The soldiers drew out their pistols and swore I should not go back. I heeded them not, but rode back and they rode after me. I cleared myself to the old man and the people, and then returned with them, and reproved them for being so rude and violent.

At night we were brought to a town called Smethick then, but since Falmouth. It being the evening of the First-day, there came to our inn the chief constable of the place, and many other people, some of whom began to inquire concerning us. We told them we were prisoners for truth's sake; and much discourse we had with them concerning the things of God. They were very sober and loving to us. Some were convinced and stood faithful ever after.

When all were gone, we went to our chamber to go to bed, and about eleven o'clock Edward Pyot said: 'I will shut the door. It may be some may come to do us some mischief.' Afterwards we understood that Captain Keat, who commanded the party, had purposed to do us some mischief that night, but the door being bolted, he missed his design.

Next morning, Captain Keat brought a kinsmen of his, a rude, wicked man, and put him into the room, he himself standing without. The evil-minded man walking huffing up and down the room, I bid him fear the Lord. Whereupon he ran upon me, struck me with both his hands; and placing his leg behind me, would have fain thrown me down. But he could not, for I stood stiff and still, and let him strike. As I looked towards the door, I saw Captain Keat look on and see his kinsman thus beat and abuse me. Whereupon I said: 'Keat, dost thou allow this?' And he said he did. 'Is this manly or civil,' said I, 'to have us under a guard and put a man to abuse and beat us? Is this manly, civil or Christian?'

I desired one of our friends to send for the constables and they came. Then I desired the captain to let the constables see his warrant or order, by which he was to carry us, which he did. And his warrant was to conduct us safe to Captain Fox, governor of Pendennis Castle. And if the governor should not be at home, he was to convey us to Launceston jail. I told him he had broken his order concerning us. For we, who were his prisoners, were to be safely conducted; but he had brought a man to beat and abuse us. So he having broken his order, I wished the constable to keep the warrant. Accordingly he did, and told the soldiers they might go, for he would take charge of the prisoners.

I showed the soldiers the baseness of their carriage towards us, and they walked up and down the house, being pitifully blank and down. The constable went to the castle, and told the officers what they had done. The officers showed great dislike of Captain Keat's base carriage towards us, and told the constables that Major-General Desborough[22] was coming to Bodmin, and that we should meet him; and it was likely he would free us. Meanwhile, our old guard of soldiers came by way of entreaty to us, and promised that they would be civil to us, if we would go with them. Thus the morning was spent till it was about eleven o'clock. And then upon the soldiers' entreaty, and promise to be more civil, the constables gave them the order again, and we went with them.

Captain Keat, who commanded our guard, understanding that Captain Fox, who was the governor of Pendennis Castle, was gone to meet Major-General Desborough, did not take us thither, but went with us directly to Bodmin. We met Major-General Desborough on the way. The captain of his troop that rode before him knew me and said: 'O, Mr Fox; what do you here?' I replied: 'I am a prisoner.' 'Alack,' said he, 'for what?' I told him I was taken up as I was travelling. 'Then,' said he, 'I will speak to my lord, and he will set you at liberty.'

So he came from the head of his troop, rode up to the coach and spoke to the major-general. We also told him how we were taken. He began to speak against the light of Christ, for which I reproved him. Then he told the soldiers they might carry us to Launceston; for he could not stay to talk with us, lest his horses should take cold.

ON NOT PUTTING OFF HATS

Next day we were brought to Launceston, where Captain Keat delivered us to the jailer. Now was there no Friend, nor friendly people, near us. And the people of the town were dark and hardened. The jailer required us to pay seven shillings a week for our horse-meat, and seven for our diet apiece. But after some time, several sober people came to see us, and some of the town were convinced. And many friendly people out of several parts of the country came to visit us, and were convinced.

Then arose a great rage amongst the professors and priests against us. And they said this people 'thou' and 'thee' all men without respect, and they will not put off their hats, nor bow the knee to any man. This made them fret. But, said they, we shall see, when the assize comes, whether they will dare to 'thou' and 'thee' the judge, and keep their hats on before him. They expected we should be hanged at the assize. But all this was little to us. For we saw how God would stain the world's honour and glory, and were commanded not to seek that honour, nor give it. But we knew the honour that comes from God only, and sought that.

It was nine weeks from the time of our commitment to the assizes, to which abundance of people came from far and near to hear the trial of the Quakers. Captain Bradden lay with his troop of horse there, whose soldiers and the sheriff's men guarded us up to the court through the multitude of people that filled the streets. And much ado they had to get us through them. Besides, the doors and windows were filled with people looking out upon us.

When we were brought into court, we stood some time with our hats on, and all was quiet. And I was moved to say: 'Peace be amongst you!' Judge Glynne, a Welshman, then Chief Justice of England, said to the jailer: 'what be these you have brought here into the court?' 'Prisoners, my lord,' said he. 'Why do you not put off your hats?' said the judge to us. We said nothing. 'Put off your hats!' said the judge again. Still we said nothing. Then said the judge: 'The court commands you to put off your hats.' Then I spoke and said, 'Where did any magistrate, king or judge, from Moses to Daniel, command any to put off their hats, when they came before them in their courts, either amongst the Jews, the people of God or amongst the heathens? And if the law of

England doth command any such thing, show me that law either written or printed.'

Then the judge grew very angry and said: 'I do not carry my law books on my back.' 'But,' said I, 'tell me where it is printed in any statute-book, that I may read it.' Then said the judge: 'Take him away, prevaricator! I'll ferk [chastise] him.' So they took us away and put us among the thieves. Presently after he calls the jailers: 'Bring them up again.'

'Come,' said he, 'where had they hats from Moses to Daniel? Come, answer me. I have you fast now.' I replied: 'Thou mayest read in the third [chapter] of Daniel that the three children were cast into the fiery furnace by Nebuchadnezzar's command, with their coats, their hose and their hats on.' This plain instance stopped him, so that not having anything else to say to the point he cried again: 'Take them away, jailer.'

Accordingly, we were taken away and thrust in among the thieves, where we were kept a great while. And then, without being called again, the sheriff's men and the troopers made way for us (but we were almost spent) to get through the crowd of people, and guarded us to the prison again, a multitude of people following us, with whom we had much discourse and reasoning to the jail. We had some good books to set forth our principles, and to inform people of the truth, which the judge and justices hearing of, they sent Captain Bradden, for them, who came into the jail to us, and violently took our books from us, some out of Edward Pyot's hands, and carried them away. So we never got them again.

CONCERNING SWEARING

In the afternoon we were had up again into the court by the jailer and the sheriff's men and troopers, who had a mighty toil to get us through the crowd of people. When we were in the court, waiting to be called, I seeing both the jurymen and such a multitude of others swearing, it grieved my life, that such as professed Christianity should so openly disobey and break the command of Christ and the apostle. And I was moved of the Lord to give forth a paper against swearing, which I had about me, to the grand and petty juries; which was as follows:

Take heed of giving people oaths to swear. For Christ our Lord and Master saith: 'Swear not at all, but let your communications be yea yea, and nay nay. For whatsoever is more than these cometh of evil'. And the apostle James saith: 'My brethren, above all things swear not, neither by heaven, nor by earth, nor by any other oath, lest ye fall into condemnation.' Hence you may see, those that swear fall into condemnation, and are out of Christ's and the apostle's doctrine.

Now if you say that the oath was the end of controversy and strife, they who are in strife are out of Christ's doctrine. For He is the covenant of peace. And the apostle brings that but as an example, as men swearing by the greater. And the oath was the end of controversy and strife among men; and said verily men swear by the greater. But God could not find a greater, but swears by Himself, concerning Christ; who, when He was come, taught not to swear at all. So such as are in Him, and follow Him, cannot but abide in His doctrine.

This paper passing among them from the jury to the justices, they presented it to the judge. So that when we were called before the judge, he bade the clerk give me that paper, and then asked me whether that 'seditious paper' was mine. I told him if they would read it up in open court, then I might hear it, if it was mine, I would own it, and stand by it. He would have had me to take it, and look upon it in my own hand, but I again desired that it might be read, that all the country might hear it, and judge whether there was any sedition in it or not. For if there were, I was willing to suffer for it. At last the clerk of the assize read it with an audible voice, that all the people might hear it. And when he had done, I told them it was my paper. I would own it, and so might they too, except they would deny the Scripture. For was not this Scripture language, and the words and commands of Christ, and the apostle, which all true Christians ought to obey?

Then they let fall that subject. And the judge fell upon us about our hats again, bidding the jailer take them off, which he did, and gave them to us; and we put them on again. Then we asked the judge and the justices what we had lain in prison for these nine weeks, seeing they now objected nothing to us but about our hats. And as for putting off our hats, I told them that was the honour which God would lay in the dust, though they made so much to do about it; the honour which is of men, and which men seek one of another, and is the mark of unbelievers. For 'how can ye believe,' saith Christ, 'who receive honour one of another, and seek not the honour that cometh from God only?' And Christ saith: 'I receive not honour from men.' And all true Christians should be of His mind.

FALSE JUSTICE

Then the judge began to make a great speech, how he represented the Lord Protector's person, who had made him Lord Chief Justice of England, and sent him to come that circuit, etc. We desired him then that he would do us justice for our false imprisonment, which we had suffered nine weeks wrongfully. But instead of that, they brought in an indictment that they had framed against us; so strange a thing and so full of lies, that I thought it had been against some of the thieves; that we came by force and arms, and in a hostile manner into the court. I told them it was false. And still we cried for justice for our false imprisonment, being taken up in our journey without cause by Major Ceely.

Then Peter Ceely spoke to the judge and said: 'May it please you, my lord, this man,' pointing to me, 'went aside with me and told me how serviceable I might be for his design; that he could raise forty thousand men at an hour's warning, and involve the nation in blood, and so bring in King Charles. I would have aided him out of the country, but he would not go. If it please you, my lord, I have a witness to swear it.'

So he called upon his witness. But the judge not being forward to examine this witness, I desired that he would be pleased to let my mittimus be read in the face of the court and country, in which my crime was signified, for which I was sent to prison. The judge said it should not be read. I said it ought to be, seeing it concerned my liberty and my life. The judge said again: 'it shall not be read'. But I said it ought to be read, 'for I have not done anything worthy of death, or of bonds, let all the country know it'.

Then seeing they would not read it, I spoke to one of my fellow prisoners. 'Thou hast a copy of it. Read it up,' said I. 'It shall not be read,' said the judge. 'Jailer,' said he, 'take him away. I will see whether he or I shall be master.' So I was taken away, and a while after, called for again. I still cried to have my mittimus read, for that signified the cause of my commitment. Wherefore I again spoke to the Friend, my fellow prisoner. He did read it, and the judge, justices and whole court were silent; for the people were eager to hear it. It was as follows:-

Peter Ceely, one of the Justices of the Peace of this County, to the Keeper of His Highness's jail at Launceston, or his lawful Deputy in that behalf, Greeting:-

I send you herewithal by the bearers hereof the bodies of Edward Pyot of Bristol, and George Fox of Drayton-in-the-Clay, in Leicestershire, and William Salt of London, which they pretend to be the places of their habitation; who go under the notion of Quakers and acknowledge themselves to be such; who have spread several papers tending to the disturbance of the public peace, and cannot render any lawful cause of coming into these parts, being persons altogether unknown, and having no pass for their travelling up and down the country, and refusing to give sureties of their good behaviour, according to the law in that behalf provided; and refuse to take the oath of abjuration, etc. These are therefore, in the name of His Highness the Lord Protector, to will and command you that when the bodies of said Edward Pyot, George Fox and William Salt shall be unto you brought, you then receive, and in His Highness's prison aforesaid you safely keep them, until by due course of law they shall be delivered. Hereof fail you not, as you will answer the contrary at your perils. Given under my hand and seal, at St Ives, the eighteenth day of January 1656. P. Ceely

When it was read, I spoke thus to the judge and justices: 'Thou sayest thou art Chief Justice of England, and you justices know that if I had put in sureties, I might have gone whither I pleased; and have carried on the design (if I had had one) which Major Ceely hath charged me with. And if I had spoken these words to him, which he hath here declared, judge ye whether bail or mainprize could have been taken in that case.'

Then turning my speech to Major Ceely I said: 'When or where did I take thee aside? Was not thy house full of rude people, and thou as rude as any of them at our examination; so that I asked for a constable or some other officer, to keep the people civil? But if thou art my accuser, why sittest thou on the bench? This is not a place for thee to sit in. For accusers do not use to sit with the judge. Thou oughtest to come down, and stand by me, and look me in the face. Besides, I would ask the judge and justices whether or not Major Ceely is not guilty of this treason, which he charges against me, in concealing it so long as he hath done? Does he understand his place, either as a soldier or as a justice of the peace? For he tells you here that I went aside with him, and told him what a design I had in hand, and how serviceable he might be for my design; that I could raise forty thousand men in an hour's time, and bring in King Charles, and involve the nation in blood. He saith, moreover, he would have aided me out of the country, but I would not go. And therefore he committed me to prison for want of sureties for the good behaviour, as the mittimus declares.

Now do not you see plainly that Major Ceely is guilty of this plot and treason he talks of, and hath made himself a party to it, by desiring me to go out of the country, and demanding bail of me, and not charging me with this pretended treason till now, nor discovering it? But I deny and abhor his words, and am innocent of his devilish design.'

So that business was let fall. For the judge saw clearly enough that instead of ensnaring me, he had ensnared himself. And the judge, finding those snares would not hold, cried: 'Take him away, jailer!' And then, when we were taken away, he fined us twenty marks apiece for not putting off our hats; and to be kept in prison till we paid it. So he sent us back to jail.

IN LAUNCESTON JAIL

The assize being over, and we settled in prison upon such a commitment that we were not likely to be soon released, we discontinued giving the jailer seven shillings a week each for our horses, and seven for ourselves, and sent our horses out into the country. Upon which he grew very wicked and devilish, and put us down into Doomsdale – a nasty, stinking place, where they put murderers after they were condemned. The place was so noisome that it was observed few that went in ever came out again in health. There was no house of office in it, and the excrements of the prisoners that from time to time had been left there had not been carried out (as we were told) for many years. So that it was all like mire, and in some places on the top of the shoes in water and urine. And he would not let us cleanse it, nor suffer us to have beds or straw to lie on.

At night some friendly people of the town brought us a candle and a little straw, and we burnt some of it to take away the stink. The thieves lay over our heads, and the head jailer in a room by them, over us also. It seems the smoke went up into the jailer's room, which put him into such a rage that he took the pots of excrements of the thieves and poured them through a hole upon our heads in Doomsdale; whereby we were so bespattered that we could not touch ourselves or one another. And the stink increased upon us, so that what with that, and what with smoke, we had nearly been choked and smothered. We had the stink under our feet before, but now we had it on our hands and backs also. And he having quenched our straw with the filth he poured down, had made a great smother in the place. Moreover, he railed at us most hideously, calling us hatchet-faced dogs and such strange names as we had never heard. In this manner we were fain to stand all night, for we could not sit down, the place was so full of filthy excrements.

A great while he kept us in this manner, before he would let us cleanse it, or suffer us to have any victuals brought in, but what we had through the grate. Once a girl brought us a little meat and he arrested her for breaking his house, and sued her in the town court for breaking the prison. Much trouble he put her to, whereby others were so discouraged that we had much to do to get water or victuals.

This head jailer, we were informed, had been a thief, and was branded in the hand and in the shoulder. His wife, too, had been branded in the hand. The under-jailer had been branded in the hand and shoulder, and his wife in the hand also. Colonel Bennet, who was a Baptist teacher, having purchased the jail and lands belonging to the castle, had placed this head jailer therein. The prisoners and some wild people talked of spirits that haunted Doomsdale, and how many had died in it; thinking, perhaps, to terrify us therewith. But I told them that if all the spirits and devils in hell were there, I was over them in the power of God, and feared no such thing. For Christ, our priest, would sanctify the walls and the house to us.

SUFFERING IS A SERVICE

By this time, the general quarter-sessions drew nigh. And the jailer still carrying himself basely and wickedly towards us, we drew up our suffering case, and sent it to the sessions at Bodmin. On reading of which the justices gave order that Doomsdale door should be opened and that we should have liberty to cleanse it, and to buy our meat in the town.

We also sent a copy of our sufferings to the Protector, setting forth how we were taken and committed by Major Ceely, and abused by Captain Keat as aforesaid. The Protector sent down an order to Captain Fox, governor of Pendennis Castle, to examine the matter about the soldiers abusing us, and striking me. There were at that time many of the gentry of the country at the castle. And Captain Keat's kinsman, that struck me, was sent for before them and much threatened. They told him that if I should change my principle, I might take the extremity of the law against him, and might recover sound damages of him. Captain Keat also was checked for suffering the prisoners under his charge to be abused. This was of great service in the country. For afterwards Friends might have spoken in any market or steeple-house thereabouts, and none would meddle with them.

I understood that Hugh Peters, one of the Protector's chaplains, told him they could not do George Fox a greater service for the spreading of his principle in Cornwall than to imprison him there. And indeed, my imprisonment there was of the Lord, and for His service in those parts. For after the assizes were over, and it was known we were likely to continue prisoners, several Friends from most parts of the nation came into the country to visit us. Those parts of the West were very dark countries at that time. But the Lord's light and truth broke forth, shone over all and many were turned from darkness to light, and from Satan's powers unto God. Many were moved to go to the steeple-houses, and several were sent to prison to us. And a great convincement began in the country. For now we had liberty to come out and to walk in the

Castle Green. And many came to us on First-days, to whom we declared the word of life.

FRIENDS STOPPED AND SEARCHED

Now in Cornwall, Devonshire, Dorsetshire and Somersetshire truth began to spread mightily, and many were turned to Christ Jesus and His free teaching. For many Friends that came to visit us were drawn forth to declare the truth in those counties; which made the priests and professors rage; and they stirred up the magistrates to ensnare Friends. They placed watches in the streets and highways, on pretence of taking up all suspicious persons; under which colour they stopped and took up the Friends that travelled in and through those counties, coming to visit us in prison. But that by which they thought to stop the truth was the means of spreading it so much the more. For then Friends were frequently moved to speak to one constable, and to the other officer, and to the justices they were brought before. And this caused the truth to spread the more amongst them in all their parishes. And when Friends got among the watches, it would be a fortnight or three weeks before they could get out of them again. For no sooner had one constable taken them and carried them before the justices, and they had discharged them, than another would take them up and carry them before other justices; which put the country to much needless trouble and charges.

The Mayor of Launceston, too, was a very wicked man, for he took up all he could get, and cast them into prison. And he would search substantial grave women, their petticoats and their head-clothes. A young man having come to see us, who came not through that town, I drew up all the gross, inhuman and unchristian actions of the mayor (for his carriage was more like a heathen than a Christian); to him I gave it, and bid him seal it up, and go out again the back way; and then come into the town through the gates. He did so, and the watch took him up, and carried him before the mayor, who presently searched his pockets and found the letter, wherein he saw all his actions characterized. This shamed him so that from that time he meddled little with the servants of the Lord.

TEACHING OTHERS TO DISPUTE

We continued in prison till the next assize. Great work we had, and service for the Lord, both between the assizes and after, amongst professors and people of all sorts. For many came to see us and to reason with us. Elizabeth Trelawney of Plymouth (who was the daughter of a baronet) being convinced, the priests and professors, and some great persons of her kindred, were exasperated, and wrote letters to her. She being a wise and tender woman, and fearing to give them any advantage, sent their letters to me. And I answered them and returned them to her again, for her to answer. Which she did; till, growing in the power and Spirit and wisdom of God, she came herself to be able to answer the wisest priest and professor of them all; and had a dominion over them in the truth, through the power of the Lord, by which she was kept faithful to her death.

CHRIST IS COME

While I was in prison here, the Baptists and Fifth Monarchy men[23] prophesied that this year Christ should come, and reign upon earth a thousand years. And they looked upon this reign to be outward; when He was come inwardly in the hearts of His people, to reign and rule there, and these professors would not thus receive Him. So they failed in their prophecy and expectation, and had not the possession of Him. But Christ *is* come, and doth dwell in the hearts of His people, and reign there. Thousands, at the door of whose hearts He hath been knocking, have opened to Him. And He is come in, and doth sup with them and they with Him. The heavenly supper with the heavenly and spiritual man. So many of these Baptist and Monarchy people became the greatest enemies of the possessors of Christ. But He reigns in the hearts of His saints over all their envy.

At the assizes, divers justices came to us and were pretty civil, and reasoned of the things of God soberly, expressing a pity towards us. Captain Fox, governor of Pendennis Castle, came and looked me in the face and said not a word; but went to his company and told them he never saw a simpler man in his life. I called after him and said: 'Stay! We shall see who is the simpler man.' But he went his way. A light, chaffy man.

TO FRIENDS IN THE MINISTRY

About this time I was moved to give forth the following exhortation to Friends in the ministry:[24]

In the power of life and wisdom, and dread of the Lord God of life and heaven and earth, dwell; that in the wisdom of God over all ye may be preserved, and be a terror to all the adversaries of God, and a dread, answering that of God in them all, spreading the truth abroad, awakening the witness, confounding deceit, gathering out of transgression into the life, the covenant of light and peace with God. Let all nations hear the sound by word or writing. Spare no place, spare no tongue nor pen; but be obedient to the Lord God. Go through the work. Be valiant for truth upon earth; and tread and trample upon all that is contrary.

Reign and rule with Christ, whose sceptre and throne are now set up, whose dominion is over all to the ends of the earth;

whose dominion is an everlasting dominion; whose throne is an everlasting throne; whose kingdom is an everlasting kingdom; and whose power is above all powers. Therefore this is the word of the Lord God to you all: keep in the wisdom of God, that spreads over all the earth; the wisdom of the creation, that is pure, from above, not destructive.

Bring all into the worship of God. Plough up the fallow ground. Thrash and get out the corn, that the seed, the wheat, may be gathered into the barn; that to the beginning all people may come to Christ, who was before the world was made. For the chaff is come upon the wheat by transgression. He that treads it out is out of transgression, and fathoms transgression; puts a difference between the precious and the vile; and can pick out the wheat from the tares, and gather into the garner; so brings to the lively hope, the immortal soul into God, out of which it came.

So the ministers of the Spirit must minister to the Spirit that is in prison, which hath been in captivity in everyone; that with the Spirit of Christ people may be led out of captivity up to God, the Father of Spirits, do service to Him, and have unity with Him, with the Scriptures, and one with another. This is the word of the Lord God to you all, and a charge to you all in the presence of the living God. Be patterns, be examples in all countries, places, islands, nations, wherever you come; that your carriage and life may preach among all sorts of people, and to them. Then you will come to walk cheerfully over the world, answering that of God in everyone; whereby in them ye may be a blessing, and make the witness of God, in them to bless you. Then to the Lord God you will be a sweet savour, and a blessing.

THE JAILER'S OWN RUIN

[One time, in prison,] we asked the jailer what doings there were at the sessions. And he said: 'Small matters; only about thirty for bastardy.' We thought it very strange, that they who professed themselves Christians should make small matters of such things. But this jailer was very bad himself. I often admonished him to sobriety. But he abused people that came to visit us.

Edward Pyot had a cheese sent him from Bristol by his wife. And the jailer took it from him, and carried it to the mayor, to search it for treasonable letters, as he said. And though they found no treason in the cheese, they kept it from us.

This jailer might have been rich if he had carried himself civilly. But he sought his own ruin; which soon after came upon him. For the next year, he was turned out of his place, and for some wickedness cast into jail himself; and there begged of our Friends. And for some unruliness in his conduct he was, by the succeeding jailer, put into Doomsdale, locked in irons and beaten; and bid to remember how he abused those good men whom he had wickedly, without any cause, cast into that nasty dungeon; and told how he deservedly should suffer for his wickedness; and the same measure he had meted to others should be meted out to himself. He became very poor, and died in prison. And his wife and family came to misery.

SET AT LIBERTY

While I was in prison in Launceston, a Friend went to Oliver Cromwell and offered himself, body for body, to lie in Doomsdale in my stead, if he would take him and let me have liberty. Which thing so struck him that he said to his great men and council: 'Which of you would do so much for me, if I were in the same condition?' And though he did not accept the Friend's offer, but said he could not do it, for that it was contrary to law, yet the truth thereby came mightily over him.

A good while after this, he sent down Major-General Desborough, pretending to set us at liberty. When he came, he offered us our liberty, if we would say we would go home and preach no more. But we could not promise him.

After this, Major-General Desborough came to the Castle Green and played at bowls with the justices and others. Several Friends were moved to go and admonish them not to spend their time so vainly; desiring them to consider that though they professed themselves to be Christians, yet they gave themselves up to their pleasures, and kept the servants of God meanwhile in prison; and telling them the Lord would plead with them, and visit them for such things. But notwithstanding what was said to him, he went away and left us in prison.

We understood afterwards that he left the business to Colonel Bennet, who had the command of the jail. For some time after, Bennet would have set us at liberty, if we would have paid his jailer's fees. But we told him we could give the jailer no fees, for we were innocent sufferers. And how could they expect fees of us, who had suffered so long wrongfully?

After a while, Colonel Bennet, coming to town, sent for us to an inn, and insisted again upon fees, which we refused. At last the power of the Lord came so over him that he freely set us at liberty, on the 13th day of the seventh month, 1656.

JAMES NAYLER

From thence we came to Exeter, where many Friends were in prison; and amongst the rest, James Nayler. For a little before we were set at liberty, James had run out into imaginations, and a company with him; which raised up a great darkness in the nation. He came to Bristol and made a disturbance there. And from thence he was coming to Launceston to see me. But he was stopped by the way, and imprisoned at Exeter; as were several others, one of whom, an honest, tender man, died in prison there, whose blood lieth on the heads of his persecutors.

The night we came to Exeter, I spoke with James Nayler. For I saw he was out and wrong. And so was his company. Next day, being First-day, we went to visit the prisoners, and had a meeting with them in the prison. But James Nayler and some of them could not stay the meeting.

The next day, I spoke to James Nayler again. And he slighted what I said, and was dark, and much out. Yet he would have come and kissed me. But I said since he had turned against the power of God, I could not receive his show of kindness. The Lord moved me to slight him, and to set the power of God over him. So after I had been warring with the world, there was now a wicked spirit risen up amongst Friends to war against. I admonished him and his company.

When he was come up to London, his resisting the power of God in me, and the truth that was declared to him by me, became one of his greatest burdens. But he came to see his out-going, and to condemn it. And after some time, he returned to truth again.

THE PROTECTOR'S CONDITION

We rode to London. When we came near Hyde Park, we saw a great concourse of people, and looking towards them, espied the Protector coming in his coach. Whereupon I rode to his coach-side; and some of his life-guards would have put me away, but he forbade them. So I rode by with him, declaring what the Lord gave me to say to him of his condition, and of the sufferings of Friends in the nation, showing him how contrary this persecution was to Christ and his apostles, and to Christianity.

When we arrived at James's Park gate, I left him. And at parting he desired me to come to his house. Next day, one of his wife's maids, whose name was Mary Saunders, came to me at my lodging and told me her master came to her and said he would tell her some good news. When she asked him what it was, he told her

George Fox was come to town. She replied that was good news indeed (for she had received truth), but she said she could hardly believe him, till he told her how I met him, and rode from Hyde Park to James's Park with him.

After a little while, Edward Pyot and I went to Whitehall. And when we came before him, Dr Owen, Vice-Chancellor of Oxford, was with him. We were moved to speak to Oliver Cromwell concerning the sufferings of Friends, and laid them before him; and directed him to the light of Christ, who enlighteneth every man that cometh into the world. He said it was a natural light. But we showed him the contrary, and manifested that it was divine and spiritual, proceeding from Christ, the spiritual and heavenly man. And that which was called the *life* in Christ the Word, was called the *light* in us.

The power of the Lord God arose in me, and I was moved in it to bid him lay down his crown at the feet of Jesus. Several times I spoke to him to the same effect. Now I was standing by the table, and he came and sat upon the table's side by me, and said he would be as high as I was; and so continued speaking against the light of Christ Jesus; and went away in a light manner.

But the Lord's power came over him, so that when he came to his wife and other company, he said: 'I never parted so from them before.' For he was judged in himself.

THE SACRAMENTS

I was moved of the Lord to travel over the nation, the truth being now spread, and finely planted in most places, that I might answer and remove out of the minds of people some objections, which the envious priests and professors had raised and spread about concerning us. For what Christ said of false prophets and anti-christs coming in the last days, they applied to us; and said we were they. Therefore was I moved to open this through the nation, and to show that they who said we were the false prophets, anti-christs and deceivers, that should come in the last days, were indeed themselves they.

[One] great objection they had: that the Quakers denied the sacrament (as they called it) of bread and wine, which, they said, they were to take and do in remembrance of Christ to the end of the world. Much work we had with the priests and professors about this, and the several modes of receiving it in Christendom, so called. For some take it kneeling, and some sitting. But none of them all, that ever I could find, take it as the disciples took it. For they took it in a chamber, after supper. But these generally take it before dinner. And some say, after the priest hath blessed it, it is Christ's body. But as to the matter, Christ said: 'Do this in remembrance of me'. He did not tell them how often they should do it, or how long. Neither did He enjoin them to do it always, as long as they lived, or that all believers in Him should do it to the world's end.

Now ye that eat and drink this outward bread and wine in remembrance of Christ's death, and have your fellowships in that, will ye come no nearer to Christ's death than to take bread and wine in remembrance of it? After ye have eaten in remembrance of His death, ye must come into His death, and die with Him, as the apostles did, if ye will live with Him. This is a nearer and further advanced state, to be with Him in the fellowship of His death, than only to take bread and wine in remembrance of His death.

You must have fellowship with Christ in His sufferings. If ye will reign with Him, ye must suffer with Him; if ye will live with Him, ye must die with Him; and if ye die with Him, ye must be buried with Him. And being buried with Him in the true baptism, ye also rise with Him. Then having suffered with Him, died with Him, and been buried with Him, if ye are risen with Christ, seek those things which are above, where Christ sitteth on the right hand of God.

Eat the bread which comes down from above, which is not outward bread. And drink the cup of salvation, which He gives in

His kingdom, which is not outward wine. And then there will not be a looking at the things that are seen (as outward bread and wine, and water are). For, as says the apostle: 'The things that are seen are temporal, but the things that are not seen are eternal'.

PATIENCE BRINGS VICTORY

In this year [1656], the Lord's truth was finely planted over the nation, and many thousands were turned to the Lord. Insomuch that there were seldom fewer than one thousand in prison in this nation for truth's testimony: some for tithes, some for going to the steeple-houses, some for contempts (as they called them), some for not swearing and others for not putting off their hats, etc.

Now after I had visited most parts of the nation, and was come to London again, finding that evil spirit at work, which had drawn [James Nayler] and his followers out from truth, to run Friends into heats about him, I wrote a short epistle to Friends, as follows:-

To all the elect seed of God called Quakers, where the death is brought into the death, and the elder is servant to the younger, and the elect is known, which cannot be deceived, but obtains victory. This is the word of the Lord God to you all: go not forth to the aggravating part, to strive with it out of the power of God, lest ye hurt yourselves and run into the same nature, out of the life. For patience must get the victory. And to answer that of God in everyone, it must bring everyone to it, to bring them from the contrary.

Let your moderation and temperance and patience be known unto all men in the Seed of God. For that which reacheth to the aggravating part without life sets up the aggravating part, and breeds confusion; and hath a life in outward strife, but reacheth not to the witness of God in everyone, through which they might come into peace and covenant with God, and fellowship one with another. Therefore that which reacheth this witness of God in yourselves, and in others, is the life and the light, which will outlast all, is over all and will overcome all. And therefore in the Seed of life live, which bruiseth the Seed of death. G.F.

A NOISY RECEPTION IN WALES

I passed into Wales. Going to Cardiff, a justice of the peace sent to me, desiring I would come with half a dozen of my friends to his house. So I took a friend or two and went up to him, and he and his wife received us very civilly. The next day we had a meeting at Cardiff, in the town hall, and that justice sent about seventeen of his family to the meeting. There came some disturbers, but the Lord's power was over them, and many were turned to the Lord. To some that had run out with James Nayler, and did not come to the meetings, I sent word that the day of their visitation was over. And they never prospered after.

We passed on through the countries till we came to Brecknock, where we set up our horses at the inn. There went with me Thomas Holmes and John-ap-John, who was moved of the Lord to speak in the streets. I walked out a little into the fields, and when I came in again, the town was in uproar. When I came into the chamber in the inn, it was full of people, and they were speaking in Welsh. I desired them to speak in English, which they did; and much discourse we had.

After a while, they went away. But towards the night the magistrates gathered together in the streets, with a multitude of people, and they bid them shout, and gathered up the town; so that for about two hours together, there was such a noise that the like we had not heard. And the magistrates set them to shout again, when they had given over. We thought it looked like the uproar, which we read was amongst Diana's craftsmen. This tumult continued till night. And if the Lord's power had not limited them, they seemed likely to have pulled down the house, and us to pieces.

At night, the woman of the house would have had us go to supper in another room, but we, discerning her plot, refused. Then she would have had half a dozen men come into the room to us, under pretence of discoursing with us. We told her no persons should come into our room that night, neither would we go to them. Then she said we should sup in another room. But we told her we would have no supper, if not in our own room. At length, when she saw she could not get us out, she brought up our supper in a great rage. So she and they were crossed in their design, for they had an intent to do us mischief; but the Lord God prevented them.

THE WATER OF LIFE

After this, we returned to England, and came to William Gandy's in Cheshire, where we had a meeting of between two and three thousand people. At this time, there was a great drought. And after this meeting was ended, there fell so great a rain that Friends said they thought we could not travel, the waters would be so risen. But I believed the rain had not extended so far, as they had come that day to the meeting. Next day, when we turned back into some parts of Wales again, the roads were dusty, and no rain had fallen there.

When Oliver Cromwell sent forth a proclamation for a fast throughout the nation for rain, it was observed that as far as truth had spread in the North, there were pleasant showers and rain enough; when in the South, in many places they were almost spoiled for want of rain. At that time I was moved to write an answer to the Protector's proclamation, wherein I told him if he had come to own God's truth, he should have had rain; and that drought was a sign unto them of their barrenness and want of the water of life.

THE RIGOURS OF TRAVEL

We went to Beaumaris [in Anglesey], a town where John-ap-John had formerly been preacher. After we had put up our horses at an inn, John went forth and spoke through the street. And there being a garrison in the town, they took him and put him in prison. The innkeeper's wife came and told me that the governor and magistrates were sending for me, to commit me to prison also. I told her they had done more than they could answer already, and had acted contrary to Christianity in imprisoning him for reproving sin in the streets and for declaring the truth.

Soon after came other friendly people, and told me if I went out into the street they would imprison me also. And therefore they desired me to keep at the inn. Upon this I was moved to go and walk up and down the streets, and told the people what an uncivil and unchristian thing they had done, in casting my friend into prison. And they being high professors, I asked them if this was the entertainment they had for strangers; if they would willingly be so served themselves; and whether they, who looked upon the Scriptures to be their rule, had any example therein from Christ or His apostles, for what they had done. So after a while they set John-ap-John at liberty,

Next day, being market-day, we were to cross a great water. And not far from the place where we were to take boat, many of the market people drew to us, amongst whom we had good service for the Lord. After the Lord's truth had been declared to them in the power of God, and Christ the free teacher set over all the hireling teachers, I bid John-ap-John get his horse into the boat, which was then ready. But there being a company of wild gentlemen, as they called them, got into it, whom we found very rude, and far from gentlemen, they, with others, kept his horse out of the boat. I rode to the boat's side and spoke to them, showing them what unmanly and unchristian conduct it was. As I spoke, I leaped my horse into the boat amongst them, thinking John's horse would have followed, when he had seen mine go in before him. But the water being deep, John could not get his horse into the boat. Wherefore I leaped out again on horseback into the water, and stayed with John on that side till the boat returned.

There we tarried from eleven in the forenoon to two in the afternoon, before the boat came to fetch us. And then we had forty-two miles to ride that evening. And when we had paid for our passage, we had but one groat left between us in money. We rode about sixteen miles, and then got a little hay for our horses. Setting forward again, we came in the night to a little ale-house, where we intended to stay and bait. But finding we could have neither oats nor hay there, we travelled on all night; and about five in the morning, got to a place within six miles of Wrexham; where that day we met with Friends, and had a glorious meeting. Very weary we were with travelling so hard up and down in Wales. And in many places we found it difficult to get meat either for our horses or ourselves.

PELTED IN MANCHESTER

Thence [in 1657] we came to Manchester; and the sessions being there that day, many rude people were come out of the country. In the meeting they threw at me coals, clods, stones and water. Yet the Lord's power bore me up over them, that they could not strike me down. At last, when they saw they could not prevail by throwing water, stones and dirt at me, they went and informed the justices in the sessions; who thereupon sent officers to fetch me before them. The officers came in while I was declaring the word of life to the people, and plucked me down, and haled me up into their court.

When I came there, all the court was in disorder and noise. Wherefore I asked where were the magistrates that they did not keep the people civil. Some of the justices said they were magistrates. I asked them why then did they not appease the people, and keep them sober. For one cried: 'I'll swear!' And another cried: 'I'll swear!'

I declared to the justices how we were abused in our meeting by the rude people who threw stones and clods, dirt and water. And how I was haled out of the meeting and brought thither, contrary to the instrument of government, which said none shall be molested in their meetings that professed God, and owned the Lord Jesus Christ, which I did. So the truth came over them, that when one of the rude fellows cried he would swear, one of the justices checked him, saying: 'What will you swear? Hold your tongue!'

At last they bid the constable take me to my lodging, and there be secured till morning, till they sent for me again. So the constable had me to my lodging; and as we went the people were exceedingly rude. But I let them see the fruits of their teachers, and how they shamed Christianity and dishonoured the name of Jesus, which they professed. At night, we went to a justice's house in the town, who was pretty moderate. And I had much discourse with him.

Next morning, we sent to the constable to know if he had anything more to say to us. And he sent us word he had nothing to say to us, but that we might go whither we would. The Lord hath since raised up a people to stand for His name and truth in that town over those chaffy professors.

SCOTTISH CURSES

I had for some time felt drawings on my spirit to go into Scotland, and had sent to Colonel William Osburn of Scotland, desiring him to come and meet me. And he, with some others, came out of Scotland to this meeting [in Cumberland]. After the meeting was over (which, he said, was the most glorious one he ever saw in his life), I passed with him and his company into Scotland; having Robert Widders with me – a thundering man against hypocrisy, deceit and the rottenness of the priests.

The noise was spread over Scotland, amongst the priests, that I was come thither. And a great cry was among them that all would be spoiled. For they said I had spoiled all the honest men and women in England already, so according to their account, the worst was left to them. Upon this they gathered great assemblies of priests together, and drew up a number of curses to be read in their several steeple-houses, that all the people might say 'Amen' to them. Some few of these I will here set down. The rest can be read in the book 'The Scotch Priests' Principles'.

The first was: 'Cursed is he that saith every man hath a light within him sufficient to lead him to salvation; and let all the people say "Amen".'

The second: 'Cursed is he that saith faith is without sin; and let all the people say "Amen".'

The third: 'Cursed is he that denieth the Sabbath day; and let all the people say "Amen".'

In this last, they make the people curse themselves. For on the Sabbath day (which is the seventh day of the week, which the Jews kept by the command of God to them), they kept markets and fairs, and so brought the curse upon their own heads.

As to the first, concerning the light, Christ saith: 'Believe in the light, that ye may become children of the light'. And 'he that believeth shall be saved; he that believeth shall have everlasting life; he that believeth passes from death to life, and is grafted into Christ.' And 'ye do well,' said the apostle, 'that ye take heed unto the light that shines in the dark place, until the day dawn and the day-star arise in your hearts.' So the light is sufficient to lead unto the day-star.

And as concerning faith, it is the gift of God; and every gift of God is pure. The faith, which Christ is the author of, is precious, divine and without sin. This is the faith which gives victory over sin, and access to God; in which faith they please God. But they are reprobates themselves concerning this faith, and are in their dead faith, who charge sin upon this faith, under pain of a curse; which faith grows victory over their curse, and returns it into their own bowels.

A PRIEST LOSES HIS SENSES

There were two Independent churches in Scotland, in one of which many were convinced. But the pastor of the other was in a great rage against truth and Friends. They had their elders, who sometimes would exercise their gifts amongst the church members, and were sometimes pretty tender. But their pastor speaking so much against the light and us, the friends of Christ, he darkened his hearers, so that they grew blind and dry, and lost their tenderness. He continued preaching against Friends, and against the light of Jesus Christ, calling it natural. At last one day in his preaching, he cursed the light, and fell down, as if dead, in his pulpit.

The people carried him out, and laid him upon a gravestone, and poured strong waters into him, which brought him to life again. And they carried him home, and he was mopish. After a while, he stripped off his clothes, put on a Scotch plaid and went into the country amongst the dairy-women.

When he had stayed there about two weeks, he came home and went into the pulpit again. Whereupon the people expected some great manifestation or revelation from him. But instead thereof, he began to tell them what entertainment he had met with; how one woman gave him skimmed milk, another gave him buttermilk and another gave him good milk. So the people were fain to take him out of the pulpit again, and carry him home.

He that gave me this account was Andrew Robinson, one of his chief hearers, who came afterwards to be convinced and received the truth. He said he never heard that he recovered his senses again. By this people may see what came upon him that cursed the light; which Light is the Life in Christ, the Word. And it may be a warning to all others that speak against the Light of Christ.

TOLD TO LEAVE SCOTLAND

Now were the priests in such a rage that they posted to Edinburgh, to Oliver Cromwell's Council there, with petitions against me. The noise was that all was gone. For several Friends were come out of England and spread over Scotland, sounding the day of the Lord, preaching the everlasting gospel of salvation, and turning people to Christ Jesus, who died for them, that they might receive His free teaching. After I had gathered the principles of the Scotch priests and the sufferings of Friends, and had seen the Friends in that part of Scotland settled, by the Lord's power, upon Christ's foundation, I went to Edinburgh; where many thousands were gathered together, with abundance of priests among them, about burning a witch. And I was moved to declare the day of the Lord amongst them.

When I had done, I went to our meeting, whither many rude people and Baptists came. The Baptists began to vaunt with their logic and syllogisms. But I was moved in the Lord's power to thrash their chaffy, light minds; and showed the people there that after that fallacious way of discoursing, they might make white seem black and black white; as that because a cock had two legs, and each of them had two legs, therefore they were all cocks. Thus they might turn anything into lightness and vanity.

Now, when I came from the meeting to the inn where I lodged, an officer belonging to the Council brought me the following order:-

> Thursday, the 8th of October 1657, at His Highness's Council in Scotland: ORDERED that George Fox do appear before the Council on Tuesday the 13th of October next, in the forenoon. E. Downing, Clerk of the Council.

When he had delivered me the order, he asked me whether I would appear or not. I did not tell him whether I would or not, but asked him if he had not forged the order. He said no, it was a real order from the Council, and he was sent as their messenger with it.

When the time came, I appeared and was conducted into a large room, where many great persons came and looked at me. After a while the door-keeper had me into the council chamber. And as I was going in, he took off my hat. I asked him why he did so, and who was there, that I might not go in with my hat on. For I told him I had been before the Protector with it on. But he hung it up and had me in before them.

When I had stood for a while, and they had said nothing to me, I was moved of the Lord to say: 'Peace be amongst you. Wait in the fear of God, that ye may receive His wisdom from above, by which all things were made and created; that by it ye may all be ordered, and may order all things unto your hands to God's glory.'

They asked me what was the occasion of my coming into the nation. I told them I came to visit the seed of God, which had long lain in bondage under corruption. And the intent of my coming was that all in the nation that professed the Scriptures, the words of Christ, and of the prophets and apostles, might come to the light, Spirit and power, which they were in, who gave them forth.

They asked me whether I had any outward business there. I said 'nay'. Then they asked me how long I intended to stay in the country. I told them I should say little to that. My time was not to be long, yet in my freedom in the Lord, I stood in the will of Him that sent me. Then they bid me withdraw, and the door-keeper took my hand and led me forth.

In a little time, they sent for me again, and told me I must depart the nation of Scotland by that day seventh night. I asked them why. What had I done? What was my transgression, that they passed such a sentence upon me, to depart out of the nation? They told me they would not dispute with me. Then I desired them to hear what I had to say to them, but they said they would not hear me. I told them Pharaoh heard Moses and Aaron, and yet he was a heathen and no Christian; and Herod heard John the Baptist and they should not be worse than these. But they cried: 'withdraw, withdraw!'. Whereupon the door-keeper took me again by the hand and led me out.

Then I returned to my inn, and continued still in Edinburgh, visiting Friends there and thereabouts, and strengthening them in the Lord. After a little time, I wrote a letter to the Council, to lay before them their unchristian dealing in banishing me, an innocent man, that sought their salvation and eternal good. When this was delivered and read amongst them, some of them, I heard, were troubled at what they had done, being made sensible that they would not be so served themselves. But it was not long before they that banished me were banished themselves, or glad to get away.

MINISTRY AMONG THIEVES

Once as I was going with William Osburn to his house, there lay a company of rude fellows by the wayside, hid under the hedges and in the bushes. Seeing them, I asked him what they were. 'O, said he, 'they are thieves.' Robert Widders, being moved to go and speak to a priest, was left behind, intending to come after. So I said to William Osburn: 'I will stay here in this valley; and do thou go look after Robert Widders.' But he was unwilling to go, being afraid to leave me there alone, because of those fellows, till I told him I feared them not.

Then I called to them, asking them what they lay lurking there for. And I bid them come to me; but they were loath to come. I charged them to come up to me, or else it might be worse with them. Then they came trembling, for the dread of the Lord had struck them. I admonished them to be honest, and directed them to the light of Christ in their hearts, that by it they might see what an evil it was to follow after theft and robbery. And the power of the Lord came over them.

I stayed there till William Osburn and Robert Widders came up, and then we passed on together. But it is likely that if we two had gone away before, they would have robbed Robert Widders when he had come after alone, there being three or four of them.

THICK, CLODDY EARTH

We passed thence through several other places, till we came to Johnstons, where were several Baptists that were very bitter, and came in a rage to dispute with us; vain janglers[25] and disputers indeed they were. When they could not prevail by disputing, they went and informed the governor against us. And next morning raised a whole company of foot, and banished me and Alexander Parker, also James Lancaster and Robert Widders, out of the town.

As they guarded us through the town, James Lancaster was moved to sing with a melodious sound in the power of God. And I was moved to proclaim the day of the Lord and preach the everlasting gospel to the people. For they generally came forth, so that the streets were filled with them. And the soldiers were so ashamed that they said they would rather have gone to Jamaica than have guarded us so. But we were put into a boat with our horses, carried over the water and there left. The Baptists, who were the cause of our being put out of this town, were themselves not long after turned out of the army. And he that was then governor was discarded also when the king came in.

Being thus thrust out of Johnstons, we went to another market town. We went to an inn and desired to have a meeting in the town, that we might preach the everlasting gospel amongst them. The officers and soldiers said we should have it in the town hall. But the Scotch magistrates in spite appointed a meeting there that day, for the business of the town. When the officers of the soldiery understood this, and perceived that it was done in malice, they would have had us go into the town hall nevertheless. But we told them by no means, for then the magistrates might inform the governor against them, and say they took the town hall from them by force, when they were to do their town business therein.

We told them we would go to the market-place. They said it was market day. We replied it was so much the better. For we would have all people to hear truth, and know our principles. Alexander Parker went and stood upon the market-cross with a Bible in his hand, and declared the truth amongst the soldiers and market people. But the Scots, being a dark, carnal people, gave little heed, and hardly took notice of what was said.

After a while, I was moved of the Lord to stand up at the cross, and declare with a loud voice the everlasting truth, and the day of the Lord that was coming upon all sin and wickedness. Whereupon the people came running out of the town hall, and they gathered so together, that at last we had a large meeting. For they sat in the court only for a pretence, to hinder us from having the hall to meet in.

Several of them were made loving to us, especially the English people, and some afterwards came to be convinced. But there was a soldier that was very envious against us. He hated both us and the truth; spoke evil of it and very despitefully against the light of Christ Jesus, to which we bore testimony. Mighty zealous he was for the priests and the hearers. As this man was hearing the priest, holding his hat before his face, while the priest prayed, one of the priest's hearers stabbed him to death. So he who had rejected the teachings of the Lord Jesus Christ, and cried down the servants of the Lord, was murdered amongst them whom he had so cried up, and by one of them.

The last meeting I had in Scotland [was in Dunbar]. The truth and the power of God was set over that nation, and many, by the power and Spirit of God, were turned to the Lord Jesus Christ, their Saviour and teacher, whose blood was shed for them. And there is since a great increase, and great there will be in Scotland. For when first I set my horse's feet upon Scottish ground, I felt the seed of God to sparkle about me, like innumerable sparks of fire. Not but that there is an abundance of thick, cloddy earth of hypocrisy and falseness above, and a briery, brambly nature, which is to be burnt up with God's word, and ploughed up with his spiritual plough, before God's seed brings forth heavenly and spiritual fruit to His glory. But the husbandman is to wait in patience.

THE CHURCH OF ROME

I had not long been in London [in 1658] before I heard that a Jesuit, who came over with an ambassador from Spain, had challenged all the Quakers to dispute with them at the Earl of Newport's house. Whereupon Friends let him know that some would meet him. Then he sent us word he would meet with twelve of the wisest and most learned men we had. A while after, he sent word he would meet with but six. And after that, he sent us word again he would have but three to come. We hastened what we could lest, after all his great boast, he should put it quite off at last.

When we were come to the house, I bid Nicholas Bond and Edward Burrough go up and enter into discourse with him; and

I would walk a while in the yard, and then come up after them. I advised them to state this question to him: whether or not the Church of Rome, as it now stood, was not degenerated from the true church, which was in the primitive times, from the life and doctrine, and from the power and Spirit that they were in. They stated the question accordingly, and the Jesuit affirmed that the Church of Rome now was in the virginity and purity of the primitive church.

By this time, I was come to them. Then we asked him whether they had the Holy Ghost poured out upon them, as the apostles had. He said 'no'. 'Then,' said I, 'if ye have not the same Holy Ghost poured forth upon you, and the same power and Spirit that the apostles had, then ye are degenerated from the power and Spirit which the primitive church was in.' There needed little more to be said to that.

Then I asked him what Scripture they had for setting up cloisters for nuns, abbeys and monasteries for men, for all their several orders; and for their praying by beads and to images; for making crosses, for forbidding meats and marriages, and for putting people to death for religion. 'If,' said I, 'ye are in the practice of the primitive church, in its purity and virginity, then let us see by Scriptures wherever they practised any such things.'

Then he brought the Scripture, where the apostle says (2 Thess. ii.5) 'when I was with you, I told you these things'. 'That is,' said he, 'I told you of nunneries and monasteries and of putting to death for religion, and of praying by beads, and to images, and all the rest of the practices of the Church of Rome, which was the unwritten word of the apostles, which they told then, and have since been continued down by tradition unto these times.'

Then I desired him to read the Scripture again, that he might see how he had perverted the apostle's words. For that which he there tells the Thessalonians he had told them before is not an unwritten word, but is there written down, namely, that the man of sin, the son of perdition, shall be revealed, before that great and terrible day of Christ, which he was writing of, should come. So this was not telling them any of those things that the Church of Rome practises.

In like manner, the apostle, in the third chapter of that epistle, tells the church of some disorderly persons he heard were amongst them: busy-bodies, who did not work at all; concerning whom he commanded them by his unwritten word, when he was among them, that if any would not work, neither should he eat; which now he commands them again in his written word in this epistle, 2 Thess. iii. So this Scripture afforded no proof for their invented traditions. And he had no other Scripture proof to offer. Therefore I told him this was another degeneration of their church into such inventions and traditions as the apostles and primitive saints never practised.

WARNINGS TO CROMWELL

During the time I was at London, many services lay upon me. For it was the time of much suffering. I was moved to write to Oliver Cromwell, and lay before him the sufferings of Friends, both in this nation and in Ireland.

There was also a rumour about this time of making Cromwell king. Whereupon I was moved to go to him, and warned him against it, and of divers dangers; which, if he did not avoid, he would bring a shame and ruin upon himself and his posterity. He seemed to take well what I said to him, and thanked me. Yet afterwards I was moved to write to him more fully concerning the matter.

About this time came forth a declaration from Oliver Cromwell, the Protector, for a collection towards the relief of divers Protestant Churches, driven out of Poland. And of twenty Protestant families, driven out of the confines of Bohemia. And there having been a like declaration published some time before, to invite the nation to a day of solemn fasting and humiliation, in order to a contribution being made for the suffering Protestants of the valleys of Lucerne, Angrona etc., who were persecuted by the Duke of Savoy, I was moved to write to the Protector and chief magistrates on this occasion, both to show them the nature of a true fast (such as God required and accepts), and to make them sensible of their injustice and self-condemnation, in blaming the Papists for persecuting the Protestants abroad, while they themselves, calling themselves Protestants, were at the same time persecuting their Protestant neighbours and friends at home.

Divers times, both in the time of the Long Parliament and of the Protector (so called), and of the Committee of Safety, when they proclaimed fasts, I was moved to write to them and tell them their fasts were like unto Jezebel's. For commonly, when they proclaimed fasts, there was some mischief contrived against us. I knew their fasts were for strife and debate, to smite with the fist of wickedness; as the New England professors soon after did, who, before they put our Friends to death, proclaimed a fast also.

Now it was a time of great suffering. And many Friends being in prisons, many other Friends were moved to go to the Parliament, to offer up themselves to lie in the same dungeon, where their friends lay, that they were in prison might go out, and not perish in the stinking jails. This we did in love to God and our brethren, that they might not die in prison; and in love to those that cast them in, that they might not bring innocent blood upon their own heads; which we knew would cry to the Lord, and bring His wrath, vengeance and plagues upon them. But little favour could we find from those professing parliaments. Instead therefore they would rage, and sometimes threaten those Friends that thus attended them, that they would whip them and send them home.

Then commonly soon after the Lord would turn them out, and send them home, who had not a heart to do good in the day of their power. But they went not off without being forewarned, for I was moved to write to them, in their several turns, as I did to the Long Parliament, unto whom I declared, before they were broken up, that thick darkness was coming over them all, even a day of darkness that should be felt.

I went to Hampton Court, to speak with the Protector about the sufferings of Friends. I met him riding into Hampton Court Park, and before I came to him, as he rode at the head of his life-guard, I saw and felt a waft (or apparition) of death go forth against him. And when I came to him, he looked like a dead man. After I had laid the sufferings of Friends before him, and had warned him, according as I was moved to speak to him, he bid me come to his house.

So next day [I] went to Hampton Court, to speak further with him. But when I came, he was sick, and one that waited on him told me the doctors were not willing I should speak with him. So I passed away, and never saw him more.

A TIME OF GREAT CONFUSION

After a while, I went to Reading, where I was under great sufferings and exercises, and in great travail of spirit for about ten weeks. For I saw there was great confusion and distraction amongst the people, and that the powers were plucking each other to pieces. And I saw how many were destroying the simplicity, and betraying the truth. Much hypocrisy, deceit and strife was got uppermost in the people, so that they were ready to sheath their swords in each other's bowels.

There had been a tenderness in many of them formerly, when they were low. But when they were got up, had killed and taken possession, they came to be as bad as others. So that we had much to do with them about our hats, and saying 'thou' and 'thee' to them. They turned their profession of patience and moderation into rage and madness. For they had hardened themselves by persecuting the innocent, and were at this time crucifying the Seed, Christ, both in themselves and others. Till at last they fell to biting and devouring one another, until they were consumed one of another.

So shortly after, God overthrew them and turned them upside down, and brought the king over them, who were often surmising that the Quakers met together to bring in King Charles; whereas Friends did not concern themselves with the outward powers or government. But at last the Lord brought him in, and many of them when they saw he would be brought in, voted for bringing him in. So with heart and voice praise the name of the Lord, to whom it doth belong; who over all hath the supremacy, and who will rock the nations, for He is over them.

I had a sight and sense of the king's return a good while before, and so had some others. I wrote to Oliver several times, and let him know that while he was persecuting God's people they whom he accounted his enemies were preparing to come upon him.

When some forward spirits that came amongst us would have bought Somerset House, that we might have meetings in it, I forbade them to do so. For I then foresaw the king's coming in again. Besides, there came a woman to me in the Strand, who had a prophecy concerning King Charles's coming in, three years before he came. And she told me she must go to him to declare it. I advised her to wait upon the Lord, and keep it to herself. For if it should be known that she went on such a message, they would look upon it as treason. But she said she must go and tell him, that he should be brought into England again. I saw her prophecy was true, and that a great stroke must come upon them in power. For they that had then got possession were so exceeding high, and such great persecution was acted by them, who called themselves saints, that they would take from Friends their copyhold lands, because they could not swear in their courts.

Sometimes when we laid these sufferings before Oliver Cromwell, he would not believe it. Wherefore Thomas Aldam and Anthony Pearson were moved to go through all the jails in England, and to get copies of Friends' commitments under the jailer's hands, that they might lay the weight of their sufferings upon Oliver Cromwell. And when he would not give order for the releasing of them, Thomas Aldam was moved to take his cap from off his head, and to rend it to pieces before him, and to say unto him: 'So shall thy government be rent from thee and thy house.'

A CALL TO PEACE

Now was there a great pother made about the image or effigy of Oliver Cromwell lying in state, men standing and sounding with trumpets over his image, after he was dead. At this my spirit was greatly grieved, and the Lord, I found, was highly offended.

Great stirs were in the nation, the minds of people being unsettled. Much plotting and contriving there was by the several factions, to carry on their several interests. And a great care being upon me, lest any young or ignorant people, that might sometimes come amongst us, should be drawn into this snare, I was moved to give forth the following epistle as a warning against all such:-

All Friends everywhere, keep out of plots and bustling, and the arm of the flesh. For all these are amongst Adam's sons in the fall, where they are destroying men's lives like dogs, beasts and swine, goring, rending and biting one another, destroying one another, and wrestling with flesh and blood. Whence arise wars and killing but from the lusts? Now all this is in Adam in the fall, out of Adam that never fell, in whom there is peace and life.

Ye are called to peace; therefore follow it. And that peace is in Christ, not in Adam in the fall. All that pretend to fight for Christ are deceived. For His kingdom is not of this world, therefore His servants do not fight. Fighters are not of Christ's kingdom, but are without Christ's kingdom. His kingdom stands in peace and righteousness, but fighters are in the lust. And all that would destroy men's lives are not of Christ's mind, who came to save men's lives.

Live in peace, in Christ the way of peace, and therein seek the peace of all men, and no man's hurt. Live all in the peaceable life, doing good to all men, and seeking the good and welfare of all men.

Not long after this [1659], George Booth rose up in arms in Cheshire, and Lambert went against him. At which time some foolish, rash spirits that came sometimes amongst us, were ready to take up arms. But I was moved of the Lord to warn and forbid them, and they were quiet. In the time of the Commitee of Safety (so called), we were invited by them to take up arms, and great places and commands were offered some of us. But we denied them all, and declared against it, both by word and writing, testifying that our weapons and armour were not carnal, but spiritual.

After I had travelled through many counties in the Lord's service, and many were convinced, notwithstanding the people in some of the places were very rude, I returned to London, when General Monk was come up thither, and the gates and posts of the city were pulling down. Long before this I had a vision, wherein I saw the city lie in heaps and the gates down. And it was then represented to me, just as I saw it several years after, lying in heaps, when it was burned.

Divers times, both by word and writing, had I forewarned the several powers, both in Oliver's time and after, of the day of recompense that was coming upon them. But they rejecting counsel, and slighting those visitations of love to them, I was moved now, before they were quite overturned, to lay their backsliding, hypocrisy and treacherous dealing before them.

DIVINE VENGEANCE

We passed into Somersetshire, where the Presbyterians and other professors were very wicked, and often disturbed Friends' meetings. One time especially there was a very wicked man, whom they got to come to the Quakers' meeting. This man put on a bear's skin on his back, and undertook with that to play pranks in the meeting. Accordingly, setting himself just opposite to the Friend that was speaking, he lolled his tongue out of his mouth, having his bear's skin on his back, and so made sport to his wicked followers, and caused a great disturbance in the meeting.

But an eminent judgement overtook him, and his punishment slumbered not. For as he went back from the meeting, there was a bull-baiting in the way which he stayed to see. And coming within the bull's reach, he struck his horn under the man's chin into his throat, and struck his tongue out of his mouth, so that it hung lolling out, as he had used it before, in derision in the meeting. And the bull's horn running up into the man's head, he swung him about upon his horn in a most remarkable and fearful manner. Thus he that came to do mischief amongst God's people was mischiefed himself. And well would it be, if such apparent examples of divine vengeance would teach others to beware.

ON SHIPWRECKS

While I was in Cornwall, there were great shipwrecks about the Land's End. Now it was the custom of that country that at such a time both rich and poor went out, to get as much of the wreck as they could, not caring to save the people's lives. And in some places, they call shipwrecks 'God's Grace'.

These things troubled me. It grieved my spirit to hear of such unchristian actions, considering how far they were below the heathen at Melita, who received Paul, made him a fire and were courteous towards him, and them that had suffered the shipwreck with him. Wherefore I was moved to write a paper, and send it to all the parishes, priests and magistrates, to reprove them for such greedy actions, and to warn and exhort them that if they could assist to save people's lives, and preserve their ships and goods, they should use their diligence therein; and consider if it had been their own condition, they would judge it hard if they should be upon a wreck, and people should strive to get what they could get from them, and not regard their lives.

Friends have endeavoured much to save the lives of the crews in times of wrecks, and to preserve the ships and goods for them. And when some that have suffered shipwreck have been almost dead and starved, Friends have taken them to their houses, to succour and recover them; which is an act to be practised by all true Christians.

YEARLY MEETING

[In 1660], I came to Balby in Yorkshire, where our Yearly Meeting[26] at that time was held in a great orchard of John Killam's, where it was supposed some thousands of people and Friends were gathered together. In the morning I heard that a troop of horse was sent from York, to break up our meeting, and that the militia, newly raised, was to join them. I went into the meeting and stood up on a great stool, and after I had spoken for some time, two trumpeters came up, sounding their trumpets near me. And the captain of the troop cried: 'Divide to the right and left, and make way.'

Then they rode up to me. I was declaring the everlasting truth and word of life, in the mighty power of the Lord. The captain bid me come down, for he was come to disperse our meeting. After some time, I told him they all knew we were a peaceable people, and used to have such great meetings. But if he apprehended that we met in a hostile way, I desired him to make search among us. And if he found either sword or pistol about any there, let such suffer.

He told me he must see us dispersed, for he came all night on purpose to disperse us. I asked him what honour it would be to him, to ride with swords and pistols amongst so many unarmed men and women as there were. If he would be still and quiet, our meeting probably might not continue above two or three hours. He said he could not stay to see the meeting ended, but must disperse them before he went.

I desired him then, if he himself could not stay, that he would let a dozen of his soldiers stay, and see the order and peaceableness of our meeting. He said he would permit us an hour's time, and let half a dozen soldiers with us. Then he went away with his troop, and Friends of the house gave the soldiers that stayed, and their horses, some meat. When the captain was gone, the soldiers that were left told us we might stay till night if we would. But we stayed but about three hours after, and had a glorious, powerful meeting.

FRIENDS' AFFAIRS

I passed to Skipton, where there was a general meeting of men Friends out of many counties, concerning the affairs of the church. A Friend went naked [down to the waist] through the town, declaring truth, and he was much beaten. Some others also came to me all bloody. To this meeting came many Friends out of most parts of the nation, for it was about business relating to the church, both in this nation and beyond the seas.

Several years before, when I was in the North, I was moved to recommend the setting up of this meeting for that service. For many Friends suffered in divers parts of the nation, their goods were taken from them contrary to the law, and they understood not how to help themselves, or where to seek redress. But after this meeting was set up, several Friends who had been magistrates, and others that understood something of the law, came thither and were able to inform Friends, and to assist them in gathering up the sufferings, that they might be laid before the justices, judges or Parliament.

This meeting had stood several years, and divers justices and captains had come to break it up. But when they understood the business Friends met about, and saw their books and accounts of collections for relief of the poor, how we took care one county to help another, and to help our friends beyond the seas, and provide for our poor, that none of them should be chargeable to their parishes etc., the justices and officers confessed we did their work, and passed away peaceably and lovingly, commending Friends' practice.

ARRESTED AT SWARTHMORE

I went to Swarthmore, Francis Howgill and Thomas Curtis being with me. I had not been long there before Henry Porter, a justice, sent a warrant by the chief constable and three petty constables to apprehend me. I had a sense of this beforehand, and being in the parlour with Margaret Fell, her servants came and told her there were some come to search the house for arms. And they went up into the chambers under that pretence. It came upon me to go out to them. And as I was going by some of them, I spoke to them. Whereupon they asked me my name. I readily told them my name. And then they laid hold on me, saying I was the man they looked for; and led me away to Ulverstone.

They kept me all night at the constable's house, and set a guard of fifteen or sixteen men to watch me, some of whom sat in the chimney, for fear I should go up it. Such dark imaginations possessed them.

Next morning, about six, I was putting on my boots and spurs to go with them before some justice; but they pulled off the latter, took my knife out of my pocket and hastened me away along the town, with a party of horse and abundance of people, not suffering me to stay till my own horse came down. When I was gone about a quarter of a mile with them, some Friends, with Margaret Fell and her children, came towards me. And then a great party of horse gathered about me in a mad rage and fury, crying out: 'Will they rescue him? Will they rescue him?' Whereupon I said unto them: 'Here is my hair, here is my back, here are my cheeks; strike on!'

Then they brought a little horse, and two of them took up one of my legs and put my foot in the stirrup, and two or three lifting over my other leg, set me upon it behind the saddle, and so led the horse by the halter. But I had nothing to hold on by. When they were come some distance out of the town, they beat the little horse, and made him kick and gallop. Whereupon I slipped off him, and told them they should not abuse the creature.

Then they led me to Lancaster. The spirits of the people being mightily up, I stood and looked earnestly upon them. And they cried: 'Look at his eyes!'

After a little time, the officers had me to Major Porter's, the justice. When I came in I said: 'Peace be amongst you.' Porter asked me why I came down into the country that troublesome time. I told him: to visit my brethren. 'Then,' said he, 'you have great meetings up and down.' I told him though we had, our meetings were known throughout the nation to be peaceable, and we were a peaceable people. He said we saw the devil in people's faces. I told him if I saw a drunkard, or a swearer, or a peevish, heady man, I could not say I saw the Spirit of God in him.

He said we could express ourselves well enough, and he would not dispute with me. But he would restrain me. I desired to know for what, and by whose order he sent his warrant for me. He told me he had an order, but would not let me see it. For he would not reveal the king's secrets. 'And besides, a prisoner,' he said, 'was not to see for what he was committed.' I told him that was not reason. For how should he make his defence then?

Then he charged me as an enemy of the king; that I endeavoured to raise a new war, and imbrue the nation in blood again. I told him I had never learned the postures of war, but was clear and innocent as a child concerning those things, and therefore was bold. Then came the clerk with the mittimus, and the jailer was sent for, and commanded to take and put me there a close prisoner, till I should be delivered by the king or parliament.

AN APPEAL TO THE KING

Margaret Fell determined to go to London, to speak with the king about my being taken, and to show him the manner of it, and the unjust dealing and evil usage I had received. When Justice Porter heard of this, he vapoured that he would go and meet her in the gap. But when he came before the king, having been a zealous man for the parliament against the king, several of the courtiers spoke to him concerning his plundering their houses; so that he quickly had enough of the court, and soon returned into the country.

Meanwhile, the jailer seemed very fearful, and said he was afraid Major Porter would hang him, because he had not put me in the dark-house. But when the jailer waited on him, after his return from London, he was very blank and down and asked how I did, pretending he would find a way to set me at liberty.

About this time, Ann Curtis, of Reading, came to see me. And understanding how I stood committed, it was upon her also to go to the king about it. Her father, who had been sheriff of Bristol, had been hung near his own door for endeavouring to bring in the king; on which consideration she had some hopes the king might hear her on my behalf.

Accordingly, when she returned to London, she and Margaret Fell went to the king together, who, when he understood whose daughter she was, received her kindly. And her request to him being to send for me up, and hear the cause himself, he promised her he would, and commanded his secretary to send down an order for bringing me up. But when they came to the secretary for the order, he, being no friend to us, said it was not in his power. He must act according to law, and I must be brought up by an habeas corpus before the judges. So he wrote to the judge of the King's Bench, signifying that it was the king's pleasure that I should be sent up by an habeas corpus.

Accordingly, a writ was sent down, and delivered to the sheriff. But because it was directed to the chancellor of Lancaster, the sheriff put it off to him. On the other hand, the chancellor would not make the warrant upon it, but said the sheriff must do that. At length both chancellor and sheriff got together. But being both enemies of the truth, they sought occasion for delay, and found, they said, an error in the writ. So the matter rested a while, and I continued in prison.

I was moved to write to the king, to exhort him to exercise mercy and forgiveness towards his enemies, and to warn him to restrain the profaneness and looseness that had got up in the nation on his return. It was thus:-

King Charles,
Thou camest not into this nation by sword, nor by victory of war, but by the power of the Lord. Now if thou live not in it, thou wilt not prosper. If the Lord hath showed thee mercy and forgiven thee, and thou dost not show mercy and forgiveness, the Lord God will not hear thy prayers, nor them that pray for thee. If thou stop not persecution and persecutors, and take away all laws that hold up persecutions about religion; if thou persist in them, and uphold persecution, that will make thee as blind as those that have gone before thee. For persecution hath always blinded those that have gone into it. Such, God by His power overthrows, doth His valiant acts upon, and bringeth salvation to His oppressed ones.

If thou bear the sword in vain, and let drunkenness, oaths, plays, may-games, with such like abominations and vanities be encouraged or go unpunished, as setting up may-poles, with the image of the crown on top of them, etc., the nations will quickly turn like Sodom and Gomorrah, and be as bad as the old world, who grieved the Lord until He overthrew them. And so He will you, if these things be not suppressed.

Hardly was there so much wickedness at liberty before as there is at this day, as though there was no terror nor sword of magistracy; which doth not grace the government, nor is a praise to them that do well. Our prayers are for them that are in authority, that under them we may live a godly life, in which we have peace, and that we may not be brought into ungodliness by them. Hear, consider, and do good in thy time, whilst thou hast power. Be merciful and forgive. This is the way to overcome, and obtain the kingdom of Christ.   G.F.

It was long before the sheriff would yield to remove me to London. At last, when they saw they could do not otherwise with me, the sheriff yielded, consenting that I should come up with some of my friends, without any other engagement than my word, to appear before the judges at London, such a day of the term if the Lord permit.

When we came to Charing Cross, multitudes of people were gathered together to see the burning of the bowels of some of the old king's judges, who had been hung, drawn and quartered.

I appeared at the King's Bench bar at the hour appointed, Robert Widders, Richard Hubberthorn and Esquire Marsh going with me. The charge against me was read openly. The people were moderate and the judges cool and loving. And the Lord's mercy was to them. But when they came to that part which said that I and my friends were embroiling the nation in blood, and raising a new war, and that I was an enemy to the king, etc., they lifted up their hands. Then, stretching out my arms, I said: 'I am the man whom that charge is against. But I am as innocent as a child concerning the charge.'

Then stood up Esquire Marsh, who was of the king's bed-chamber, and told the judges it was the king's pleasure that I should be set at liberty, seeing no accuser came up against me. They asked me whether I would put it to the king and council; I said yes, with a good will. Thereupon they sent the sheriff's return, which he made to the writ of habeas corpus, containing the matter charged against me in the mittimus, to the king, that he might see for what I was committed.

On perusal of this, and consideration of the whole matter, the king, being satisfied of my innocency, commanded his secretary to send an order to Judge Mallet for my release, which he did. Thus, after being a prisoner more than twenty weeks, I was freely set at liberty by the king's command.

THE FIFTH MONARCHISTS

The everlasting power of the Lord was over all, and His blessed truth, life and light shone over the nation. And great and glorious meetings we had, and very quiet. And many flocked in unto the truth. Richard Hubberthorn had been with the king, who said none should molest us, so long as we lived peaceably; and promised this to us upon the word of a king, telling him we might make use of his promise.

Some Friends also were admitted into the House of Lords, and had liberty to declare their reasons why they could not pay tithes, swear or go to the steeple-house worship, or join with others in worship; and they heard them moderately. And there being about seven hundred Friends in prison in the nation, who had been committed under Oliver's and Richard's[27] government, upon contempts (as they call them), when the king came in, he set them all at liberty. There seemed at that time an inclination and intention in the government to grant Friends' liberty, because they were sensible that we had suffered as well as they under the former powers. But still, when anything was going forward in order thereto, some dirty spirits or other threw something in the way to stop it.

It was said there was an instrument drawn up for confirming our liberty, and that it only wanted signing; when, suddenly, that wicked attempt of the Fifth Monarchy people broke out, and put the city and nation in an uproar. This was a First-day night, and very glorious meetings we had that day. But about midnight, or soon after, the drums beat and the cry was: 'Arm! Arm!'

I got up out of bed, and in the morning took boat, and landing at Whitehall stairs, walked through Whitehall. They looked strangely at me there, but I passed through them and went to Pall Mall, where divers Friends came to me, though it had now become dangerous passing the streets. For by this time, the city and suburbs were up in arms, and exceedingly rude the people and soldiers were. Insomuch that Henry Fell, going to a Friend's house, the soldiers knocked him down and he would have been killed, had not the Duke of York come by.

I stayed at Pall Mall, intending to be at the meeting there. But on the Seventh-day night, a company of troopers came and knocked at the door. The servant letting them in, they rushed into the house, and laid hold of me. And there being amongst them one that had served under the parliament, he put his hand to my pocket and asked whether I had any pistols. I told him he knew I did not carry pistols. Why therefore ask such a question of me, whom he knew to be a peaceable man?

Others of the soldiers ran into the chambers, and there found in bed Esquire Marsh who, though he was one of the king's bedchamber, out of his love to me came and lodged where I did. When they came down again, they said: 'Why should we take this man away with us? We will let him alone.' 'O,' said the parliament soldier, 'he is one of the heads and a chief ringleader.' Upon this the soldiers were taking me away, but Esquire Marsh hearing of it sent for him that commanded the party, and desired him to let me alone, for he would see me forthcoming in the morning.

In the morning, before they could fetch me, and before the meeting was gathered, there came a company of footsoldiers to the house and one of them drawing his sword, held it over my head. I asked him why he drew his sword at an unarmed man. At which his fellows, being ashamed, bid him put up his sword.

These footsoldiers took me away to Whitehall, before the troopers came for me.

When I was brought to Whitehall, the soldiers and people were exceedingly rude, yet I declared the truth to them. But some great persons coming by, who were full of envy: 'What!' said they, 'Do you let him preach? Put him into prison, where he may not stir.' So into that place they put me, and the soldiers watched over me. After I had been kept there two or three hours, Esquire Marsh spoke to Lord Gerrard, and he bid them set me at liberty.

On this insurrection of the Fifth Monarchy men, great havoc was made both in city and country, so that it was dangerous for sober people to stir abroad for several weeks after. Men or women could hardly go up and down the streets to buy provisions for their families without being abused. In the country, they dragged men and women out of their houses, and some sick men out of their beds by the legs. Nay, one man in a fever the soldiers dragged out of bed to prison, and when he was brought there he died.

Margaret Fell went to the king and told him what sad work there was in the city and nation, and showed him we were an innocent, peaceable people, and that we must keep our meetings as heretofore, whatever we suffered; but that it concerned him to see that peace was kept, that no innocent blood might be shed. The prisons were now everywhere filled with Friends and others, in the city and country, and the posts were so laid for the searching of letters, that none should pass unsearched. We heard of several thousands of our Friends being cast into prison in several parts of the nation, and Margaret Fell carried an account of them to the king and council.

THE PEACE TESTIMONY

Having lost our former declaration in the press, we hastily drew up another against plots and fighting, got it printed and sent some copies to the king and council. Others were sold in the streets and at the Exchange.

A Declaration from the harmless and innocent people of God, called Quakers, against all sedition, plotters and fighters in the world; for removing the ground of jealousy and suspicion from magistrates and people concerning wars and fightings.

Our principle is, and our practices have always been, to seek peace and ensue it; to follow after righteousness and the knowledge of God; seeking the good and welfare, and doing that which tends to the peace of all. We know that wars and fightings proceed from the lusts of men, as James iv. 1-3, out of which the Lord hath redeemed us, and so out of the occasion of war. The occasion of war, and war itself (wherein envious men, who are lovers of themselves more than lovers of God, lust, kill and desire to have men's lives or estates) ariseth from lust. All bloody principles and practices, as to our own particulars, we utterly deny; with all outward wars and strife, and fightings with outward weapons, for any end, or under any pretence whatsoever. This is our testimony to the whole world.

We do earnestly desire and wait that, by the Word of God's power, and its effectual operation in the hearts of men, the kingdoms of this world may become the kingdoms of the Lord, and of His Christ; that He may rule and reign in men by His Spirit and truth; that there by all people, out of every profession, may be brought into love and unity with God, and one with another; and that they may all come to witness the prophet's words, who said: 'Nation shall not lift up sword against nation, neither shall they learn war any more' (Isa. ii.4, Mic. iv.3).

Whereas men come against us with clubs, staves, drawn swords, pistols cocked, and beat, cut and abuse us, yet we never resisted them; but to them our hair, backs and cheeks have been ready. It is not an honour to manhood or nobility to run upon harmless people, who lift not up a hand against them, with arms and weapons.

Therefore consider these things, ye men of understanding. For plotters, raisers of insurrections, tumultuous ones and fighters, running with swords, clubs, staves and pistols, one against another; these, we say, are of the world, and have their foundation from this unrighteous world, from the foundation of which the Lamb hath been slain; which Lamb hath redeemed us from this unrighteous world. And we are not of it, but are heirs of a world of which there is no end, and of a kingdom where no corruptible thing enters. Our weapons are spiritual and not carnal, yet mighty through God, to the pulling down of the strongholds of sin and Satan, who is the author of wars, fighting, murder and plots. Our swords are broken into ploughshares, and spears into pruning-hooks, as prophesied in Micah iv. Therefore we cannot learn war any more, neither raise up against nation or kingdom with outward weapons, though you have numbered us amongst the transgressors and plotters. The Lord knows our innocency herein, and will plead our cause with all people on earth, at the day of their judgement, when all men shall have a reward according to their works.

O Friends! Offend not the Lord and His little ones, neither afflict His people, but consider and be moderate. Do not run out hastily, but consider mercy, justice and judgement. That is the way for you to prosper and obtain favour of the Lord.

Our meetings were stopped and broken up in the days of Oliver, under pretence of plotting against him. In the days of the Committee of Safety we were looked upon as plotters to bring in King Charles. And now our peaceable meetings are termed seditious. O that men should lose their reason, and go contrary to their own conscience! We have suffered all along, because we would not take up carnal weapons to fight, and are thus made a prey, because we are the innocent lambs of Christ, and cannot avenge ourselves! These things are left on your hearts to consider. But we are out of all those things, in the patience of the saints. And we know, as Christ said: 'He that takes the sword shall perish with the sword'.

WILLIAM SYMPSON

William Sympson was moved of the Lord to go, several times for three years, naked and barefoot before [professors], as a sign to them, in markets, courts, towns, cities, to priests' and great men's houses, telling them so should they be stripped naked, as he was stripped! And sometimes he was moved to put on sackcloth and besmear his face, and tell them so would the Lord God besmear all their religion, as he was besmeared. Great sufferings did the poor man undergo. Sore whippings with horse-whips and coach-whips on his bare body, grievous stonings and imprisonments, that they might have taken warning. But they would not. They rewarded his love with cruel usage. Only the Mayor of Cambridge did nobly to him, for he put his gown about him and took him into his house.

FRIENDS IN NEW ENGLAND

We received account from New England that the government there had made a law to banish the Quakers out of their colonies, upon pain of death, in case they returned; and that several Friends, having been so banished, and returning, were taken and actually hung; and that many more were in prison, in danger of the like sentence being executed upon them. When those were put to death, I was in prison in Lancaster, and had a perfect sense of their sufferings, as though it had been myself, and as though the halter had been put about my own neck, though we had not at that time heard of it.

But as soon as we heard of it, Edward Burrough went to the king and told him there was a vein of innocent blood opened in his dominions, which, if not stopped, would overrun all. To which the king replied: 'But I will stop that vein.' Edward Burrough said: 'Then do it speedily, for we do not know how many may soon be put to death.' The king answered: 'As speedily as ye will. Call,' said he to some present, 'the secretary and I will do it presently.' The secretary being called, a mandamus was forthwith granted.

A day or two after, Edward Burrough going again to the king, to desire the matter might be expedited, the king said he had no occasion at present to send a ship thither, but if we would send one, we might do it as soon as we chose. Edward Burrough then asked the king if it would please him to grant his deputation to one called a Quaker, to carry the mandamus to New England. He said: 'Yes, to whom ye will.' Whereupon E.B. named Samuel Shattock, who, being an inhabitant of New England, was banished by their law, to be hung if he came again. And to him the deputation was granted.

Then he sent for Ralph Goldsmith, an honest Friend, who was master of a good ship, and agreed with him for £300, goods or no goods, to sail in ten days. He forthwith prepared to set sail and, with a prosperous gale, in about six weeks arrived before the town of Boston, in New England, upon a First-day morning. Many passengers went with him, both of New and Old England: Friends, whom the Lord moved to go to bear testimony against those bloody persecutors, who had exceeded all the world in that age in their persecutions.

The townsmen at Boston, seeing a ship come into the bay with English colours, soon came on board and asked for the captain. Ralph Goldsmith told them he was the commander. They asked him if he had any letters. He said 'yes'. They asked if he would deliver them. He said: 'No, not today.' So they went on shore and reported there was a ship full of Quakers, and that Samuel Shattock was among them, who, they knew, was by their law to be put to death, for coming again after banishment. But they knew not his errand, nor his authority.

So all being kept close that day, and none of the ship's company suffered to land, next morning Samuel Shattock, the king's deputy, and Ralph Goldsmith, the commander of the vessel, went on shore. And sending back to the ship the men that landed them, they two went through the town to the governor's (John Endicott's) door, and knocked.

He sent out a man to know their business. They sent him word their business was from the king of England, and they would deliver their message to none but the governor himself. They were then admitted, and the governor came to them. And having received the deputation and the mandamus, he put off his hat and looked upon them. Then going out, he bid the Friends follow him. He went to the deputy-governor, and after a short consultation, came out to the Friends and said: 'We shall obey His Majesty's commands.'

After this, the master gave liberty to the passengers to land. And presently the noise of the business flew about the town, and the Friends of the town and the passengers of the ship met together, to offer up their praises and thanksgivings to God, who had so wonderfully delivered them from the teeth of the devourer. While they were thus met, a poor Friend came in, who, being sentenced by their bloody law to die, had lain some time in irons, expecting execution. This added to their joy, and caused them to lift up their hearts in high praises to God, who is worthy forever to have the praise, the glory and the honour. For He only is able to deliver, to save and to support all that sincerely put their trust in Him.

AGAINST THE FIFTH MONARCHY MEN

As for the Fifth Monarchy men, I was moved to give forth a paper, to manifest their error to them. For they looked for Christ's personal coming in an outward form and manner, and fixed the time to the year 1666. At which time some of them prepared themselves when it thundered and rained, thinking Christ was then come to set up His kingdom. And they imagined they were to kill the whore without them. But I told them the whore was alive within them, and was not burned with God's fire, nor judged in them with the same power and Spirit the apostles were in. And their looking for Christ's coming outwardly to set up His kingdom was like the Pharisees' 'Lo here' and 'Lo there'. But the Christ was come and had set up His kingdom above sixteen hundred years ago (according to Nebuchadnezzar's dream and Daniel's prophecy) and He had dashed to pieces the four monarchies, the great image with its head of gold, breast and arms of silver, belly and thighs of brass, legs of iron and feet part of iron and part of clay. And they were all blown away with God's wind, as the chaff in the summer threshing-floor.

And when Christ was on earth, He said His kingdom was not of this world. If it had been, His servants would have fought, but it was not. Therefore His servants did not fight. Therefore all the Fifth Monarchy men, that are fighters with carnal weapons, are none of Christ's servants, but the beast's and the whore's. Christ said: 'All power in heaven and in earth is given to me.' So then His kingdom was set up above sixteen hundred years ago, and He reigns. 'And we shall see Christ reign,' said the apostle. And He shall reign till all things be put under His feet; though all things are not yet put under His feet, nor subdued.

MISSIONARY WORK

This year [1661], several Friends were moved to go beyond the seas, to publish truth in foreign countries. John Stubbs and Henry Fell and Richard Costrop were moved to go towards China and Prester John's country. But no masters of ships would carry them. With much ado they got a warrant from the king. But the East India Company found ways to avoid it, and masters of their ships would not carry them. Then they went into Holland, hoping to get passage there. But none could they get there either.

Then John Stubbs and Henry Fell took shipping for Alexandria in Egypt, intending to go by the caravans from thence. [They] reached Alexandria. But they had not been there long before the English consul banished them. Yet before they came away, they dispersed many books and papers, for opening the principles and way of truth to the Turks and Grecians. They gave the book called 'The Pope's Strength Broken' to an old friar, for him to give or send to the Pope; which when the friar had perused, he placed his hand on his breast and confessed what was written therein was truth. 'But,' said he, 'if I should confess it openly, they would burn me.'

John Stubbs and Henry Fell, not being suffered to go further, returned to England, and came to London again. John had a vision that the English and the Dutch, who had joined together not to carry them, would fall out one with the other. And so it came to pass.

FRIENDS' MARRIAGES

Among the exercises and troubles Friends had from without, one was regarding Friends' marriages, which sometimes were called in question. This year there was a cause tried at the assize in Nottingham concerning one. The case was thus. Some years before, two Friends were joined together as man and wife about two years. Then the man died, leaving his wife with child, and an estate in lands of copyhold. When the woman was delivered, the jury presented the child heir to its father's lands, and accordingly the child was admitted. Afterwards, another Friend married the widow.

After that, a man that was near of kin to her former husband brought his action against the Friend that had last married her, endeavouring to dispossess them, and deprive the child of the inheritance, and to possess himself thereof as next heir to the woman's first husband. To effect this, he endeavoured to prove the child illegitimate, alleging the marriage was not according to law.

In opening the cause, the plaintiff's counsel used unseemly words concerning Friends, saying they went together like brute beasts, with other ill expressions.

After the counsels on both sides had pleaded, the judge took the matter in hand, and opened it to the jury, telling them that there was a marriage in Paradise when Adam took Eve, and Eve took Adam, and that it was the consent of the parties that made a marriage. As for the Quakers, he said he did not know their opinions, but he did not believe they went together as brute beasts, as had been said of them, but as Christians. And therefore he believed the marriage was lawful, and the child lawful heir. The jury gave in their verdict for the Friend's child, against the man that would have deprived it of its inheritance.

TROUBLE OVER SWEARING

[In 1662], we came to Swannington in Leicestershire. At night, as I was sitting in the hall [of a Friend's house], speaking to a widow woman and her daughter, there came one called Lord Beaumont, with a company of soldiers, who, slapping their swords on the door, rushed into the house with swords and pistols in their hands crying: 'Put out the candles and make fast the doors!' Then they seized upon the Friends of the house and asked if there were no more about the house. The Friends told them there was one man more in the hall. There were some Friends out of Derbyshire, one of whom was named Thomas Fauks. And this Lord Beaumont, after he had asked all their names, bid his man set down that man's name Thomas Fox. But the Friend said his name was not Fox but Fauks.

In the meantime, some of the soldiers came and brought me out of the hall to him. He asked me my name. I told him my name was George Fox, and that I was well known by that name. 'Ay,' said he, 'you are known all the world over.' I said I was known for no hurt, but for good. Then he put his hand into my pockets to search them, and pulled out my comb-case, and afterwards commanded one of his officers to search further for letters, as he pretended. I told him I was no letter-carrier, and asked him why he came amongst a peaceable people with swords and pistols, without a constable, contrary to the king's proclamation, and to the late Act. For he could not say there was a meeting, I being only talking with a poor widow woman and her daughter. By reasoning thus with them, he came somewhat down. Yet sending for the constables, he gave them charge of us, and to bring us before him next morning. Accordingly, the constables set a watch of the town's-people upon us that night, and had us next morning to his house, about a mile from Swannington.

When we came before him, he told us we met contrary to the Act. I desired him to show us the Act. 'Why,' says he, 'you have it in your pocket.' I told him he did not find us in a meeting. Then he asked us whether we would take the oaths of allegiance and supremacy. I told him I never took any oaths in my life, nor engagement, nor covenant. Yet still he would force the oath upon us. I desired him to show us the oath, that we might see whether we were the persons it was to be tendered to, and whether it was not for the discovery of Popish recusants. At length, he brought us a little book. But we called for the statute-book. He would not show us that, but caused a mittimus to be made, which mentioned that we were to have had a meeting. With this he delivered us to the constables to convey us to Leicester jail.

But when they had brought us back to Swannington, being harvest time, it was hard to get anybody to go with us. For the people were loath to go with their neighbours to prison, especially in such a busy time. They would have given us our mittimus, to carry it ourselves to the jail. For it had been usual for constables to give Friends their own mittimuses (for they durst trust Friends), and they have gone themselves with them to the jailer. But we told them though our Friends had sometimes done so, yet we would not take this mittimus, but some of them should go with us to the jail.

At last they hired a poor labouring man to go with us, who was loath to go, though hired. So we rode to Leicester, being five in number. Some carried their Bibles open in their hands, declaring the truth to the people as we rode, in the fields and through the towns, and telling them we were prisoners of the Lord Jesus Christ, going to suffer bonds for His name and truth's sake. One woman Friend carried her wheel on her lap, to spin on in prison. And the people were mightily affected.

LEICESTER JAIL

[The jailer at Leicester] had been a very wicked, cruel man. Six or seven Friends being in prison before we came, he had taken some occasion to quarrel with them and thrust them into the dungeon among the felons, where there was hardly room for them to lie down.

We stayed all that day in the prison-yard and desired the jailer to let us have some straw. He surlily answered: 'you do not look like men that would lie on straw.' After a while, William Smith, a Friend, came to me and he being acquainted with the house, I asked him what rooms there were in it, and what rooms Friends had usually been put into before they were put into the dungeon. I asked him also whether the jailer or his wife was master. He said the wife was master. And though she was lame, and sat mostly in her chair, being only able to go on crutches, yet she would beat her husband when he came within her reach, if he did not do as she would have him.

I considered, probably, many Friends might come to visit us, and that if we had a room to ourselves, it would be better for them to speak to me, and me to them, as there should be occasion. Wherefore I desired William Smith to go speak with the woman and acquaint her, if she would let us have a room, suffer our Friends to come out of the dungeon, and leave it to us to give her what we would, it might be better for her. He went, and after some reasoning with her, she consented, and we were had into a room.

Then we were told the jailer would not suffer us to have any drink out of the town into the prison, but what beer we drank we must take of him. I told them I would remedy that, for we would get a pail of water and a little wormwood once a day, and that might serve us. So we should have none of his beer, and the water he could not deny us.

Before we came, when the few Friends that were prisoners there met together on First-days, if any of them was moved to pray to the Lord, the jailer would come up with his quarter-staff in his hand, and his mastiff dog at his heels, and pluck them down by the hair of the head, and strike them with his staff. But when he struck Friends, the mastiff dog, instead of falling upon them, would take the staff out of his hand.

When the First-day came, I spoke to one of my fellow prisoners, to carry a stool and set it in the yard, and give notice to the debtors and felons that there would be a meeting in the yard, and they that would hear the word of the Lord declared might come thither. So the debtors and prisoners gathered in the yard, and we went down and had a very precious meeting, the jailer not meddling. Thus every First-day we had a meeting as long as we stayed in prison. And several came in out of the town and country. Many were convinced and some received the Lord's truth there, who have stood faithful witness for it ever since.

SUDDEN LIBERTY

When the sessions came, we were brought before the justices, with many more Friends sent to prison whilst we were there, to the number of about twenty. Being brought into the court, the jailer put us into the place where the thieves were put, and then some of the justices began to tender the oaths of allegiance and supremacy to us. I told them I never took any oath in my life, and they knew we could not swear, because Christ and his apostle forbade it. Therefore they put it but as a snare to us. We told them, if they could prove that after Christ and the apostle had forbid swearing, they did ever command Christians to swear, then we would take these oaths. Otherwise we were resolved to obey Christ's command and the apostle's exhortation. They said we must take the oath, that we might manifest our allegiance to the king. I told them I had been formerly sent up a prisoner by Colonel Hacker from that town to London, under pretence that I held meetings to plot to bring in King Charles.

I also desired them to read our mittimus, which set forth the cause of our commitment to be that we were to have had a meeting. And I said Lord Beaumont could not by that Act send us to jail, unless we had been taken at a meeting, and found to be such persons as the Act speaks of. Therefore we desired they would read the mittimus and see how wrongfully we were imprisoned. They would not take notice of the mittimus, but called a jury, and indicted us for refusing to take the oaths of allegiance and supremacy.

While we were standing where the thieves used to stand, a cut-purse had his hand in several Friends' pockets. Friends declared it to the justices, and showed them the man. They called him up before them, and upon examination he could not deny it, yet they set him at liberty.

It was not long before the jury returned, and brought us in guilty. And then, after some words the justices whispered together, and bid the jailer take us down to prison again. But the Lord's power was over them and His everlasting truth, which we declared boldly amongst them. There being a great concourse of people, most of them followed us, so that the cryer and bailiffs were fain to call the people back again to the court.

We declared the truth as we went down the streets, all along till we came to the jail, the streets being full of people. When we came in our chamber again, after some time the jailer came to us and desired all to go forth that were not prisoners. When they were gone, he said: 'Gentlemen, it is the court's pleasure that ye all should be set at liberty, except those that are in for tithes. And you know there are fees due to me. But I shall leave it to you to give to me what you will.'

Thus we were all set at liberty suddenly, and passed everyone into his service.

THE DEVIL

Joseph Hellen and G[eorge] Bewley had been to Loo to visit Blanch Pope, a Ranting woman, under pretence to convince and convert her. But before they left her, she had so darkened them with her principles that they seemed to be like her disciples, especially Joseph Hellen. For she had asked them who made the devil. Did not God? This idle question so puzzled them that they could not answer her.

They afterwards asked me that question. I told them 'no'. For all that God made was good and was blessed. So was not the devil. He was called a serpent before he was called a devil and an adversary, and then he had the title of devil given to him. Afterwards he was called a dragon, because he was a destroyer. The devil abode not in truth, and by departing from the truth, he became a devil. So the Jews, when they went out of the truth, were said to be of the devil, and were called serpents.

Now there is no promise of God to the devil, that ever he should return to truth again. But to man and woman, who have been deceived by him, the promise of God is that the Seed of the woman shall bruise the serpent's head; shall break his power and strength to pieces. Now when these things were opened more at large to the satisfaction of Friends, those two who had yielded to the spirit of that Ranting woman were judged by the truth. And one of them, Joseph Hellen, ran quite out, and was disowned by Friends. But George Bewley was recovered, and afterwards became serviceable.

THE ORIGINAL GOSPEL

[In 1663, we went] to Truro, where we had a meeting. Next morning, some of the chief of the town desired to speak with me. I went and had much discourse with them concerning the things of God. In their reasoning they said the Gospel was the four books of Matthew, Mark, Luke and John. And they called it natural. I told them the Gospel was the power of God, which was preached before Matthew, Mark, Luke and John, or any of them were printed or written. And it was preached to every creature (of which a great part might never see or hear of those four books), so that every creature was to obey the power of God. For Christ, the spiritual man, would judge the world according to the Gospel, that is, according to His invisible power.

When they heard this, they could not gainsay. For the truth came over them. I directed them to their teacher, the Grace of God, and showed them the sufficiency of it, which would teach them how to live, and what to deny. And being obeyed, would bring them salvation. So to that grace I recommended them, and left them.

THE NORTHERN PLOT

When I came [back to Swarthmore], they told me Colonel Kirby had sent his lieutenant thither to take me, and that he had searched trunks and chests for me. That night, as I was in bed, I was moved of the Lord to go next day to Kirby Hall, which was Colonel Kirby's house, about five miles off, to speak with him, and I did so.

When I came thither, I found the Flemings and several others of the gentry (so called) of the country, come to take their leave of Colonel Kirby, he being about to go up to London to the parliament. I was shown into the parlour amongst them. Presently [Colonel Kirby] came in, and I told him that understanding he was desirous to see me, I came to visit him, to know what he had to say to me, and whether he had anything against me. He said, before all the company, as he was a gentleman, he had nothing against me. 'But,' said he, 'Mistress Fell must not keep great meetings at her house, for they meet contrary to the Act.'

I told him that Act did not take hold on us, but on such as met to plot and contrive, and to raise insurrections against the king; whereas we were no such people. For he knew that they that met at Margaret Fell's house were his neighbours, and a peaceable people. After many words had passed, he shook me by the hand and said again he had nothing against me. And others of them said I was a deserving man. So we parted, and I returned to Swarthmore.

Shortly after, when Colonel Kirby was gone to London, there was a private meeting of the justices and deputy-lieutenants at Holker Hall, where Justice Preston lived. And there they were granted a warrant to apprehend me. I heard overnight both of their meeting and of the warrant, and so could have escaped out of their reach if I would. But I considered, there being a noise of a plot in the North, if I should go away, they might fall upon Friends. But if I gave up myself to be taken, it might stop them, and the Friends should escape the better.

Next day, an officer came with sword and pistols to take me. I told him I knew his errand before, and had given up myself to be taken. For if I would have escaped their imprisonment, I could have gone forty miles off before he came. But I was an innocent man, and so cared not what they could do to me. He asked me how I heard of it, seeing the order was made privately in a parlour. I said it was no matter; it was sufficient that I heard of it. I asked him to let me see his order. Whereupon he laid his hand on his sword and said I must go with him before the lieutenants, to answer such questions as they should propose to me. I told him it was but civil and reasonable for him to let me see his order. But he would not. 'Then,' said I, 'I am ready.' So I went along with them, and Margaret Fell accompanied us to Holker Hall.

When we came thither, there was one Rawlinson, a justice, and one called Sir George Middleton, and many more that I did not know, besides old Justice Preston who lived there. They brought Thomas Atkinson, a Friend of Cartmel, as a witness against me, for some words which he had told to one Knipe, who had informed them; which words were that I had written against the plotters, and knocked them down. These words they could not make much of, for I told them I had heard of a plot, and had written against it.

Then said George Middleton: 'You deny God, and the Church and the faith.' I replied: 'Nay, I own God, and the true Church and the truth faith. But what Church dost thou own?' said I (for I understood he was a Papist). Then he turned against me and said: 'You are a rebel and a traitor!' I asked him to whom he spoke, or whom did he call rebel. He was so full of envy that for a while he could not speak. But at last he said he spoke it to me.

With that I struck my hand on the table and told him I had suffered more than twenty such as he, or than any that was there. For I had been cast into Derby dungeon for six months together, and had suffered much because I would not take up arms against this king before Worcester fight. I had been sent up prisoner out of my own country by Colonel Hacker to Oliver Cromwell, as a plotter to bring in King Charles in the year 1654. And I had nothing but love and goodwill to the king, and desired the eternal good and welfare of him and all his subjects.

Then they asked me whether I had heard of the plot, and I said yes, I had heard of it. They asked me how I had heard of it. I told them I had heard of it through the high sheriff of Yorkshire, who had told Dr Hodgson that there was a plot in the North. And as for knowing any in the plot, I was as a child in that, for I knew none of them. Then said they: 'Why would you write against it, if you did not know some that were in it?' I said: 'my reason was because you are so forward to mash the innocent and guilty together, therefore I wrote against it to clear the truth from such things, and to stop all forward, foolish spirits from running into such things.' One of them said: 'O, this man hath great power!'

Then George Middleton cried: 'Bring the book and put the oaths of allegiance and supremacy to him.' Now he himself being a Papist, I asked him whether he had taken the oath of supremacy. As for us, we could not swear at all, because Christ and the apostle had forbidden it. Some of them would not have had the oath put to me, but have set me at liberty. But the rest would not agree to that. For this was their last snare, and they had no other way to get me into prison. All other things had been cleared to them.

JUSTICE AND LAW

In the sixth month [in 1664], the assizes were held at Lancaster. Judge Turner then sat on the crown bench, and so I was brought before him. Before I was called to the bar, I was put among the murderers and felons for about two hours, the people, the justices and the judge also gazing upon me. After they had tried several others, they called me to the bar, and empanelled a jury. Then the judge asked the justices whether they had tendered me the oath at the [previous] sessions. They said they had. The judge asked me whether I had not refused the oath at the last assizes. I said I never took an oath in my life, and Christ, the Saviour and Judge of the world, said 'Swear not at all'. The judge said he was not at that time to dispute whether it was lawful to swear, but to inquire whether I had refused to take the oath or not. I told him those things mentioned in the oath, as plotting against the king, and owning the Pope's – or any other foreign – power, 'I utterly deny'.

'Well,' said he, 'you say well in that, but did you deny to take the oath? What say you?' 'What wouldst thou have me say?' said I, 'for I have told thee before what I did say.' Then he asked me if I would have these men to swear, that I had taken the oath. I asked him if he would have those men to swear that I had refused the oath. At which the court burst out into laughter. I was grieved to see so much lightness in a court, where such solemn matters are handled, and thereupon asked them if this court was a play-house. 'Where is gravity and sobriety? For this behaviour does not become you.'

Then the clerk read the indictment and I told the judge I had something to speak to it. For I had informed myself of the errors that were in it. He told me he would hear afterwards any reasons I could allege why he should not give judgement. Then I spoke to the jury and told them that they could not bring me in guilty according to that indictment, for the indictment was wrong laid, and had many gross errors in it. The judge said I must not speak to the jury, but he would speak to them. And he told them I had denied to take the oath at the last assizes. 'And,' said he, 'I can tender the oath to any man now and praemunire[28] him for not taking it.' And he said they must bring me in guilty, seeing I refused to take the oath.

Next day, I having put by others from pleading for me, the judge asked me what I had to say, why he should not pass sentence upon me. I told him I was no lawyer, but I had much to say, if he would have the patience to hear. At that he laughed and others laughed also, and said: 'Come! What have you to say? He can say nothing!'

'Yes,' said I, 'I have much to say, have but the patience to hear me.' Then I asked him whether the oath was to be tendered to the king's subjects, or to the subjects of foreign princes. He said to the subjects of this realm. 'Then,' said I, 'look at the indictment, and ye may see that ye have left out the word "subject". So, not having named me in the indictment as a subject, ye cannot praemunire me for not taking the oath.' Then they looked over the statute and the indictment and saw that it was as I said. And the judge confessed it was an error.

I told him I had something else to stop his judgement, and I desired him to look what day the indictment said the oath was tendered to me at the sessions there. They looked and said it was the eleventh day of January. 'What day of the week were the sessions held on?' said I. 'On a Tuesday,' said they. 'Then,' said I, 'look at your almanacs and see whether there were any sessions held at Lancaster on the eleventh day of January, so called.' So they looked and found that the eleventh was the day called Monday, and that the sessions were on the day called Tuesday, which was the twelfth day of that month. Then the judge said this was a great mistake and an error. Some of the justices were in a great rage at this, and were ready to quit the bench. They stamped and said: 'Who hath done this? Somebody hath done it on purpose!'

[After exposing other errors], said I: 'I have something further to allege.' 'Nay,' said the judge, 'I have had enough. You need say no more.' 'If,' said I, 'thou hast enough, I desire nothing but law and justice at thy hands, for I don't look for mercy.' 'You must have justice,' said he, 'and you shall have law.' Then I asked: 'Am I at liberty and free from all that hath ever been done against me in this matter?' 'Yes,' said the judge, 'you are free from all that hath been done against you. But then,' starting up in a rage, he said, 'I can put the oath to any man here, and I will tender you the oath again.'

Then I turned me about and said: 'All people, take notice. This is a snare, for I ought to be set free from the jailer and from this court.' But the judge cried: 'Give him the book!' Then the power of darkness rose up in them, like a mountain, and a clerk lifted up a book to me. I took it and looked into it, and said: 'I see it is a Bible. I am glad of it.'

PRIVATIONS IN LANCASTER CASTLE

After some further discourse, they committed me to prison again, there to lie to the next assize. And Colonel Kirby gave order to the jailer to keep me close, and suffer no flesh alive to come at me, for I was not fit, he said, to be discoursed with men.

Then I was put into a tower, where the smoke of the other prisoners came up so thick that it stood as dew upon the walls, and sometimes it was so thick that I could hardly see the candle when it burned. And I being locked under three locks, the under-jailer, when the smoke was great, would hardly be persuaded to come up to unlock one of the uppermost doors, for fear of the smoke, so that I was almost smothered. Besides, it rained in upon my bed, and many times, when I went to stop out the rain in the cold winter season, my shirt was wet through with the rain that came in upon me, while I was labouring to stop it out. And the place being high and open to the wind, sometimes as fast as I stopped it, the wind blew it out again. In this manner did I lie, all that long, cold winter, till the next assize; in which I was so starved with cold and rain that my body was greatly swelled, and my limbs much benumbed.

[At the next assize], they recorded me as a praemunired person, though I was never brought to hear the sentence or knew of it, which was very illegal. For they ought not only to have had me present to hear the sentence given, but also to have asked me first what I could say why sentence should not be given against me. But they knew I had so much to say, that they could not give sentence, if they heard it.

While I was a prisoner in Lancaster Castle, there was a great noise and talk of the Turk's over-spreading Christendom, and great fears entered many. But one day as I was walking in my prison chamber, I saw the Lord's power turn against him, and that he was turning back again. And I declared to some what the Lord had let me see, when there were such fears of his over-running

Christendom. And within a month after the news came, that they had given him a defeat.

Another time, as I was walking in my chamber, with my eye to the Lord, I saw an angel of the Lord with a glittering drawn sword stretched southward, as though the court had been all on fire. Not long after, the wars broke out with Holland, the sickness[29] broke forth and after the Fire of London. So the Lord's sword was drawn indeed.

By reason of my long and close imprisonment in so bad a place, I was become very weak in body. But the Lord's power was over all, supported me through all and enabled me to do service for Him, and for His truth and people, as the place would admit. For while I was in Lancaster prison, I answered several books, as the Mass, the Common Prayer, the Directory and the Church Faith, which are the four chief religions that are got up since the apostles' days.

After the assize, Colonel Kirby and some other justices were very uneasy with my being at Lancaster. For I had galled them sore at my trials there, and they laboured much to get me removed to some remote place. Colonel Kirby threatened I should be sent far enough, and sometimes said I should be sent beyond sea. About six weeks after the assizes, they got an order from the king and council to remove me from Lancaster. And with it they brought a letter from the Earl of Anglesea, wherein was written that if those things were found true against me, which I was charged withal, I deserved no clemency or mercy.

SCARBOROUGH CASTLE

When they had prepared for my removal, the under-sheriff and the head sheriff's man, with some bailiffs, came and fetched me out of [Lancaster] Castle, when I was so weak with lying in that cold, wet and smoky prison that I could hardly go or stand. They lifted me upon one of the sheriff's horses. When I was on horseback in the street, the townspeople being gathered to gaze upon me, I told the officers I had received neither Christianity, civility nor humanity from them.

They hurried me away about fourteen miles to Bentham, though I was so very weak I was hardly able to sit on horseback. And my clothes smelt so of smoke that they were loathsome to myself. The wicked jailer, a young fellow, would come behind and give the horse a lash with his whip, and make him skip and leap. So that I, being weak, had difficulty to sit on him. And then he would come and look me in the face and say: 'How do you do, Mr Fox?' I told him it was not civil of him to do so. The Lord cut him off soon after.

Next night, we came to York, [where they] kept me two days. Then the marshal and four or five soldiers were sent to convey me to Scarborough Castle. Indeed, these were very civil men. When we were come to Scarborough, they had me to an inn, and gave notice to the governor, who sent six soldiers to be my guard that night.

Next day, they conducted me into the castle, put me into a room, and set a sentry on me. Being very weak and subject to fainting, they let me go out sometimes into the air with the sentry. They soon removed me out of this room, and put me into an open one, where the rain came in; and smoked exceedingly, which was very offensive to me.

One day the governor, Sir J. Crossland, came to see me, and brought with him Sir Francis Cobb. I desired the governor to go into my room and see what a place I had. I had got a little fire made in it, and it was so filled with smoke that when they were in it, they could hardly find their way out again. And he being a Papist, I told him that was his Purgatory which they had put me into.

I was forced to lay out about fifty shillings to stop out the rain, and keep the room from smoking so much. When I had been at that charge, and made it somewhat tolerable, they removed me into a worse room, where I had neither chimney nor fire-hearth.

This being to the sea-side and lying much open, the wind drove in the rain forcibly, so that the water came over my bed, and ran about the room, that I was fain to skim it with a platter.

And when my clothes were wet, I had no fire to dry them, so that my body was benumbed with cold and my fingers swelled, that one was grown as big as two.

They would suffer few Friends to come to me, and many times not any, no, not so much as to bring me a little food. But I was forced for the first quarter to hire one, not a Friend, to bring me necessaries. Sometimes the soldiers would take it from her, and she would scuffle with them for it. Afterwards, I hired a soldier to fetch me water and bread, and something to make a fire of, when I was in a room where a fire could be made. Commonly a threepenny loaf served me three weeks, and sometimes longer, and most of my drink was water with wormwood steeped or bruised in it.

One time, when the weather was very sharp, and I had taken great cold, I got a little elecampane beer, and I heard one of the soldiers say to the other that they would play me a trick, for they would send for me up to the deputy-governor, and in the meanwhile drink my strong beer out. And so they did. When I came back, one of the soldiers came to me in a jeer and asked me for some strong beer. I told him they had played their pretty trick. And so I took no further notice of it.

A HAPPY MAN

At last, the governor [of Scarborough Castle] came under some trouble himself. For he having sent out a privateer to sea, they took some ships that were not enemies' ships, but their friends'. Whereupon he was brought into trouble, after which he grew somewhat more friendly to me.

Before, I had a marshal set over me, on purpose to get money out of me. But I was not free to give him a farthing. And when they found they could get nothing from me, he was taken away again. The officers often threatened that I should be hanged over the wall. Nay, the deputy-governor told me once that the king, knowing I had a great interest in the people, had sent me thither, that if there should be any stirring in the nation, they should hang me over the wall to keep the people down. But I told them, if that was what they desired, and it was permitted them, I was ready. For I never feared death nor sufferings in my life, but I was known to be an innocent, peaceable man, free from all stirrings and plottings, and one that sought the good of all men.

Afterwards, the governor growing kinder, I spoke to him when he was going to London to the Parliament, and desired him to speak to Esquire Marsh, Sir Francis Cobb (so called) and some others, and let them know how long I had lain in prison, and for what. And he did so. When he came down again, he told me that Esquire Marsh said he would go a hundred miles barefoot for my liberty; he knew me so well. And several others, he said, spoke well of me. From which time the governor was very loving to me.

There were, amongst the prisoners, two very bad men, that often sat drinking with the officers and soldiers. And because I would not sit and drink with them too, it made them the worse against me. One time, when these two prisoners were drunk, one of them came to me and challenged me to fight with him. Seeing what condition he was in, I got out of his way. And next morning, when he was more sober, showed him how unmanly it was in him to challenge a man to fight, whose principle, he knew, it was not to strike; but if he was stricken on one ear, to turn the other. I told him if he had a mind to fight, he should have challenged some of the soldiers, that could have answered him in his own way. But however, seeing he had challenged me, I was now come to answer him with my hands in my pockets and – reaching my head towards him – 'here,' said I, 'here is my hair, here are my cheeks, here is my back'. With that he skipped away from me, and went into another room; at which the soldiers fell a-laughing. And one of the officers said: 'you are a happy man, that can bear such things.'

A SUCCESSFUL APPEAL

After I had lain prisoner above a year in Scarborough Castle, I sent a letter to the king, in which I gave him an account of my imprisonment and the bad usage I had received in prison; and also that I was informed that no man could deliver me but he. After this, John Whitehead being at London, and being acquainted with Esquire Marsh, went to visit him, and spoke to him about me. And he undertook, if John Whitehead would get the state of my case drawn up, to deliver it to the master of releases, Sir John Birkenhead, and endeavour to get a release for me.

So John Whitehead and Ellis Hookes drew up an account of my imprisonment and sufferings, and carried it to Marsh. And he sent it to the master of requests, who procured an order from the king for my release. The substance of the order was that the king being certainly informed that I was a man principled against plotting and fighting, and had been ready at all times to discover plots, rather than to make any, etc., therefore his royal pleasure was that I should be discharged from my imprisonment. As soon as this order was obtained, John Whitehead came to Scarborough with it, and delivered it to the governor, who, upon receipt thereof, gathered his officers together, and without requiring bonds or sureties for my peaceable living, being satisfied that I was a man of a peaceable life, he discharged me freely.

After I was released, I would have made the governor a present for the civility and kindness he had of late shown me. But he would not receive anything, saying whatever good he could do for me and my friends, he would do it, and never do them any hurt. And afterwards, if at any time the mayor of the town sent to him for soldiers to break up Friends' meetings, if he sent any down, he would privately give them a charge not to meddle.

THE GREAT FIRE OF LONDON

The very next day after my release, the fire broke out in London, and the report of it came quickly down into the country. Then I saw the Lord God was true and just in His word, which He had showed me before in Lancaster jail, when I saw the angel of the Lord with a glittering sword drawn southwards, as before expressed. The people of London were forewarned of this fire. Yet few laid it to heart, or believed it; but rather grew more wicked, and higher in pride. For a Friend was moved to come out of Huntingdonshire a little before the fire, to scatter his money, and turn his horse loose in the streets, to untie the knees of his breeches, let his stockings fall down, and to unbutton his doublet, and tell the people so should they run up and down, scattering their money and their goods, half undressed, like mad people, as he was a sign to them. And so they did, when the city was burning.

Thus hath the Lord exercised His prophets and servants by His power, showed them signs of His judgements, and sent them to forewarn the people. But instead of repenting, they have beaten and cruelly entreated some, and some they have imprisoned, both in the former power's days and since. But the Lord is just, and happy are they that obey His word.

The Elder Statesman

THE AUTHORITY OF QUAKER MEETINGS

I WAS WEAK with lying almost three years in cruel and hard imprisonment. My joints and body were so stiff and benumbed that I could hardly get on my horse or bend my joints. Nor could I well bear to be near the fire or to eat warm meat, I had been kept so long from it.

Being come to London, I walked a little among the ruins, and took good notice of them. Then I was moved of the Lord to recommend the setting up of five monthly meetings of men and women in the city of London (besides the women's meetings and the quarterly meetings), to take care of God's glory, and to admonish and exhort such as walked disorderly or carelessly, and not according to truth. For whereas Friends had had only quarterly meetings, now truth was spread, and Friends were grown more numerous, I was moved to recommend the setting up of monthly meetings throughout the nation[30].

And the Lord opened to me what I must do, and how the men's and women's monthly and quarterly meetings should be ordered and established in this and in other nations; and that I should write to those where I did not come, to do the same.

So the Lord's power came over all, and the heirs of it came to inherit it. For the authority of our meetings is the power of God, the gospel, which brings life and immortality to light, that all may see over the devil that hath darkened them, and that all the heirs of the gospel may walk according to the gospel, and glorify God with their bodies, souls and spirits, which are the Lord's. For the order of the glorious gospel is not of man nor by man.

Thus [in 1667–8] were the men's monthly meetings settled through the nation. The quarterly meetings were generally settled before. I wrote also into Ireland by faithful Friends, and into Scotland, Holland, Barbados and several parts of America, advising Friends to settle their men's monthly meetings in those countries. For they had their general quarterly meetings before. But now that truth was increased amongst them, they should settle those men's monthly meetings in the power and Spirit of God, that first convinced them.

IRELAND

[In 1669] was I moved of the Lord to go over to Ireland, to visit the seed of God in that nation. There went with me Robert Lodge, James Lancaster, Thomas Briggs and John Stubbs. We waited near Liverpool for shipping and wind. After waiting some days, we sent James Lancaster to take passage, which he did, and brought word the ship was ready, and would take us in at Black Rock. We went thither on foot; and it being some distance, and the weather very hot, I was much spent with walking.

When we arrived, the ship was not there. So we were obliged to go to the town and take shipping. When we were on board, I said to the rest of my company: 'Come, ye will triumph in the Lord, for we shall have fair wind and weather.' Many passengers in the ship were sick, but not one of our company. The captain and many of the passengers were very loving; and we being at sea on the first day of the week, I was moved to declare truth among them; whereupon the captain said to the passengers: 'Here are things that you never heard in your lives!'

When we came before Dublin, we took boat and went ashore. And the earth and air smelt, methought, of the corruption of the nation, so that it yielded another smell to me than England did; which I imputed to the Popish massacres that had been committed, and the blood that had been spilt in it, from which a foulness ascended.

We passed through among the officers of the customs four times, yet they did not search us. For they perceived what we were. Some of them were so envious they did not care to look at us. We did not soon find Friends, but went to an inn, and sent out to inquire for some; who, when they came to us, were exceedingly glad of our coming, and received us with good joy.

He that was then Mayor of Cork was very envious against truth and Friends, and had many Friends in prison. And knowing that I was in the country, he had issued four warrants to take me. Wherefore Friends were desirous that I might not ride through Cork. But there appeared to me in a vision a very ugly visaged man, of a black and dark look. My spirit struck at him in the power of God. And it seemed to me that I rode over him with my horse; and my horse set his foot on the side of his face. When I came down in the morning, I told a Friend that was with me that the command of the Lord was to me to ride through Cork, and bade him tell no man.

So we took horse, many Friends being with me. And when we came near the town, they would have showed me a way on the backside of the town. But I told them my way was through the streets. Wherefore taking one of them along with me, to guide me through the town, I rode on. And as we rode through the market-place, and by the mayor's door, he seeing me ride by said: 'There goes George Fox!' But he had not power to stop me.

When we had passed through the sentinels, and were come over the bridge, we went to a Friend's house and alighted. There the Friends told me what a rage was in the town, and how many warrants were granted to take me. While I was sitting there with Friends, I felt the evil spirit at work in the town, stirring up mischief against me. And I felt the power of the Lord strike at that evil spirit.

Great was the rage that the mayor and others of Cork were in, that they had missed me. And great pains they afterwards took to take me, having their scouts abroad upon the roads, as I understood, to observe which way I went. Afterwards there was scarcely a public meeting I came to but spies came in to watch if I were there. And the envious magistrates and priests sent information one to another concerning me, describing me by my hair, hat, clothes and horse, so that when I was near a hundred miles from Cork, they had an account concerning me, and description of me, before I came amongst them.

To James Hutchinson's in Ireland came many great persons, desiring to discourse with me about election and reprobation. I told them though they judged our principle foolish, it was too high for them; they could not with their wisdom comprehend it. Therefore I would discourse with them according to their capacities. 'You say,' said I, 'that God hath ordained the greatest part of men for Hell, and that they were ordained so before the world began; for which your proof is in Jude. You say Esau was reprobated, and the Egyptians and the stock of Ham. But Christ saith to His disciples: "go teach all nations" and "go into all nations and preach the gospel of life and salvation". Now, if they were to go to all nations, were they not to go to Ham's stock and Esau's stock? Did not Christ die for all?'

After I had travelled over Ireland, and had visited Friends in their meetings, as well for business as for worship, and had answered several papers and writings from monks, friars and Protestant priests (for they all were in a rage against us, and endeavoured to stop the work of the Lord; and some Jesuits swore in a hearing of some of us that we came to spread our principles in that nation, but we should not do it), I returned to Dublin to take passage for England.

A COUNTERFEIT GEORGE FOX

There was one John Fox, a Presbyterian priest, who used to go about preaching. And some changing his name (as was reported) from John to George, gave out that George Fox had changed his religion and was turned from a Quaker to be a Presbyterian, and would preach at such a place such a day. This begot so great a curiosity in the people that many went thither to hear this Quaker turned Presbyterian, who would not have gone to hear John Fox himself. By this means, it was reported, they had got together above a thousand people. But when they came there, and perceived they had a trick put upon them, and that he was a counterfeit George Fox, and understood that the real George Fox was hard by, several hundreds of them came to our meeting, and were sober and attentive. I directed them to the grace of God in themselves, which would teach them and bring them salvation.

When the meeting was over, some of the people said they liked George Fox the Quaker's preaching better than George Fox the Presbyterian's. Thus, by my providential coming into those parts [Gloucestershire] at that time, was this false report discovered. And shame came over the contrivers of it.

MARRIAGE TO MARGARET FELL

We travelled till we came to Bristol, where I met with Margaret Fell, who was come to visit her daughter Yeomans. I had seen from the Lord a considerable time before that I should take Margaret Fell to be my wife. And when I first mentioned it to her, she felt the answer of Life from God thereunto. But though the Lord had opened this thing to me, yet I had not received a command from the Lord for the accomplishing of it then. Wherefore I let the thing rest and went on in the work and service of the Lord as before, according as He led me, travelling up and down in this nation and through Ireland.

But now being at Bristol, and finding Margaret Fell there, it opened in me from the Lord that the thing should be accomplished. After we had discoursed the matter together, I told her if she also was satisfied with the accomplishment of it now, she should first send for her children, which she did. When the rest of her daughters[31] were come, I asked both them and her sons-in-law if they had anything against it, or for it. And they all severally expressed their satisfaction therein.

Then I asked Margaret if she had fulfilled and performed her husband's will to her children. She replied the children knew that. Whereupon I asked them whether, if their mother married, they should not lose by it. And I asked Margaret whether she had done anything in lieu of it, which might answer it to the children. The children said she had answered it to them, and desired me to speak no more of it. I told them I was plain, and would have all things done plainly. For I sought not any outward advantage to myself.

So after I had thus acquainted the children with it, our intention of marriage was lain before Friends, both privately and publicly, to their full satisfaction, many of whom gave testimony thereunto that it was of God. Afterwards, a meeting being appointed for the accomplishing thereof, in the meeting house at Broad Mead in Bristol, we took each other, the Lord joining us together in the honourable marriage, in the everlasting covenant and immortal Seed of life. In the sense whereof living and weighty testimonials were borne thereunto by Friends in the movings of the heavenly power which united us together. Then was a certificate relating both to the proceedings and the marriage openly read and signed by the relations, and by most of the ancient Friends of that city, besides many others from divers parts of the nation.

We stayed about a week in Bristol, and then went together to Olveston, where, taking leave of each other in the Lord, we parted, betaking ourselves to our several services: Margaret returning homewards to the North, and I passing on in the work of the Lord, as before.

THE CONVENTICLE ACT

[In 1670], some Members of Parliament took advantage [of a tumultuous meeting in a steeple-house] to get an Act passed against seditious conventicles[32]; which soon after came forth and was turned against us, who of all people were free from sedition and tumult.

On the First-day after the Act came into force, I went to the meeting in Gracechurch Street [in London], where I expected the storm was most likely to begin. When I came there, I found the street full of people, and a guard set to keep Friends out of their meeting house. I went to the other passage out of Lombard Street, where also I found a guard. But the court was full of people, and a Friend was speaking amongst them, but he did not speak long. When he had done, I stood up and was moved to say: 'Saul, Saul, why persecutest thou me? It is hard for thee to kick against that which pricks thee!' Then I showed that it is Saul's nature that persecutes still, and that they who persecute Christ in His members now, where He is made manifest, kick against that which pricks them; that it was the birth of the flesh that persecuted the birth born of the Spirit; and that it was the nature of dogs to tear and devour the sheep; but that we suffered as sheep that bite not again. For we were a peaceable people, and loved them that persecuted us.

After I had spoken a while to this effect, the constable came with an informer and soldiers. And as they pulled me down, I said: 'Blessed are the peacemakers.' The commander of the soldiers put me among the soldiers and bid them secure me, saying to me: 'You are the man I looked for.'

As we went along the streets, the people were very moderate.

Some of them laughed at the constable and told him we would not run away. [We were taken] to the mayor's house. When the mayor came, we were brought into the room where he was, and some of his officers would have taken off our hats, which he perceiving, called to them and bid them let us alone, and not meddle with our hats. 'For,' said he, 'they are not yet brought before me in judicature.'

So we stood by while he examined some Presbyterian and Baptist teachers, with whom he was somewhat sharp, and convinced them. After he had done with them, I was brought up to the table where he sat. And then the officers took off my hat, and the mayor said mildly to me: 'Mr Fox, you are an eminent man amongst those of your profession. Pray, will you be instrumental to dissuade them from meeting in such great numbers? For, seeing Christ hath promised that where two or three are met in His name, He will be in the midst of them, and the king and parliament are graciously pleased to allow of four to meet together to worship God, why will not you be content to partake both of Christ's promise to two or three, and the king's indulgence to four?'

I answered to this purpose: Christ's promise was not to discourage many from meeting together in His name, but to encourage the few, that the fewest might not forbear to meet, because of their fewness. But if Christ hath promised to manifest His presence in the midst of so small an assembly, where but two or three were gathered in His name, how much more would His presence abound where two or three hundred are gathered in His name? I wished him to consider whether this Act would not have taken hold of Christ, with His twelve apostles and seventy disciples, if it had been in their time, who used to meet often together, and that with great numbers.

After some more discourse, he took our names and the places where we lodged, and at length set us at liberty.

STRICKEN BY THE PERSECUTION

We passed towards Rochester. On the way, as I was walking down a hill, a great weight and oppression fell upon my spirit. I got on my horse again, but the weight remained so that I was hardly able to ride. At length we came to Rochester, but I was much spent, being so extremely laden and burdened with the world's spirits that my life was oppressed under them.

After, I rode with great uneasiness to Stratford, to a Friend's house. Here I lay exceedingly weak, and at last lost both hearing and sight. Several Friends came to me from London. And I told them that I should be as a sign to such as would not see, and such as would not hear the truth. In this condition I continued some time. Divers Friends who practised physic came to see me, and would have given me medicines. But I would not meddle with any, for I was sensible I had a travail to go through, and therefore desired none but solid, weighty Friends might be about me. Under great sufferings and travails, sorrows and oppressions, I lay for several weeks, whereby I was brought so low and weak in body that few thought I could live.

I went to the widow Dry's at Enfield, where I lay all that winter, warring in spirit with the evil spirits of the world, that warred against truth and Friends. For there were great persecutions at this time. Some meeting houses were pulled down, and many were broken up by soldiers. Sometimes a troop of horse, or a company of foot came. And some broke their swords, carbines, muskets and pikes with beating Friends. And many they wounded, so that their blood lay in the streets. Amongst others that were active in this cruel persecution at London, my old adversary Colonel Kirby was one; who, with a company of foot, went to break up several meetings. And he would often enquire for me at the meetings he broke up.

Now, though it was a cruel, bloody, persecuting time, yet the Lord's power went over all, and His everlasting Seed prevailed. And Friends were made to stand firm and faithful in the Lord's power. Some sober people of other professions would say if Friends did not stand, the nation would run into debauchery.

After some time, it pleased the Lord to allay the heat of this violent persecution. And I felt in spirit an overcoming of the spirits of those man-eaters that had stirred it up, and carried it on to that height of cruelty, though I was outwardly very weak. And I plainly felt, and those Friends that were with me, and that came to visit me, took notice, that as the persecution ceased, I came from under the travails and sufferings that had lain with such weight upon me; so that towards the Spring, I began to recover, and to walk up and down, beyond the expectation of many, who did not think I could ever have gone abroad again.

THE NEW JERUSALEM

Whilst I was under this spiritual suffering, the state of the New Jerusalem, which comes down out of Heaven, was opened to me; which some carnal-minded people had looked upon to be like an outward city dropped out of the elements. I saw the beauty and glory of it; the length, the breadth and the height thereof, all in complete proportion. I saw that all who are within the light of Christ, and in His faith, which He is the author of, and in the Spirit, the Holy Ghost, which Christ and the holy prophets and apostles were in, and within the grace and truth and power of God, which are the walls of the city: such are within the city, are members of it, and have the right to eat of the tree of life, which yields her fruit every month, and whose leaves are for the healing of the nations.

But they that are out of the grace, truth, light, Spirit and power of God, they who resist the Holy Ghost, quench, vex and grieve the Spirit of God, who hate the light, turn the grace of God into wantonness, and do despite to the Spirit of Grace, they who have erred from the faith, and made shipwreck of it and of a good conscience, who abuse the power of God and despise prophesying, revelation and inspiration: these are the dogs and unbelievers that are without the city. These make up the great city Babylon, confusion and her cage, the power of darkness. And the evil spirit of error surrounds and covers them over. In this great city Babylon are: the false prophets, in the false power and false spirit; the beast, in the dragon's power; and the whore that is gone a-whoring from the Spirit of God, and from Christ her husband. But the Lord's power is over all this power of darkness, false prophets and their worshippers, who are for the lake which burns with fire.

VOYAGE TO AMERICA

It was upon me from the Lord to go beyond the seas to visit America. I went to Gravesend on the 12th of 6th month [1671], and there we found the Friends that were bound for the voyage with me. The vessel was a yacht, called the *Industry* and the number of passengers about fifty.

When we had been about three weeks at sea, one afternoon we spied a vessel about four leagues astern of us. Our master said it was a Sallee[33] man-of-war, that seemed to give us chase. Our master said: 'Come, let us go to supper, and when it grows dark, we shall lose him.' This he spoke to please and pacify the passengers, some of whom began to be very apprehensive of the danger. But Friends were well satisfied in themselves, having faith in God, and no fear upon their spirits.

When the sun was gone down, I saw the ship out of my cabin, making towards us. When it grew dark, we altered our course to miss her. But she altered also, and gained upon us. At night the master and others came into my cabin and asked me what they should do. I told them I was no mariner. And I asked them what they thought was best to do. They said there were but two ways:

either to out-run him, or to tack about, and hold the same course we were going before. I told them if he were a thief, they might be sure he would tack about too. And as for out-running him, it was no purpose to talk of that, for they saw he sailed faster than we. They asked me again what they should do. 'For,' they said, 'if the mariners had taken Paul's counsel, they had not come to the damage they did.'

I answered it was a trial of faith, and therefore the Lord was to be waited on for counsel. So retiring in spirit, the Lord showed me that His life and power was placed between us and the ship that pursued us. I told this to the master and the rest, and that our best way was to tack about and steer our right course. I desired them also to put out all their candles but the one they steered by, and to speak to all the passengers to be still and quiet.

About eleven at night, the watch called and said they were just upon us. That disquieted some of the passengers, whereupon I sat up in my cabin, and looking through the porthole, the moon being not quite down, I saw them very near us. I was getting up to go out of the cabin; but remembering the word of the Lord, that His life and power was placed between us and them, I lay down again. The master and some of the seamen came again and asked me if they might steer such a point. I told them they might do as they would. By this time the moon was quite down, a fresh gale arose and the Lord hid us from them. And we sailed briskly on and saw them no more.

I was not sea-sick during the voyage, as many of the Friends and other passengers were. But the many hurts and bruises I had formerly received, and the infirmities I had contracted in England by extreme cold and hardships that I had undergone in many long imprisonments, returned upon me at sea; so that I was very ill in my stomach and full of violent pains in my bones and limbs. I perspired abundantly, chiefly my head, and my body broke out in pimples, and my legs and feet swelled extremely, so that my stockings and slippers could not be drawn on without difficulty and great pain.

Suddenly, the sweating ceased, so that when I came into the hot climate, where others perspired most freely, I could not perspire at all. But my flesh was hot, dry and burning. And that which broke out in pimples struck in again to my stomach and heart, so that I was very ill and weak beyond expression. Thus I continued during the rest of the voyage, which was about a month. For we were above seven weeks at sea.

THE WEST INDIES

On the third of the eighth month, early in the morning, we discovered the island of Barbados. We got on shore as soon as we could, and I, with some others, walked to a Friend's house, above a quarter of a mile from the bridge. But being very ill and weak, I was so tired with that little walk that I was in a manner spent by the time I got thither. There I abode very ill for several days, and though they several times gave me things to make me perspire, they could not effect it. But what they gave me did rather parch and dry up my body, and made me probably worse than otherwise I might have been. Thus I continued about three weeks after I landed, having much pain in my bones, joints and whole body, so that I could hardly get any rest. Yet I was pretty cheerful and my spirit kept above it all. Neither did my illness take me off from the service of truth, but both while I was at sea and after I came to Barbados, before I was able to travel about, I gave forth several papers (having a Friend to write for me), some of which I sent by the first conveyance for England to be printed.

My weakness continued the longer on me by reason that my spirit was much pressed down at first with the filth and dirt and unrighteousness of the people, which lay as a heavy weight and load upon me. But after I had been above a month upon the island, my spirit became somewhat easier, and I began to recover in some measure my health and strength. Because I was not well able to travel, the Friends of the island concluded to have their men's and women's meeting for the service of the church at Thomas Rous's, where I lay; by which means I was present at each of their meetings, and had very good service for the Lord in both.

As to their blacks or negroes, I desired [Friends] to endeavour to train them up in the fear of God, those that were bought and those born in their families, that all might come to the knowledge of the Lord. I desired them also that they would cause their overseers to deal mildly and gently with their negroes, and not use cruelty towards them, as the manner of some hath been and is; and that after certain years of servitude, they would make them free.

But the rage and envy in our adversaries did not cease. They endeavoured to defame Friends with many false and scandalous reports, which they spread abroad through the island. Whereupon we drew up a paper, to go forth in the name of the people called Quakers, for the clearing of truth and Friends from those false reports. [One] wicked slander, of our endeavouring to make the negroes rebel, our adversaries took occasion to raise; from our having had some meetings with and amongst the negroes. For both I and other Friends had several meetings with them in several plantations, wherein we exhorted them to justice, sobriety, temperance, chastity and piety, and to be subject to their masters and governors; which was altogether contrary to what our envious adversaries maliciously suggested against us.

Having been three months or more in Barbados, and having visited Friends, thoroughly settled meetings and despatched the service which the Lord had brought me thither, I felt my spirit clear of that island, and found drawings to Jamaica. We had a quick and easy passage to Jamaica, where we met with our Friends James Lancaster, John Cartwright and George Pattison again, who had been labouring there in the service of truth; into which we forthwith entered with them, travelling up and down through the island, which is large. And a brave country it is, though the people are, many of them, debauched and wicked.

When we had been about seven weeks in Jamaica, had brought

Friends into pretty good order and settled several meetings amongst them, we embarked for Maryland, leaving Friends and truth prosperous in Jamaica, the Lord's power being over all, and His blessed Seed reigning.

AMERICA

We went on board on the 8th of [March 1672], and having contrary winds, were a full week sailing forwards and backwards before we could get out of sight of Jamaica. A difficult voyage this proved, and dangerous, especially in passing through the Gulf of Florida, where we met with many trials by winds and storms. We were between six and seven weeks in this passage from Jamaica to Maryland.

Here we found John Burnyeat, intending shortly to sail for England. But on our arrival, he altered his purpose and joined us in the Lord's service. He had appointed a general meeting for all the Friends in the provinces of Maryland, that he might see them together, and take his leave of them, before he departed out of the country. And it was so ordered by the good providence of God that we landed just in time to reach that meeting. A very large meeting this was, and held four days.

After, we parted company, dividing ourselves unto several coasts, for the service of truth. I, with several Friends of the province, went over by boat to the eastern shore, and had a meeting there on the First-day. It was upon me from the Lord to send to the Indian emperor and his kings to come to that meeting. The emperor came and was at it. But his kings, lying further off, could not reach in time. Yet they came after with their cocka-rooses[34]. I had in the evening two good opportunities with them. They heard the word of the Lord willingly, and confessed to it. What I spoke to them, I desired them to speak to their people; and let them know that God was raising up His tabernacle of witness in their wilderness country, and was setting up His standard and glorious ensign of righteousness. They carried themselves very courteously and lovingly, and inquired where the next meeting would be, and they would come to it.

Next day we began our journey by land to New England; a tedious journey through the woods and wilderness, over bogs and great rivers. When we were over [the River Delaware], we were troubled to procure guides, who were hard to get and very chargeable. Then had we that wilderness country to pass through since called West Jersey, not then inhabited by English; so that we have travelled a whole day together, without seeing man or woman, house or dwelling-place. Sometimes we lay in the woods by a fire, and sometimes in the Indians' wigwams or houses. We came one night to an Indian town, and lay at the king's house, who was a very worthy man. Both he and his wife received us very lovingly, and his attendants (such as they were) were very respectful to us. They laid us mats to lie on. But provisions were very short with them, having caught but little that day.

The Yearly Meeting for all the Friends of New England and the other colonies adjacent was held in [Rhode Island]; to which, besides very many Friends who lived in those parts, came John Stubbs from Barbados, and James Lancaster and John Cartwright from another way. This meeting lasted six days, the first four days being general public meetings for worship, to which abundance of other people came; for they having no priest in the island, and so no restriction to any particular way of worship, and both the governor and deputy-governor, with several justices of the peace daily frequenting the meetings, this so encouraged the people that they flocked in from all parts of the island. Very good service we had amongst them, and truth had a good reception. I have rarely observed people, in the state wherein they stood, hear with more attention, diligence and affection, than generally they did, during the four days together.

At another place, I heard some of the magistrates said among themselves if they had money enough, they would hire me to be their minister. This was where they did not well understand us and our principles. But when I heard of it, I said it was time for me to be gone. For if their eye was so much to me, or any of us, they would not come to their own teacher. For this thing (hiring ministers) had spoiled many, by hindering them from improving their own talents; whereas our labour is to bring all men to their own teacher in themselves.

A MIRACULOUS CURE

While we were at Shrewsbury [in East Jersey], an accident befell. John Jay, a Friend of Barbados, who came with us from Rhode Island, and intended to accompany us through the woods to Maryland, being to try a horse, got upon his back. And the horse fell a-running, and cast him down upon his head, and broke his neck, as the people said. They that were near him took him up as dead, carried him a good way and laid him on a tree.

I got to him as soon as I could. And feeling him, concluded he was dead. As I stood by him, pitying him and his family, I took hold of his hair, and his head turned any way, his neck was so limber. Whereupon I took his head in both my hands, and setting my knees against the tree, I raised his head and perceived there was nothing out or broken that way. Then I put one hand under his chin, and the other behind his head, and raised his head two or three times with all my strength, and brought it in. I soon perceived his neck began to grow stiff again, and then he began to rattle in the throat, and quickly after to breathe.

The people were amazed. But I bid them get him something warm to drink and put him to bed. After he had been in the house a while he began to speak. But he did not know where he had been. The next day, we passed away (and he with us, pretty well), about sixteen miles to a meeting at Middletown, through woods and bogs and over a river; where we swam our horses, and got over ourselves upon a hollow tree. Many hundred miles did he travel with us after this.

THE LORD IS OVER ALL

Having visited the north part of Carolina, and made a little entrance for truth upon the people there, we set forward for Virginia again, travelling through the woods and bogs, as far as we could well reach that day; and at night lay by a fire in the woods. Next day we had a tedious journey, through bogs and swamps, and were exceedingly wet and dirty all the day, but dried ourselves at night by a fire.

We got that night to Sommertown. When we came near the house, the woman of the house, seeing us, spoke to her son to fasten up their dogs (for both in Virginia and Carolina they generally keep great dogs to guard their houses, living lonely in the woods). But the son said he need not, for the dogs did not use to meddle with these people. Whereupon, when we were come into the house she told us we were like the children of Israel, whom the dogs did not move their tongues against.

Here we lay in our clothes by the fire, as we had done many a night before. Next day, before we went away, we had a meeting. For then people having heard of us had a great desire to hear us. And a very good meeting we had among them, where we never had one before. Praised be the Lord for ever! After the meeting was over, we hasted away.

When we had rode about twenty miles, calling at a house to inquire the way, the people desired us to tarry all night with them, which we did. Next day we came among Friends, after we had travelled about a hundred miles from Carolina into Virginia; in which time we observed a great variety of climates, having passed in a few days from a very cold to a warm and spring-like country.

But the power of the Lord is the same in all, is over all, and doth reach the good in all. Praised be the Lord for ever!

OPPOSITION TO WOMEN'S MEETINGS

[Back in England, in 1673], at Slaughterford, in Wiltshire, we had a very good meeting, though we met there with much opposition from some who had set themselves against women's meetings, which I was moved of the Lord to recommend to Friends, for the benefit and advantage of the Church of Christ: that faithful women who were called to the belief of the truth, being made partakers of the same precious faith, and heirs of the same everlasting gospel of life and salvation that men are, might in like manner come into the possession and practice of the gospel order, and therein be meet-helps unto the men in the restoration, in the service of truth, in the affairs of the church, as they are outwardly in civil or temporal things. That so all the family of God, women as well as men, might know, possess, perform and discharge their offices and services in the house of God, whereby the poor might be better taken care of, the younger instructed, informed and taught in the way of God; the loose and disorderly reproved and admonished in the fear of the Lord; the clearness of persons proposing marriage more closely and strictly inquired into in the wisdom of God; and all the members of the spiritual body, the church, might watch over and be helpful to each other in love.

But after these opposers had run into much contention and wrangling, the power of the Lord struck down one of the chief of them, so that his spirit sunk, and he came to be sensible of the evil he had done in opposing God's heavenly power, and confessed his error before Friends; and afterwards gave forth a paper of condemnation, wherein he declared that he did wilfully oppose (although I often warned him to take heed), until the fire of the

Lord did burn within him. And he saw the angel of the Lord with his sword in his hand, ready to cut him off.

THE LAST IMPRISONMENT

We travelled into Worcestershire, and went to John Halford's at Armscott, where we had a very large and precious meeting in his barn. After the meeting, Friends being most of them gone, as I was sitting in the parlour, discoursing with some Friends, Henry Parker, a justice, came to the house, and with him one Rowland Hains, a priest. This justice heard of the meeting by means of a woman Friend, who being nurse to a child of his, asked leave of her mistress to go to the meeting to see me. And she, speaking of it to her husband, he and the priest plotted together to come and break it up and apprehend me. But from their sitting long at dinner, it being the day on which his child was sprinkled, they did not come till the meeting was over, and Friends mostly gone. But though there was no meeting when they came, yet I being in the house, who was the person they aimed at, Henry Parker took me, and Thomas Lower for company with me; and though he had nothing to lay to our charge, sent us both to Worcester jail.

When we had been some time in jail, we thought fit to lay our case before the Lord Windsor, who was Lord Lieutenant of Worcestershire, and before the deputy lieutenants and magistrates, which we did by letter. But no enlargement did we receive by our application to the Lord Windsor (so called).

We were not called till the last day of the sessions. When we came in, they were stricken with paleness in their faces, and it was some time before anything was spoken; insomuch that a butcher in the hall said: 'What, are they afraid? Dare not the justices speak to them?'

[After hearing my case], the chairman stood up and said: 'You, Mr Fox, are a famous man, and all this may be true which you have said. But, that we may be the better satisfied, will you take the oaths of allegiance and supremacy?' 'Ye know,' said I, 'in your own consciences that we, the people called Quakers, cannot take an oath, or swear in any case, because Christ hath forbidden it.' While I was speaking, they cried: 'Give him the book!' And I said: 'The book saith "swear not at all".' Then they cried: 'Take him away, jailer!'

Soon after the sessions, the term coming on, an habeas corpus was sent down to Worcester for the sheriff to bring me up to the King's Bench bar. Whereupon the under-sheriff having made Thomas Lower his deputy to convey me to London, we set out. [In London] I appeared before Judge Wild, and both he and his lawyers were pretty fair, so that I had time to speak, to clear my innocency and show my wrong imprisonment. But after this, Justice Parker, or some other of my adversaries, moved the court that I might be sent back to Worcester.

I stayed in and about London till toward the latter end of the 1st month 1674, and then went down leisurely (for I was not able to bear hasty and hard travelling). After I was returned to prison, several came to see me; and amongst others, the Earl of Salisbury's son, who was very loving, and troubled that they had dealt so wickedly by me. He stayed about two hours.

My wife came out of the North to be with me. And the assizes coming on, in the sixth month, the state of my case being drawn up in writing, she and Thomas Lower delivered it to Judge Wild. In it were set forth the occasion of my journey, the manner of my being taken and imprisoned, the proceedings of the several sessions against me and the errors in the indictment by which I had been praemunired. When the judge had read it, he shook his head and said we might try the validity or invalidity of the errors, if we would. And that was all they could get from him.

About this time, I had a fit of sickness, which brought me very low and weak in my body. And I continued so a pretty while, insomuch that some Friends began to doubt of my recovery. I seemed to myself to be amongst the graves and dead corpses. Yet the invisible power did secretly support me, and conveyed refreshing strength into me, even when I was so weak, that I was almost speechless. One night, as I was lying awake upon my bed in the glory of the Lord, which was over all, it was said unto me that the Lord had a great deal more work for me to do for Him, before He took me to Himself.

Endeavours were used to get me released, at least for a time, till I was grown stronger. But the way of effecting it proved difficult and tedious. For the king was not willing to release me by any other way than a pardon, being told he could not legally do it. And I was not willing to be released by a pardon, which he would readily have given me, because I did not look upon that as agreeable with the innocency of my cause.

We came to London and I was brought before the judges of the King's Bench. The errors of the indictment were so many and gross that the judges were all of opinion that the indictment was quashed and void, and that I ought to have my liberty. Thus after I had suffered imprisonment a year and almost two months for nothing, I was fairly set at liberty upon a trial of the errors in my indictment, without receiving any pardon, or coming under any obligation or engagement at all. And the Lord's everlasting power went over all, to His glory and praise.

A NEW PACE OF LIFE

The illness I got in my imprisonment at Worcester had so much weakened me that it was long before I recovered my natural strength again. For which reason, and as many things lay upon me to write, both for public and private service, I did not stir much abroad during the time that I now stayed in the North. But when Friends were not with me, [I] spent much time in writing for truth's service. While I was at Swarthmore, I gave several books to be printed.

I took notice also of those who had run out from truth, drawn others out after them and turned against truth and Friends at several times since the first breaking forth of truth in this latter age, and what became of them; noting particularly the repentance and return of such of them as came back to truth again. Some ran quite out and never returned, but were cut off in their gainsaying and rebellion, for the word and power of God hath blasted and is blasting them, and the holy seed hath ground and is grinding them to pieces. I have observed that they who have been convinced, and have not lived and walked in the truth, have been the worst enemies to the truth and do most hurt amongst Friends in the truth, and to others.

In 1676, while I was at Swarthmore, died William Lampitt, the old priest of Ulverstone (which parish Swarthmore is in). He was an old deceiver, a perverter of the right way of the Lord, and a persecutor of the people of God. Much contest I had with him, when I first came into those parts. He had been an old false prophet. For in 1652 he prophesied that the Quakers would all vanish, and come to nought within half a year. But he came to nought himself. For he continued in his lying and false accusing of God's people, till a little before he died, and then he cried for a little rest. To one of his hearers that came to visit him before he died he said: 'I have been a preacher a long time, and thought I had lived well. But I did not think it had been so hard a thing to die.'

HOLLAND AND GERMANY

[In 1677] it was upon me from the Lord to go into Holland, to visit Friends and to preach the gospel there, and in some parts of Germany. Wherefore setting things in order for my journey as fast as I could, I took leave of Friends at London, and with several other Friends went down to Colchester, in order to [take] my passage for Holland. The Friends that went over with me [included] William Penn, Robert Barclay, George Keith and his wife, John Furly and his brother, and Isabel Yeomans, one of my wife's daughters.

About one in the morning we weighed anchor, having a fair brisk wind, which by next morning brought us within sight of Holland. But that day proving very clear and calm, we got forward little, till about four in the afternoon, when a fresh gale arose, which carried us within a league of land. Then being becalmed again, we cast anchor for that night, it being between the hours of nine and ten in the evening. But William Penn and Robert Barclay, understanding that Benjamin Furly was come from Rotterdam to the Briel to meet us, got two of the boatmen to let down a small boat that belonged to the packet, and row them to shore. But before they could reach, the gates were shut. And there being no house without the gates, they lay in a fisherman's boat all night.

As soon as the gates were opened in the morning, they went in and found Benjamin Furly, with other Friends of Rotterdam, that were come thither to receive us. And they sent a boat, with three young men in it, that lived with Benjamin Furly, who brought us to the Briel, where Friends received us with great gladness.

[After travelling through Rotterdam, Amsterdam, Friesland and Hamburg, we] set out for Oldenburg. It was a lamentable sight to see so great and brave a city burnt down. We went to an inn, and though it was a First-day, the soldiers were drinking and playing at shovel-board. And at the few houses that were left, the shops were open and the people trading one with another. I was moved to declare the truth among them, and warn them of the judgements of God. And though they heard me quietly, and were civil, yet I was burdened with their wickedness. Many times in mornings, noons and nights, at the inns and on the ways as I travelled, I spoke to the people, preaching the truth to them, warning them of the day of the Lord, and exhorting them to turn to the light and Spirit of God in themselves, that thereby they might be led out of evil.

[Back in Holland,] we went to the Hague, where the Prince of

Orange kept his court. And we visited one of the judges of Holland, with whom we had pretty much discourse. He was a wise, tender man, and put many objections and queries to us; which, when we had answered, he was satisfied, and parted with us in much love. Leaving the Hague, we went to Delft, and thence to Rotterdam for the night, where we stayed some days, and had several meetings. While I was here I gave forth a book for the Jews, with whom, when I was in Amsterdam, I had a desire to have some discourse; but they would not. Here also I reviewed several other books and papers which I had given forth before, and which were now transcribed.

SUFFERINGS IN NEW ENGLAND

About this time, I received letters from New England, which gave account of the magistrates' and rulers' cruel and unchristianlike proceedings against Friends there, whipping and abusing them very shamefully. For they whipped many women Friends. One woman they tied to a cart, and dragged her along the street, stripped above the waist. They whipped some masters of ships that were not Friends, only for bringing Friends thither. And at that very time, while they were persecuting Friends in this barbarous manner, the Indians slew three-score of their men, took one of their captains and flayed the skin off his head while he was alive, and carried it away in triumph; so that the sober people said the judgements of God came upon them for persecuting the Quakers. But the blind, dark priests said it was because they did not persecute them enough.

Great exercise I had in seeking relief here for our poor suffering Friends there, that they might not live under the rod of the wicked. Upon this and other services for truth, I stayed in London a month or five weeks, visiting meetings and helping and encouraging Friends to labour for the deliverance of their suffering brethren in other parts.

A SUIT ABOUT TITHES

About this time [1681], I had occasion to go to several judges' chambers upon a suit about tithes. For my wife and I and several other Friends were sued in Cartmel-Wapenstake Court in Lancashire for small tithes; and we had demurred to the jurisdiction of that court. Whereupon the plaintiff prosecuted us in the Exchequer Court at Westminster, where they run us up to a writ of rebellion, for not answering the bill upon oath; and got an order of court to the sergeant, to take me and my wife into custody.

This was a little time before the Yearly Meeting, at which time it was thought they would have taken me up. And according to outward appearances, it was likely, and very easy for him to have done it, lodging at the places where I used to do, and being very public in meetings. But the Lord's power was over them, and restrained them; so they did not take me. Yet understanding there was a warrant out against me, as soon as the Yearly Meeting was over, I went to several judges' chambers, to speak with them about it; and to let them understand both the state of the case and the ground and reason of our refusing to pay tithes.

The first I went to was Judge Gregory, to whom I tendered mine and my wife's answer to the plaintiff's bill; in which was set forth that she had lived three and forty years at Swarthmore and in all that time there has been no tithe paid or demanded. And an old man, who had long been a tithe-gatherer, had made an affidavit, that he never gathered tithe at Swarthmore Hall in Judge Fell's time, or since. There were many particulars in our answer, but it would not be accepted without an oath.

I told the judge that both tithe and swearing among Christians came from the Pope, and it was a matter of conscience to us not to pay tithes, nor to swear. For Christ bid His disciples, who had freely received, give freely. And He commanded them not to swear at all. The judge said there was tithe paid in England before Popery was. I asked him by what law or statute they were paid then. But he was silent. Then I told him there were eight poor men brought up to London out of the North about two hundred miles for small tithes, and one of them had no family but himself and his wife, and kept no living creature but a cat. I asked him also whether they could take a man and his wife and imprison them both for small tithes, and so destroy a family. And if they could, I desired to know by what law. He did not answer me, but only said that was a hard case.

When I found there was no help to be had there, we left him, and went to Judge Montague's chamber; and with him I had much discourse concerning tithes. Whereupon he sent for our adversary's attorney; and when he came, I offered him our answer. He said if we would pay the charges of the court, and be bound to stand trial, and abide by the judgement of the court, we should not have the oath tendered to us. I told him that they had brought those charges upon us, by requiring us to put in our answer upon oath; which they knew before we could not do for conscience's sake. And as we could not pay any tithe nor swear, so neither should we pay any of their charges. Upon this he would not receive our answer.

So we went from thence to Judge Atkyns's chamber, and he being busy, we gave our answers and our reasons against tithes and swearing to his clerk. But neither could we find any encouragement from him to expect redress. Wherefore leaving him we went to one of the most noted counsellors, and showed him the state of our case and our answers. He was very civil to us and said this way of proceeding against us was somewhat like an inquisition.

SECOND JOURNEY TO HOLLAND

Now [in 1684] had I drawings in Spirit to go into Holland, to visit the Seed of God there. We had a very good passage. And about five in the afternoon next day, we landed at the Briel in Holland, where we stayed that night. Early next morning we went to Rotterdam, where we abode some days.

The day after we came to Rotterdam, one William Frouzen, a burgomaster and kinsman of Aarent Sunneman's, hearing I was there, invited me to his country house, having a desire to speak with me about some business relating to Aarent Sunneman's daughters. The burgomaster received us very kindly, and was very glad to see me. And entering into discourse about his kinsman's daughters, I found he was apprehensive that, their father being dead, and having left them considerable portions, they might be stolen and married to their disadvantage.

Wherefore I told him that it was our principle and practice that none should marry amongst us unless they had a certificate of the consent of their relations or guardians. For it was our Christian care to watch over and look after all young people that came among us; especially those whose natural relations were dead. And as for his kinsman's daughters, we should take care that nothing should be offered to them but what should be agreeable to truth and righteousness, and that they might be preserved in the fear of God, according to their father's mind.

This seemed to give him great satisfaction. While I was with him there came a great many people to me, and I exhorted them all to keep in the fear of God, and to mind His good Spirit in them, to keep their minds to the Lord. After I had stayed two or three hours, and had conversed with him on several things, I took my leave of him and he very kindly sent me to Rotterdam in his chariot.

EASING FRIENDS' SUFFERINGS

[In 1685 I was in] London, but made no long stay there, my body not being able to bear the closeness of the city long together. While I was in town, besides the usual services of visiting Friends and looking after their sufferings to get them eased, I assisted Friends of the city in distributing certain sums of money, which our Friends of Ireland had charitably and very liberally raised, and sent over for the relief of their brethren, who suffered for the testimony of a good conscience; which money was distributed amongst poor, suffering Friends in the several countries, in proportion as we understood their need.

Before I left the city, I heard of a great doctor lately come from Poland, whom I invited to my lodging, and had much discourse with him. After I had informed myself by him of such things as I had a desire to know, I wrote a letter to the King of Poland on behalf of Friends at Danzig, who had long been under grievous sufferings.

I came back to London in the 1st month, 1686, and set myself with all diligence to look after Friends' sufferings, from which we had now some hopes of getting relief. The sessions came on in the 2nd month at Hick's Hall, where many Friends had appeals to be tried; with whom I was from day to day, to advise and see that no opportunity were slipped, nor advantage lost; and they generally succeeded well.

Soon after also the king was pleased, upon our often laying our sufferings before him, to give order for the releasing of all prisoners for conscience's sake that were in his power to discharge. Whereby the prison-doors were opened and many hundreds of Friends, some of whom had been long in prison, were set at liberty.

THE WEIGHT OF TROUBLES

In [October 1688] I returned to London, having been near three months in the country for my health's sake, which was very much impaired; so that I was hardly able to stay in a meeting the whole time; and often after a meeting had to lie down on a bed. Yet did not my weakness of body take me off from the service of the Lord, but I continued to labour in and out of meetings, in His work, as He gave me opportunity and ability.

I had not been long in London before a great weight came upon me, and a sight the Lord gave me of the great bustles and troubles, revolutions and change, which soon after came to pass.[35] In the sense whereof, and in the movings of the Spirit of the Lord, I wrote a general epistle to Friends, to forewarn them of the approaching storm, that they might all retire to the Lord, in whom safety is.

About this time great exercise and weights came upon me (as had usually done before the great revolutions and changes of government), and my strength departed from me; so that I reeled, and was ready to fall, as I went along the streets. At length I could not go abroad at all, I was so weak for some time, till I felt the power of the Lord to spring over all, and had received an assurance from Him that He would preserve His faithful people to Himself through all.

LOBBYING ON BEHALF OF FRIENDS

About the middle of [March 1689], I went to London, the parliament then sitting, and engaged about the Bill for Indulgence. Though I was weak in body, and not well able to stir about, yet so great a concern was upon my spirit on behalf of truth and Friends that I attended continually for many days, with other

Friends, at the parliament house, labouring with the Members, that the thing might be done comprehensively and effectually.

In this, and other services, I continued till towards the end of [April], when, being much spent with continual labour, I got out of town for a little while as far as Southgate. While I was there, I wrote a letter to a Friend at Amsterdam, in which I enclosed an epistle to the Friends at Danzig, who at this time were under great persecution. And as I wrote to encourage and strengthen them in their testimony, and comfort them in their sufferings for the truth, so also I wrote a paper to their persecutors, the magistrates of Danzig, laying before them the evil of persecution, and persuading them to Christian moderation, and to do unto others in matters of religion as they would be done unto.

[In 1690], I remained in London till the beginning of [November], being continually exercised in the work of the Lord, either in public meetings, opening the way of truth to people and building up and establishing Friends therein, or in other services relating to the church of God. For the parliament now sitting, and having a bill before them concerning oaths, and another concerning clandestine marriages, several Friends attended the House, to get those bills so worded that they might not be hurtful to Friends. In this service I also assisted, attending on the parliament and discoursing with several of the members.

POSTSCRIPT

Thus, reader, thou hast had some account of the life and travels, labours, sufferings and manifold trials and exercises of this holy man of God, from his youth to almost the time of his death, of which he himself kept a journal; out of which the foregoing sheets were transcribed. It remains that an account be added of the time place and manner of his death and burial.

The day after he had written [an] epistle to Friends in Ireland, he went to the meeting in Gracechurch Street, which was large, being the First-day of the week. And the Lord enabled him to preach the truth fully and effectually, opening many deep and weighty things with great power and clearness. After which having prayed, and the meeting being ended, he went to Henry Goldney's, in White Hart Court, near the meeting house. And some Friends going with him there, he told them he thought he felt the cold strike to his heart, as he came out of the meeting. 'Yet,' he added, 'I am glad I was here. Now I am clear, I am fully clear.'

As soon as the Friends withdrew, he lay down upon a bed (as he sometimes used to do, through weariness after meeting), but soon rose again; and in a little time lay down again, complaining still of cold. And his strength sensibly decaying, he was soon obliged to go into bed; where he lay in much contentment and peace, and very sensible to the last.

And as in the whole course of his life, his spirit, in the universal love of God, was bent upon the exalting of truth and righteousness, and the making known the way thereof to the nations and people afar off, so now, in the time of his outward weakness, his mind was intent upon, and (as it were) wholly taken up with, that. And some particular Friends he sent for, to whom he expressed his mind and desire for the spreading of Friends' books, and truth thereby in the world. Divers Friends came to visit him in his illness; to some of whom he said: 'All is well. The Seed of God reigns over all, and over death itself. And though,' said he, 'I am weak in body, yet the power of God is over all, and the Seed reigns over all disorderly spirits.'

Thus lying in a heavenly frame of mind, his spirit wholly exercised towards the Lord, he grew weaker and weaker in his natural strength. And on the third day of the week, between the hours of nine and ten in the evening, he quietly departed this life in peace, and sweetly fell asleep in the Lord, whose blessed truth he had lovingly and powerfully preached in the meeting but two days before. Thus ended he his day in his faithful testimony, in perfect love and unity with his brethren, and in peace and goodwill to all men, on the 13th. of [January 1691], being in the 67th year of his age.

On the day appointed for the interment of George Fox, a very great concourse of Friends and others assembled at the meeting house in White Hart Court, near Gracechurch Street, about the middle of the day, to attend his body to the grave. The meeting held about two hours, with great and heavenly solemnity, manifestly attended with the Lord's blessed presence and glorious power; in which divers living testimonials were given, from a lively remembrance and sense of the blessed ministry of this dear and ancient servant of the Lord, his early entering into the Lord's work at the breaking forth of this gospel-day, his innocent life, long and great travels, and unwearied labours of love in the everlasting gospel, for the turning and gathering of many thousands from darkness to the light of Christ Jesus, the foundation of true faith; the manifold sufferings, afflictions and oppositions, which he met withal for his faithful testimony, both from his open adversaries, and from false brethren; and his preservations, deliverances and dominion in, out of and over them all, by the power of God; to whom the glory and honour always was by him, and is, and always ought to be, by all ascribed.

After the meeting was ended, his body was borne by Friends and accompanied by very great numbers, to Friends' burying-ground, near Bunhill Fields; where, after a solemn waiting upon the Lord, amd several living testimonies borne, recommending the company to the guidance and protection of that Divine Spirit and power, by which this holy man of God had been raised up, furnished, supported and preserved, to the end of his day, his body was committed to the earth; but his memorial shall remain, and be everlasting blessed among the righteous.

THE EPISTLES

To the Ringers of the Bells in the Steeple-house called St Peter's in Derby (1650):

Friends,
Take heed of pleasures and prize your time now, while you have it. And do not spend it in pleasures or earthliness. The day may come that you will say you had time, when it is past. Therefore look at the love of God now, while you have time. For it bringeth to loathe all vanities and worldly pleasures. O consider! Time is precious. Fear God, and rejoice in Him who hath made heaven and earth.

A Few Lines for the Comfort and Encouragement of the Faithful (1650):

Come, ye blessed of the Lord, and rejoice together! Keep in unity and oneness of spirit. Triumph above the world! Be joyful in the Lord, reigning above the world, and above all things that draw from the Lord; that in clearness, righteousness, pureness and joy you may be preserved to the Lord. O hear! O harken to the call of the Lord! Come out of the world and keep out of it for evermore! Come, sing together, ye righteous ones, the song of the Lord, the song of the Lamb; which none can learn but they who are redeemed from the earth, and from the world.

To the Judges (1650):

I am moved to write unto you that ye do true justice to every man; and see that none be oppressed or wronged, or any oaths imposed. For the land mourneth because of oaths and adulteries and sorceries and drunkenness and profaneness. O consider, ye that are men set in authority: be moderate, and in lowliness consider these things. Show mercy to the fatherless, to the widows and to the poor. And take heed of rewards or gifts, for they blind the eyes of the wise. The Lord doth loathe all such. Love mercy and true judgement, justice and righteousness, for the Lord delighteth therein.

To Father and Mother (1652):

Dear Father and Mother in the flesh,
To that of God in both of you I speak; and do beseech you both for the Lord's sake to return within and wait to hear the voice [of] the Lord there. Waiting there and keeping close to the Lord, a discerning will grow, that you may distinguish the voice of the stranger when you hear it.

To Adam Sands, a Very Wicked, False Man (1652):

Adam Sands,
To the Light in thy conscience I appeal, thou child of the Devil, thou enemy of righteousness. The Lord will strike thee down, though now for a while in thy wickedness thou mayest reign. The plagues of God are due to thee, who hardenest thyself in thy wickedness against the pure truth of God. With the pure truth of God, which thou hast resisted and persecuted, thou art to be thrashed down; which is eternal, and doth comprehend thee. And

with the Light, which thou despisest, thou art seen. And it is thy condemnation.

To Friends (1652):

Friends,
Whatever you are addicted to, the Tempter will come in that thing. When he can trouble you, then he gets advantage over you; and then you are gone. Stand still in that which is pure; and then mercy comes in. After you see your thoughts and the temptations, do not think but submit. Then the power comes. Stand still in the Light and submit to it, and the other will be hushed and gone. Then contentment comes. When temptations and troubles appear, sink down in that which is pure, and all will be hushed and fly away. Your strength is to stand still.

To Friends (1652):

Friends,
If you love the Light and walk in it, you love Christ and will all walk in unity together. If you hate the Light, you hate Christ.

To Friends (1652):

Dear Friends,
Mind that Light in you that shows you sin and evil, which checks you when you speak an evil word, and tells you that you should not be proud, nor wanton nor fashion yourselves like unto the world. For the fashion of this world passes away. And if you harken to [the Light], it will keep you in humbleness of mind and loneliness of heart and turn your minds within to wait upon Him for teaching, till an entrance thereof be made to your souls.

To Friends (1652):

To all my dear brethren, whom the God of power has enlightened
with His eternal Light,
It has discovered to you His way of Truth, and brought you out of
the dark ways wherein you had walked. Where the pure Light of
God is witnessed, it guides to Himself. The Light is but one,
which leads out of darkness and the dark's world into the world
which is without end. Therefore, all Friends, brethren in the
eternal Truth: walk in it up to God. Be not sayers only, nor
backsliders, for the backslider is a sayer and not a doer. There arise
ambition, pride and presumption out of that nature. But dwell in
the pure Light, which God has made manifest. Turn your minds
to Him and walk as Children of the Day and as Children of the
Light, and 'let your light shine before men, that they may glorify
your Father which is in heaven' (Matt. 5,26).

To Friends (1653):

Friends,
Fear not the powers of darkness, but keep your meetings and meet
in that which keeps you over them. And in the power of God you
will have unity. Dwell in love and unity, one with another; and
know one another in the power of the endless life, which does not
change. And know the Word of God abiding in you, which was in
the beginning, and brings to the beginning; which Word, being
ingrafted, it saves the soul and hammers down, throws down and
burns up that which wars against it.

To Friends in the Ministry (1653):

Stand up, you prophets of the Lord, for the truth upon the earth.
Quench not your prophecy, neither heed them that despite it. But

in that stand which brings you through to the end. Heed not the eyes of the world, you prophets of the Lord. Answer that in them all which they have closed their eyes to, that you may to them tell of things to come, answering that of God in them. Quench not the Spirit, by which you may prove all things. That which is good, hold fast. For if the Spirit be quenched, then light is put for darkness, darkness for light, and evil is put for good. But when the Spirit is not quenched, then with the Spirit you may see the good, to take the good, and the evil to shun.

To Friends Everywhere, Scattered Abroad (1653):

In the measure of the life of God, wait for wisdom from God, even from Him from whom it comes. And all ye who are children of God, wait for living food from the living God, to be nourished up to eternal life, from the one fountain, whence life comes; that ye may all be guided and walk in order: servants in your places, young men and women in your places, and rulers of families; that everyone, in your respective places, may adorn the Truth, in the measure of it. With it let your minds be kept up to the Lord Jesus, from which it comes, that ye may be a sweet savour to God, and in wisdom ye may all be ordered and ruled. And that no strife, bitterness or self-will may appear amongst you. But with the Light, in which is unity, all these may be condemned.

To All Professors of Christianity (1654):

Where pride is thrown down, earth and the fleshly will is thrown down, and the pure is raised up. There alone is the Lord exalted. Let the heavens bow down to Him, and the earth reel to and fro, and stagger up and down. The Lord is setting up His throne and His crown, and throwing down the crown of man. And He alone will be glorified. To whom be all honour and glory, all praises and all thanks! Who gives His children wisdom and strength, knowledge and virtue, power and riches, blessings and durable substance; an eye to discern, and an ear to hear things singly; and brings down the pride of man's heart.

An Exhortation and Warning to the Pope and All Kings and Rulers in Europe (1654):

Friends,

Ye heads and rulers, kings and nobles of all sorts: be not bitter nor hasty in persecuting the lambs of Christ, neither turn yourself against the visitation of God, and His tender love and mercies from on high, who sent to visit you; lest the Lord's hand, arm and power take hold swiftly upon you; which is now stretched over the world. It is turned against kings, and shall turn wise men backward, and will bring their crowns to the dust, and lay them low and level with the earth. The Lord will be king, who gives crowns to whomsoever obey His will. This is the age wherein the Lord God of heaven and earth is staining the pride of man and defacing his glory. You that profess Christ and do not love your enemies, but on the contrary shut up and imprison those who are His friends; these are marks that you are out of His life, and do not love Christ, who do not the things He commands. The day of the Lord's wrath is kindling, and His fire is going forth to burn up the wicked.

To Churches Gathered into Outward Forms, upon the Earth (1655):

All ye churches gathered into outward forms upon the earth, the Son of God is come to reign. He will tread and trample, will shake and make you quiver, you that are found out of His light, without His life and power. His day hath appeared. Mortar and clay will you be found. Breaking, shaking and quaking are coming among you! Your high building is to be laid desolate. Your professed liberty shall be your bondage. The mouth of the Lord of Hosts hath spoken it. Tremble, ye hypocrites, ye notionists!

To Friends, Concerning Priests (1655):

All Friends,
Now the Beast opens his mouth in blasphemy, speaking 'great swelling words'. Now is the cage of the unclean birds and unclean spirits seen. Now are the locusts seen and the caterpillars known. Now are the seven thunders uttering their voices. Now are the hailstones falling, and 'the vials of wrath pouring out upon the Beast and the false prophet' (Rev. 15, 10, & 15). Now are the whited walls seen and the painted sepulchres, full of dead men's bones. Now are the thistles, briars and thorns, where the figs do not grow, seen. And now they are seen, which make merchandise of words of the prophets, Christ and the Apostles, and through pretence make long prayers, who devour widows' houses.

To the Protector [Oliver Cromwell] (1655):

To the measure of the life of God in thee I speak. Many lie in jails, because they cannot pay the priests' tithes. Many have their goods spoiled and treble damages taken of them. And many are whipped and beaten in the house of correction, without breach of law. These things are done in thy name, in order to protect them in these actions. To the measure of God's Spirit in thee I speak, that thou mayest answer that which is of God in every man's conscience; for this is that which bringeth to honour all men in the Lord. Therefore consider for whom thou dost rule, that thou mayest come to receive power from God to rule for Him. And all that is contrary to God may by His light be condemned.

To a Friend in the Ministry (1656):

Dear Brother,
Mind the Lord and stand in His will and counsel. Look not forth at time nor place, but at thy Father's house, wheresoever thou art. And dwell in the pure measure of God in thee. There thou wilt see the Lord God present with thee. For the bringing of many out of prison art thou there set. Behold the Word of the Lord cannot be bound. The Lord God of Power give thee wisdom, courage, manhood and boldness, to thrash down all deceit. Dear heart, be valiant and mind the pure Spirit.

To Friends (1656):

Keep your meetings in the power of the Lord, which is over all that is in the fall and must have an end. Therefore be wise in the wisdom of God, which is from above, by which all things were made and created; that that may be justified among you, and you all kept in the solid life, which was before death was; and in the Light, which was before the darkness was, with all its works. In which Light and life ye all may feel, and have the heavenly unity and peace, possessing the gospel fellowship, that is everlasting.

To Friends in Business (1656):

Friends,
Take heed of striving about earthly things. After riches increase, take heed of setting your hearts upon them, lest they become a curse and a plague to you. For when you were faithful at the first, the world would refrain from you and not have commerce with you. But after, when they saw you were faithful and just in things, and righteous and honest in your tradings and dealings, then they came to have commerce and trade with you the more, because they

know you will not cozen them nor cheat them. Then you came to have greater trading, double than ever you had, and more than the world. But there is the danger and temptation to you of drawing your minds into your business and clogging them with it. So that you can hardly do anything to the service of God, but there will be crying 'my business, my business!'. Your minds will go into the things, and not over the things. And so therein you do not come into the image of God, in which is dominion.

To Friends (1657):

Friends,
None owns the Light as it is in Jesus except he that owns the Light that Jesus lighteth him withal. None owns the Truth, but who owns the Light that comes from Christ, the Truth. And none comes to the Father, but who owns the Light that comes from Christ, which leads to Him.

To All Friends and Brethren Everywhere (1657):

Friends, be careful how ye set your feet among the tender plants that are springing up out of God's earth, lest ye tread upon them, hurt, bruise or crush them in God's vineyard.

To Friends (1657):

All Friends everywhere that are in any sufferings, let your sufferings be gathered up together in every county; you that have suffered by justices, constables or bailiffs, let your names be set to your sufferings, a name or two to witness them and the names of them that cause you to suffer. In the county where the judges come, let your sufferings be laid before them. God, who is just, is ready to plead their cause and to judge and cast out the unjust judges. For He that judges among the judges gives true judgement, and gives judgement on the unjust. And that a copy of your sufferings be kept and sent up to the head in the nation, that he may see, measure and weigh how unrighteously they have judged, and what his servants have done.

To Friends, to Know One Another in the Light (1657):

All Friends everywhere,
Meet together and in the measure of God's Spirit wait. That with it all your minds may be guided up to God, to receive wisdom from God, that you may all come to know how you may walk up to Him in His wisdom. And Friends, meet together and know one another in that which is eternal, which was before the world was. For knowing one another only in the letter and flesh, differs you little from the beast of the field. If you turn from this Light, you grow strange; and so neglecting meetings, you grow cold. Your minds run into the earth and grow weary, slothful, careless, heavy, sottish, dull and dead. Therefore in the Light wait and walk, that you may have fellowship one with another.

To Friends (1657):

O Friends! Keep out of that state which is out of and below the chaste nature. For all unchastity by the power of the Lord is to be judged. Therefore live in the Truth, in the Light of God, that keeps you all chaste. Keep down the unchaste, keep down the adulterous eye and keep down the lust of the flesh, which is not of the Father but of the world. Lust is against the spiritual fellowship, spiritual union and spiritual dominion. Keep down the lustful heart and eye, for that leads from God and joins with the adulterate in anything, or with anything, that is evil. Keep

Truth and a pure conscience. There you have an unspotted life, in which you may see over the spotted life, where no chastity nor purity is. Therefore live in that which keeps you chaste. Then you follow Christ, the Lamb.

To Friends (1658):

My dear Friends,
You that have denied the world's giving thanks and their saying of grace and living out of it, do you in everything give thanks to the Lord through Jesus Christ. And you that have denied the world's praising God with their lips, whilst their hearts are far off, do you always praise the Lord night and day. And you that have denied the world's fastings, keep the fast of the Lord, that breaks the bond of iniquity and lets the oppressed go free, that your health may grow and your Light shine, as the morning.

To the Saints Scattered in Old and New England, Germany, Holland, Ireland, Scotland, Barbados and Virginia (1659):

Friends,
We need no Mass to teach us, for the Spirit that gave forth the Scripture teaches us how to pray, sing, fast, give thanks, to praise and worship, and how to honour and glorify God. And so the Spirit of Truth, which gave forth the Scriptures, is our director, guide, leader and comforter. And we are a people redeemed from the earth and the world, and need none of your Church-made faith, which you have framed. For Christ is the author of our Faith, which is the gift of God.

To All Friends (1661):

There is a summer religion, which appears when the sun shines upon them. In the summertime, all the venomous creatures creep out of their holes, corners and dens: the flies, wasps and snakes. But when the winter is come, and the storms and tempests come, then the venomous, viperous creatures, religion and words are gone. But the religion that is the Power of God stands, which was before the power of darkness was.

To Friends in New England and the Islands beyond the Sea (1662):

To all my dear Friends and brethren among whom the precious Truth and Power of God has been declared and joyfully received,

Fetters, irons, whippings, stripes and spoilings of goods have not daunted you. Your courage, valiantness and boldness for Truth has much appeared among a crooked and perverse generation that professed Christ, among whom He has not had so much place of entertainment as in their manger. Their hearts are dens of dragons and places of darkness. You, in the power of God stand. All your feet are sure. Which power goes over all that which brings the curse, wrath, woe, misery, thraldom, bondage and captivity. You all have unity, peace, concord, love and fellowship in the Gospel, which goes over the enmity.

To Justice Fleming (1663):

O, Justice Fleming!
Mercy, compassion, love and kindness adorn and grace men and magistrates. O! Dost thou not hear the cry of the widows, and the cry of the fatherless, who were made so through persecution! Were they not driven like sheep, from constable to constable, as

though they had been the greatest transgressors or malefactors in the land? Which grieved and tendered the hearts of many sober people, to see how their innocent neighbours and countrymen, who were of a peaceable carriage, and honest in their lives and conversations amongst men, were used and served! One more is dead whom thou sent to prison, having left five children, both fatherless and motherless. How canst thou do otherwise than take care of these fatherless infants, and also of the other's wife and family?

To Friends (1663):

Sing and rejoice, you Children of the Day and of the Light. For the Lord is at work in this thick night of darkness that may be felt. Truth does flourish as the rose, the lilies do grow among the thorns, the plants a-top the hills, and upon them the lambs do skip and play. Never heed the tempests nor the storms, floods or rains, for the Seed, Christ, is over all and does reign. And so, be of good faith and valiant for the Truth. The Truth can live in the jails. Fear not the loss of the fleece, for it will grow again. And follow the Lamb, if it be under the beast's horns or under the beast's heels. For the Lamb shall have the victory over them all.

To Friends (1664):

All my dear Friends,
In the everlasting Power, Life and Truth, live. For you cannot live without it, in the winds and storms. And though the hills and mountains are burnt, the trees are become fruitless, winter has devoured the former fruits, you do see that persecution has choked them, the heat has scorched them; whereby the untimely figs are fallen, the corn is withered on the house top, the night is come and the evil beasts go out of their den; but Truth lives and

the Power of God is over them all. Christ rules. There is Bread of Life and Water of Life in Him and His house, though the caterpillars and locusts are agreed to eat up all the green.

To Friends (1666):

Friends,
Concerning the women's meetings: encourage all the women of families that are convinced, mind virtue, love Truth and walk in it, that they may come up into God's service; that they may be serviceable in their generation, in the creation, and come into the practice of the pure religion; that everyone may come to know their duty in it and their service in the power and wisdom of God. For now the practical part is called for; for people must not be always talking and hearing, but they must come into obedience.

To Friends and All People (1667):

We say that the Word of God is the original, which fulfils the Scriptures. The Word is it which makes a divine, which is called a hammer; but it is a living hammer, and is called a sword and fire; but it is a living sword and a living fire, to hammer, to cut down and burn up that which separated and kept men from God. By this Word are men and women sanctified and made clean. This is the Word that makes both men and women divine, and brings them into the divine nature, which hammers and cuts down that which corrupted their nature.

To Friends (1668):

Dear Friends,
All who from the beginning have been convinced of God's Truth

and are turned to the world or gone into drunkenness, swearing, pleasure and looseness, or to the old Mass House, or have sold the Truth for a wife or husband, and gone to the priests covertly to be married; these all must be admonished to come to the Light that did first convince them, and give forth a paper of condemnation; and so clear the Truth, that none may make a jest of their transgressions, so that the house may be swept.

To *Friends in the Ministry* (1669):

Sound your trumpets all abroad, ye angels of the Lord, sons and daughters, prophets of the highest; that all who are dead and asleep in their graves, who have been long dreaming and slumbering, may be awakened, and hear the voice of the Lamb; that all who have long heard the voice of the beast may now hear the voice of the bridegroom and the voice of the bride; that they may now hear the voice of the great prophet and king – the shepherd and bishop of their soul. Sound, sound it all abroad, ye trumpets, among the dead in Adam; for Christ is come, the second Adam, that they might have life, yea have it abundantly.

To *Ministering Friends* (1669):

Friends,
All you that are become Children of the Light and of the Day: do not judge one another in public meetings, for that hurts the hearers. You do more hurt than you do good, and that makes confusion. For if you have anything to say, have patience. Let the gift be exercised and speak to one another by yourself alone. That will show the spirit of order and government, the spirit of love, patience and humility, and keep down passion.

To Friends (1669):

Friends, see that all apprentices that are bound amongst you may serve out their times faithfully, according to covenant, that all may know their places. For youth, if they be let loose, are like wild asses and wild heifers. Through a foolish pity of some, they let up a great deal of airiness and wildness in them; all which should be kept under by the Power of God.

To Friends (1671):

Friends,
When you are met together in the name of Jesus your Saviour, let your minds be over all of Him; and up to Him that is invisible, the Lord God, and His Son Jesus Christ; that you may see Him and feel Him among you, in your meetings, in His life, Light, Power and Spirit. That you may know that God is, and that He is the rewarder of all them that diligently seek Him.

To Margaret Fell (1671):

My dear heart,
To whom is my love, and to all the children in the Seed of Life that changeth not, but is over all; blessed be the Lord for ever. I have undergone great sufferings in my body and spirit, beyond words. But the God of heaven be praised, His truth is over all. I am now well. And if the Lord permit, within a few days I pass from Barbados towards Jamaica. And I think to stay but little there. I desire that ye may be all kept free in the Seed of Life, out of all cumbrances. Friends are generally well. Remember me to Friends that enquire after me. So no more, but my love in the Seed and Life that changeth not.

To Friends (1673):

Friends,
The Truth is above all, and will stand over all them that hate it, who labour in vain against it, and will bring their old house on their own heads. And in the winter, when their house is down, and their religion is frozen, their rivers are dried up, their husks are gone, the swine begin to cry, the vermin runs up and down amongst their old rubbish, their sparks and candles are gone out, and hail and storms light upon the head of the wicked; then woe to all the wicked who have no covering. No peace with God can be enjoyed, but in the covenant of Light; without it, trouble.

To the Men's and Women's Meetings in Barbados (1674):

Take heed, Friends, in laying open one another's weaknesses. If anyone has anything to say, let [him] speak to the person concerned. If they will not hear, take two or three more before they are brought into public. And so let brotherly love continue; kindness, affableness, courteousness and whatsoever is decent, comely and of a good report in the eyes of God.

To Friends (1674):

Some men may say men must have the power and superiority over the woman, because God says the man must rule over his wife, and that man is not of woman but woman is of the man (Gen. 3,16). Indeed, after man fell, that command was. But before man fell, there was no such command. For they were both meet-helps. They were both to have dominion over all that God made. So then the man is not without the woman, neither the woman without the man in the Lord.

To Friends in Nevis and the Caribbean Islands (1675):

If any should come to burn your house, rob you or come to ravish your wives and daughters, or a company should come to fire a city, or come to kill people, don't you watch against all such actions? And won't you watch against such evil things in the Power of God in your own way? You cannot but discover such things to the magistrates, who are to punish such things. Therefore the watch is kept and set to discover such, that they may be punished.

To Princess Elizabeth [grand-daughter of James I] (1677):

Princess Elizabeth,
I have heard of thy tenderness towards the Lord and His holy truth, by some Friends that have visited thee; and also by some of thy letters, which I have seen. It is indeed a great thing for a person of thy quality to have such a tender mind after the Lord and His precious truth, seeing so many are swallowed up with voluptuousness and the pleasures of this world. Yet all make an outward profession of God and Christ, one way or other; but without any deep, inward sense and feeling of Him. Feel the grace and truth in thy heart, that is come by Jesus Christ, that will teach thee how to live, and what to deny. It will establish thy heart, season thy words, and bring thy salvation.

To Friends (1677):

In love to God, and in love to your persecutors, you can pray for them who persecute you. This suffering is above all the sufferings in the world, which are without love and charity. Such are not the sufferers for the true Lord Jesus, who suffered, though He was above all. And the Lamb overcame and had the victory, and His

sanctified ones, following Him, are partakers thereof. Glory to
His name forever, Amen.

To Johannes III, King of Poland (1678):

O King!
We desire thy prosperity, both in this life and that which is to
come. And we desire that we may have our Christian liberty to
serve and worship God under thy dominion. For our principle
leads us not to do anything prejudicial to the king or his people.
We are a people that exercise a good conscience towards God
through His Holy Spirit; and in it do serve, worship and honour
Him. That which we desire of thee, O king, is that we may have
liberty of conscience to serve and worship God, and to pray unto
Him in our meetings together in the name of Jesus, as He
commands, with a promise that He will be in the midst of them.

*To Friends in America, Concerning Their Negroes and Indians
(1679):*

All Friends everywhere that have Indians or Blacks, you are to
preach the Gospel to them and other servants, if you be true
Christians, for the gospel of salvation was to be preached to every
creature under heaven. Christ commands it to His disciples: 'Go
and teach all nations, baptizing them into the name of the Father,
Son and Holy Ghost' (Matt. 28,19). You must instruct and teach
your Indians and Negroes and all others how Christ, by the Grace
of God, tasted death for every man, gave Himself a ransom for all
men, and is the propitiation not for the sins of Christians only, but
for the sins of the whole world.

To the Captives Who Met Together to Worship God in Algiers (1681):

Dear Friends,
I understand by a letter from a Friend, a captive among you, that you have a meeting there in Algiers of about twenty. I am glad to hear you meet. My desire is that the Lord may preserve you all, that do meet in the name of Jesus; that in your lives, conversations and words you may preach righteousness, holiness and godliness, and the life of truth; so that you may answer the Spirit of God, both in the Turks and Moors, and the rest of the captives.

To Friends in New Jersey and Pennsylvania (1682):

Dear Friends,
Now in your settling of plantations and provinces, and especially in woody countries as these are, you may have many trials and troubles. But if you keep in the wisdom of God, that will keep you both gentle, kind and easy to be entreated one of another; that will preserve you out of heats, extremes of passions; and that all Friends that come over be with speed settled in their plantations.

To All Planters and Such Who Are Transporting Themselves into Foreign Plantations (1682):

My Friends, that are gone and going over to plant and make outward plantations in America, keep your own plantations in your hearts with the Spirit and Power of God; that your own vines and lilies be not hurt. And in all places where you do outwardly live, and settle; invite all the Indians and their kings, and have meetings with them or they with you. And so by it you may make heavenly plantations in their hearts for the Lord, and so beget them to God.

To All Vintners and Innkeepers (1682):

First, all you vintners that sell wine, that keep taverns or suchlike houses; and all you innkeepers, and you that keep victualling-houses, ale-houses, strong-water shops etc: see that you never let any man or woman have any more wine, ale, strong drink, brandy or strong waters than what is for their health and their good. But if you do give or let men or women have so much wine, brandy, strong liquors, strong beer or ale, till they be drunk, you destroy the good creatures of God; you destroy them that have not power over their lusts, no more than a rat or a swine, who will drink till they are drunk; you are a great cause of ruining them in their health, purses and estates.

To the Suffering Friends of Danzig (1684):

Dear Friends,
We do hear and understand that the magistrates have cast you into prison again in Danzig. And that they have proferred you your liberty upon condition that you would go away, or forsake your common meeting-place, or divide yourselves into several little meetings. Truly, Friends, we have had many of these proffers made to us within this twenty or thirty years, but we never durst make such bargains or covenants, to forsake the assembling of ourselves together, as we used to do; but did leave our suffering cause wholly to the Lord Christ Jesus, in whose name we were gathered, who has all power in heaven and earth given to Him. And the Lord at last did and has tendered the hearts of many of our prosecutors, both in England and other places.

Lines to Be Dispersed amongst Friends Everywhere (1687):

Dear Friends and Brethren in the Lord Jesus Christ,
The Lord, by His eternal arm and power, having supported you in all your sufferings, and great spoiling of goods and tedious imprisonments, only for serving and worshipping the living God that made you; the Lord, by His infinite power and mercy, having been pleased to open the king's heart towards you, by which you are set at liberty from jails, and the spoilers of your goods are stopped, whereby ye may follow your callings, confess Christ Jesus and call Him Lord by the Holy Ghost: a great concern lies upon me from the Lord to write unto you, dear brethren, that none may abuse this liberty, nor the mercies of the Lord, but praise them. For there is great danger in the time of liberty, of getting up into ease, looseness and false liberty.

Notes

1. *Drayton-in-the-Clay:* Now called Fenny Drayton.
2. *Stock of the martyrs:* His mother probably had an ancestor who was a victim of religious persecution, possibly one of the Mancetter Martyrs, from Mancetter nearby.
3. *Creatures:* Not just animals and people, but material creation.
4. *Priest:* Any paid minister.
5. *Professor:* Someone who would consider himself a practising Christian.
6. *Seventh month:* Under the old calendar, the year began in March; so 'seventh month' would be September. On occasions, I have substituted the more conventional months' names, to avoid confusion.
7. *Tender:* Receptive to teaching and the truth.
8. *First-days:* George Fox objected to the pagan origin of the names of the days of the week, so opted for neutral numbers, beginning with Sunday.
9. *Friends:* It is not entirely clear when George Fox started referring to his followers by this name, which is incorporated in the formal title of Quakers: the Religious Society of Friends.
10. *Steeple-house:* Churches in the physical sense. A major tenet of George Fox's beliefs was that the true church was not a matter of bricks and mortar.
11. *Common-prayer-men:* What we today would tend to call Anglicans.
12. *Quakers:* Although it is a charming story that Quakers were so named because a judge mocked their passionate tremblings,

it seems that the word had been used earlier to describe other religious types who trembled before the Lord.

13. *Worcester fight:* The Battle of Worcester, 1651.

14. *Man in leather breeches:* George Fox was much ridiculed for his leather suit, which made him highly conspicuous, but which he justified on the grounds of practicality and hard-wearing.

15. *Mazed or fond:* Crazy or simple-minded.

16. *Richard Farnsworth:* Convinced in 1651, he became one of George Fox's most tireless helpers.

17. *James Nayler:* Left his Independent church to become a Quaker, but subsequently got carried away with strange notions, leading to one of the most serious crises in early Quaker history.

18. *Moss-troopers:* Remnants of raiding bands of free-booters, who infested the border areas of England and Scotland.

19. *Isaiah liv,17:* 'No weapon that is fashioned against you shall prosper, and you shall confute every tongue that rises against you in judgement. This is the heritage of the servants of the Lord and their vindication from me, says the Lord.'

20. *Colonel Hacker:* Colonel Hacker and his troops superintended the execution of King Charles I.

21. *Alchymy:* A much baser metal alloy.

22. *Major-General Desborough:* He was in charge of Wiltshire, Somerset, Devon and Cornwall from 1655, and was much appreciated by Oliver Cromwell.

23. *Fifth Monarchy men:* A fanatical group which interpreted Nebuchadnezzar's dream as a promise of a new reign on earth by Christ – the fifth monarchy – now due. They attempted unsuccessfully to take London in 1661, which led to renewed persecution of religious groups, including Friends.

24. *Friends in the ministry:* Quakers who are moved to go out into the world, or travelling among Quakers, sharing their experiences and insights.

25. *Janglers:* Ranting believers who disputed in a way of which George Fox disapproved.

26. *Yearly Meeting:* This eventually became the main administrative framework of Friends, e.g. London Yearly Meeting, which groups Friends in Great Britain.

27. *Richard:* Oliver Cromwell's son and named successor.

28. *Praemunire:* Originally a writ charging a sheriff to summon a person accused of asserting papal jurisdiction in England. It was used frequently at this time as a way of keeping people like Quakers in jail.

29. *The sickness:* The Great Plague of the mid 1660s.

30. *Monthly meetings:* Now the most important intermediate administrative layer for Friends' business, where representatives of all the meetings for worship within an area discuss issues.

31. *Daughters:* As is recorded in the diary, there was a son too, called George. Unlike his sisters, he was not a supporter of George Fox.

32. *Conventicles:* Clandestine religious meetings.

33. *Sallee:* A sea-port in Morocco, after which notorious pirates were named.

34. *Cockarooses:* According to Rufus M. Jones, a local word for Indian headmen.

35. *Revolution and change:* The advent of William and Mary.

Index